MAVERICKS

MAVERICKS

Canadian Rebels, Renegades and Antiheroes

P E T E R   C .   N E W M A N

HarperCollins*PublishersLtd*

FIRST EDITION

HarperCollins books may be purchased for educational, business, or sales
promotional use through our Special Markets Department.

HarperCollins Publishers Ltd
2 Bloor Street East, 20th Floor
Toronto, Ontario, Canada
M4W 1A8

www.harpercollins.ca

Library and Archives Canada Cataloguing in Publication
Newman, Peter C., 1929–
Mavericks : Canadian rebels, renegades and antiheroes / Peter C.
Newman.

ISBN 978-1-55468-420-5

1. Canada–Biography. I. Title.
FC25.N494 2010   971.009'9   C2010-903100-8

Printed and bound in the United States

RRD 9 8 7 6 5 4 3 2 1

With love for my charming grandson, Adon Kerr,
a maverick at heart who, when he comes into his own,
will surpass all our expectations

Contents

MAVERICKS

INTRODUCTION
The Hard-Ass Mavericks Who Turned
Entrepreneurial Canada into a Moveable Feast

POWER IS FOR PRINCES. Yet there is no man or woman worthy of princedom in this volume—which ranges from chronicling Conrad Black's zeal to establish his innocence and regain some semblance of legitimacy (plus a hitchhiker's earlier tour of the formidable workings his mind), to recounting the last desperate days of John Diefenbaker, the fierce renegade of Tory politics, as he went wacko in his final bid for glory.

Their qualities and fallibilities, and those of the other characters who occupy this book, inevitably concern power—seeking it, using it, abusing it and losing it—and very occasionally, regaining it. Far more telling than any of the brooding fantasies contemplated by the bravest of princes were the adventures and misadventures of this posse of mavericks. They fought like hell for their share of the spoils—or more—and since they weren't heroes, their survival instinct was more aggressive and power-fully spiked than that of their antagonists.

Maverick is a western term, originally meaning an unbranded range animal separated from its herd. In its urban connotation, it applies to anyone with a highly developed sense of indepen-dence who rejects or resists the dictates of adhering to a group. That rogue quality is what provides the narrative arc for the disparate characters in this book. They were masters of their fates, made life-changing decisions regardless of the conse-quences and perpetuated a new way of looking at the world: to a remarkable degree, they substituted deep-rooted character with personal style. They welcomed risk and never hesitated to overstep their personal prerogatives. Constantly in flight and flux and obsessed by the determination to control their busi-ness environment, they were citizens more of their age than of their country.

Of course not all the mavericks in this volume are concerned with finances. The political section is dominated by a profile of the Rt. Hon. John Diefenbaker, the most radical prime minis-ter in the country's history—even though he was a Tory—who became known for his maverick ideas about Canadian conserva-tism. Coincidentally, the original title of my political biography of him was *Maverick in Power: The Diefenbaker Years.* Publisher Jack McClelland, hardened the title to *Renegade in Power,* which he felt more closely defined his stance. Other mavericks in this book are of interest because they similarly followed no predictable pat-terns, but found their own path to making a difference.

The Protestant ethic that built Canada was not part of the mission statements of these mavericks, and unlike their predecessors, they believed that wealth, instead of being guarded, ought to be spent—lavished, really—on their favourite charities: themselves. I will never forget standing in the luxurious treehouse bedroom that fashion mogul Peter Nygard had built on his private Caribbean island. He was trying to persuade me that the tropical pleasure dome was just an extension of his primitive Robinson Crusoe approach to relaxing in the sun and appreciating nature. "Gee, I don't know," I said, looking around, trying to get into the spirit of the place. "Somehow I doubt that Robinson Crusoe had a mirror over his bed," I said, and Nygard did his best to imitate a Trudeau shrug. Then we went down to meet twenty-five of his best naked friends in his oversize sauna.

———

MAN HAS ALWAYS been alive to the itching in his palm. But only a few remarkable Canadians evolved their acquisitive impulses into economic influence so immense that it grew beyond their control, like a forest fire that feeds on itself. Sir Herbert Holt is a good example: he owned a greater share of Canadian business than anyone before or after him, remaining obsessively anonymous throughout. An unremembered man without friends, his monomaniacal pursuit of money and power culminated in his becoming the richest Canadian who ever lived. During his reign there was scarcely a productive agency in the country he did not own—or that didn't feel the bite of his rivalry. Then there was Sir Harry Oakes, the gritty, intolerably nasty gold seeker who accidentally found "the richest half mile on Earth" under an Ontario lake, only to be hacked to death in his Bahamian paradise. No one was ever charged with the crime, since there were too many people who wanted him dead.

The compulsive drive for economic success has been a dominant shaping force in Canadian history, and the hyper mavericks in this book transformed this country from a community of traders and land tillers into one of the world's most economically animated nation-states. Good examples were E.P. Taylor, who became not only Canada's largest brewer and the owner of our most prized racehorses, but also the founding genius of Argus Corporation, the forerunner of Conrad Black's Hollinger empire. When I published a fairly critical reconstruction of some of his deals, and he was asked about me, he purred: "Well, we all know that Newman is a communist, but I'm not going to take him off my Christmas card list, just yet."

My perfect epitaph.

More colourful and more daring was Nelson Skalbania, who was the only one of my Gonzo capitalists who actually papered his bedroom ceiling with $100,000 worth of gold leaf. He bought and flipped million-dollar apartment and office buildings within minutes of each other—and never even bothered to inspect the properties. Then there was the big-city impresario, Garth Drabinsky, who flew too close to the sun too many times. He spent a lifetime yearning for legitimacy and seriously demanded to be sentenced as a mentor for prisoners wishing to learn his tricks of the trade. His conviction and prison sentence were being appealed when this book went to press.

The mania of financial empire building dislodged satisfaction with common achievement. The men in this book were unable to transact business deals without becoming embroiled in them. In the process, they set themselves beyond the prosaic strivings and fallibilities of ordinary citizens—and that was what made them interesting. They shared a common strain: being mavericks meant that they obeyed their own laws, and while they viewed the free enterprise system as a beneficial discipline, they were not averse to bending it so it would reward the most deserving— namely, themselves. They shared a deadly act of faith, equating their self-worth with their net worth—which turned out to be a fatal miscalculation.

While some succeeded brilliantly as individuals, they failed as a class. They could not adjust quickly enough to the new economic environment. Once, business tycoons were social heroes—proof to an invidiously competitive society that ability and application could be spectacularly repaid. But as environmental and ethical concerns developed, it became clear that private fortunes did not represent the peak of human evolution.

Because they were mavericks, theirs was a paradoxical kin- ship—maintained through incessant jousting and pulling rugs out from under competitors' feet—of such characters as Victor Rice, who was head of Canada's most venerable company, fired fifty-two thousand of his employees and skipped out on multimillion-dollar government loans, and the puffed-up Eaton boys, who carelessly drove the country's marquee department store into the ground.

That was mild compared to former Ottawa house builder Robert Campeau's wild gambles on the pride of American department stores, which he stripped of usable capital, devastating their shareholders. His record was so shoddy and played on such a grand scale that he was blamed for causing the 1987 market crash. The most apt comment on his mental state was that he appointed his private shrink to his company's board of directors, so that somebody could keep track of his bizarre behaviour.

————

ACOLYTES IN TOMORROW'S temples of business will be faced with a drastically altered and increasingly complex set of rules. The wrench beyond the elementary rungs of responsibility will take metal in the soul. The competent and ruthless will manipulate themselves upward much faster than rivals who are only competent. They will have to identify themselves with their economic ambitions so thoroughly that they'll accept corporate actions and philosophies as genuine extensions of their personal feelings.

Such iron-hearted loyalty will not extend to the successful executive's superiors. Disagreement with presidential decisions will be expressed in deliberate authority-destroying rebellion. Some of these restless aggressors will be fired; others will become—until they, in turn, are deposed—the most imaginative managers this country has ever had. Executives tugging for success in the super-competitive environment of the evolving Canadian corporation will have to sit perpetually on the edge of their chairs—prepared, when their clairvoyance fails, to be buried where they fall. They will have to pay in full measure for every new foothold on their upward climb, in terms of loss of privacy, the inability to plan according to personal feeling, and loneliness. Decisions formerly taken following friendly consultation with equals will have to be made in the personal isolation of a Holt struggling to contain his beleaguered business empire.

As in the other arts, the results of successful management are obvious, its means mysterious. The most unusual character in the pages that follow was Donald Smith, the primitive fur trader who spent the first thirty years of his working life in the Labrador wilderness. Back in civilization, he rose to become governor of the Hudson's Bay Company, helped settle one of the Riel Rebellions and for nearly thirty years, headed the Bank of Montreal. Elevated to become Lord Strathcona, he was the main source of funds for building the CPR, and as a parliamentarian, he cast the vote that defeated Sir John A. Macdonald's Conservative government.

What changes a man or a woman into one of the anointed in the business world is not their move to a seat behind a polished mahogany desk. It is a magical transformation when their hearts and brains no longer have the energy to stay out of constant economic embroilment. This inner frenzy burns so brightly because the entrepreneurs who dominate this book maintained one common faith: they believed that man loses his opportunity for business greatness only when he abandons his quest.

I've drawn the profiles in this unruly collection of mavericks from my chronicles of their adventures and misadventures over my fifty-year career as a muck-raking journalist—an honourable and useful profession yet to be recognized by Canada's controversial national census. All but one is Canadian: Kinky Friedman, of course, was not. He would never have passed his citizenship test, even if he had cheated. But our conversation did take place in Vancouver, and he was such a raw example of Jewish humour on the hoof that he is certainly part of my psyche—and thus belongs in this book.

Maverick is also a subspecies invented for Conrad Black. His life—in or out of jail—has been dedicated to claiming the sense of limitless entitlement that forms his character, governs his actions, propels his pronouncements and allows him to feel superior to everyone except his peers, certain in the knowledge that he has none. When he didn't approve of the charges under which he was convicted at his trial in Chicago, Conrad had the goddamn law changed. That's chutzpah of a rare vintage.

These are snapshots in time, capturing many of these larger-than-life characters as I found them when I first wrote these pieces. Some subsequently changed their lives—and became boringly ordinary. But I am happy to report that none has yet been nominated for sainthood.

PART 1: BUSINESS

A Hitchhiker's Guide to the Mind of Conrad Black

I have been an avid chronicler of Conrad Black's ventures and misadventures for most of three decades, going back to the biography I wrote about him in 1982. He was only 38 then but was flying high, having just completed his daring takeover of Argus Corporation, Hollinger's predecessor that escalated his $7 million inheritance into control over corporate assets worth $4 billion. I called him The Establishment Man, and concluded that his future had no limits, except any he might choose to impose on himself. At the time, Conrad seemed to be an audacious Knight Templar spreading enlightenment on Planet Earth. His later exploits turned him into a brawling metaphor of global media wealth and influence. He claimed iconic status on two continents, bestowing his presence in the manner of latter-day royalty. When his empire came under grinding pressure from unhappy shareholders voicing raucous complaints, he insisted that he was sinless, blameless and as innocent as a baby lamb chewing organic greens on the back of a turnip truck. With singular

*determination and the will not merely to survive but to prevail, Conrad
has fought back from what appeared to almost everyone else as beyond the
brink. Having commented freely on Conrad's convictions, which at press
time were close to being lifted, we must treat his successful bid for freedom
with equal respect. I believe Black leaves his American jail as a better man
with a higher appreciation for Canada. What follows is adapted from my
book* The Establishment Man.

———

EVEN ON THOSE odd occasions when Conrad Black is unexpectedly attuned to other people's sensitivities, he has trouble
differentiating between knowing and feeling, between solitude
and loneliness, between repeating Toronto Club *bons mots* and
forcing the lock of his true emotions. As he moved from being
the upstart megadeal maker to wearing the ermine as Lord Black
of Crossharbour to being imprisoned in an American penitentiary as 18330-424, he exhibited three distinct personalities—his
prison incarnation being the most impressive.

The common denominator of his astonishing life and tur-
bulent times is his uncommon brain. The uncanny ability with
which he can recall at will almost anything he has read, seen
or experienced is a daunting natural gift, like a singer's perfect
pitch or a tightrope walker's sense of balance. Everything he says
and does is monitored through his dazzling talent for remembering obscure facts and fussy details. He reduces casual visitors
and intense acolytes with such bravura sleights-of-mind as rhym-

ing off the tonnages of every ship in the Spanish Armada and the names of their captains; reconstructing John Diefenbaker's 1957 cabinet or reeling off daily casualty reports on both sides of Hitler's bloody siege of Leningrad.

But more often he will resurrect historical incidents, thoughts and examples like a pop archaeologist, evaluating the depth of other people's knowledge by sifting for clues in their reactions to his flights of recall. He is also possessed of an alarmingly accurate ability to imitate friends' and critics' voices, to the point where he can have conversations with himself, sounding exactly like the people he is imitating.

Each of his acquaintances and associates has his own favourite list of items that Black has dredged up from his memory bank, including the salary of each of Sterling Newspapers' six hundred employees; the MPs (by constituency name) who have won Quebec's federal elections since Confederation; the latest ranking of cardinals in the Vatican's Byzantine pecking order; and the fact that Spencer Perceval was the only British prime minister to have been assassinated in office.

John Finlay, one of Conrad's early Hollinger associates, remembered a dinner they had at the Toronto's York Club with Pierre Gousseland, the French-born chairman of Amax, a giant U.S. metal-extracting firm. "Conrad absolutely dazzled him," Finlay recalled, "by going through France's five republics in perfectly fluent French, not just by dates and individual ministers, but their accomplishments and downfalls. This fellow just sat back and listened, spellbound. But after dinner Gousseland had to leave, and we withdrew to the club's drawing room with an Englishman who was the Amax senior vice-president of finance. When it turned out he had served aboard a Royal Navy battle cruiser during the Second World War, Conrad started to go through the British fleet, gun by gun, inch by inch. At one point they were talking about a particularly tense period and Conrad demanded, 'Where were you when that took place?' The Englishman said, 'August 1943? I can't remember.' So Conrad asked him, 'What ship were you on?' As soon as he found out it had been HMS *Renown*, Black shrugged and said, 'Oh, well, you must have been stationed in Gibraltar.' The fellow just wilted."

Jonathan Birks, then the most interesting of the carriage-trade store's inheritors, recalled trying to test his friend's memory. Birks had just finished reading a book on the Bonapartes and, with the volume's family chart before him, telephoned Conrad on the spur of the moment. "Since I had just finished the book and had the Bonaparte family lists on my desk," Birks said, "I figured there was no way I couldn't remember more about Napoleon than he did. So I coyly started in on the subject of Bonaparte, where his family came from, which prince had married what princess and stuff like that. Within twenty minutes, he had exhausted my chart. Obviously talking off the cuff, he went on for another half hour, not only reciting what each man had done but how his later absence would affect the history of the Austro-Hungarian Empire. It was a very humiliating experience."

Peter White, one of Black's original partners in the Sterling newspaper chain, recalled a similar incident when they were

both living in Knowlton and a relative from Britain who had
served as commanding officer of a Royal Navy cruiser dropped
in for a visit. "The subject of some battle that had taken place
in the theatre of war that my uncle had been in came up, and
Conrad said, Oh, yes, such and such ships were in that engagement, weren't they? Uncle Hank disagreed and named the
battle line he thought had fought that long-ago engagement.
But Conrad was adamant. 'I don't think you're right, sir,' he
maintained. They looked it up. Of course, Conrad turned out
to be right, and my uncle, the naval captain who was there,
turned out to be wrong. The longer you know him, the more
often you come across this ability of Conrad's to drag up events,
dates and conversations. He can probably remember every telephone number any of his friends ever had."

Nick Auf der Maur, Conrad's Montreal *bon vivant* friend,
spent most of the 1960s enlisting himself in various radical causes,
including the setting up of a Cuban press office in Canada. "I
recruited this Argentinian guy I knew to be our manager of their
Montreal bureau, and when the head of the Cuban press agency
was in town, I asked them if they'd like to have dinner with a real
live capitalist press baron," he recalled. "I'd built up Conrad as
the owner of a big chain of newspapers, and the Cuban was quite
enthralled by the whole idea. We were chatting away, and at one
point Conrad went to the washroom. So I said, 'You know, Mr.
Black is quite knowledgeable about your part of the world. Just
ask him what he knows about the Argentinian navy, for example.' So when he came back, the Latin visitor asked him about

naval activities surrounding the time of Juan Perón's overthrow. Conrad promptly proceeded not only to reel off the entire fleet and the names of every ship's captain but also where each vessel was manoeuvring on the day of Perón's ouster. The two Latin Americans just sat there, stunned that this weird guy in an Italian Montreal restaurant in 1971 could recite precisely what had happened sixteen years before off Buenos Aires in the Rio de la Plata."

Brian McKenna, another Montreal friend, recalled sitting in on arguments Conrad had with Patrick Brown, who had covered the Vietnam War for the CBC, was married to a Vietnamese woman and had spent years boning up on that strife-torn country's postcolonial history. "Conrad would hold forth not just on the complex politics of Saigon, but he knew the home provinces where each of the various players came from and the details of their political circumstances," McKenna remembered. "It was just as if he were discussing the parish politics of east-end Montreal." When Scott Abbott, sports editor of the *Sherbrooke Daily Record*, spontaneously challenged Conrad to recite the final major league baseball standings for 1953, he spun them off in reverse order, giving the won-lost record of each team and making only one mistake. (Abbott vividly recalled his first meeting with Conrad: "He greeted me by saying, 'I understand you're an American presidential history buff.' When I allowed that I could name all the U.S. presidents with the dates of their administrations, he shot back: 'Yes, but can you do it backwards in thirty seconds?' I gather he could, but I didn't ask.")

The late Igor Kaplan, Conrad's lawyer, had a similar experience when he invited Black to his house during a visit of his European-born mother. "They were discussing the politics of the Weimar Republic when she casually mentioned that it was too bad Gustav Stresemann, the foreign minister of the Weimar Republic, had died so suddenly. Conrad enthusiastically agreed but reminded her that he'd been responsible for almost destroying the Treaty of Locarno. Mother was flabbergasted. 'My God, I'd forgotten that,' she said. 'I was about seventeen when Stresemann came to power. Today there are very few of *my* contemporaries who would remember him because Hitler was the most dominating name in German politics, which makes it even more remarkable that Conrad, who was not even born then, would know details of what the man had been trying to achieve.'"

Kaplan's explanation for Black's phenomenal memory was that Conrad listens and reads with as much energy as most people use for stage acting or orating: "When you're talking to him, Conrad looks directly at you, he never glances away, and he never appears ready to interrupt or answer you." Brian Stewart, a friend from Black's university days, claims that when Conrad is reading, "there's an almost physical sense of concentration that comes over his face. His brows get furrowed—it's as if he was burning up each page."

It is a mental feat implanted during his youth by the habits of Conrad's family. "He used to challenge his father on general questions a lot," Stewart recalled. "I was quite interested in bull-fighting at the time, and even though Conrad had told me that his father knew nothing about it, I asked George Black who he thought the greatest bullfighter of all time had been. He was damned if he was going to admit he wasn't sure. He must have sat there and thought for ten solid minutes before he said: 'I have it: *Manolete*, of course.' It was a good answer, and I vividly remember the two of them, father and son, continually challenging each other on some pretty obscure stuff."

———

PHYSICALLY, IT IS HIS EYES that are Black's most compelling feature. When he gets bored, they grow as blank as the gaze of a Las Vegas croupier—but during negotiations on percentage spreads or while he is trying to dredge up the details of command in the Children's Crusade, they glint with Cromwellian intensity. Their colour is a matter of minor dispute. "I think they're hazel," he contends. "I'm not sure. Even Sir Nevile Henderson in his memoirs refers to Adolf Hitler's eyes as being surprisingly blue, so blue one could become quite lyrical about them if one were a woman. Hitler, of course, had brown eyes. And Henderson's embassy wasn't very successful, in any case." (In any case, Black's eyes are periwinkle grey, a hue found mostly inside gun muzzles.)

His body language is his strongest suit. Anger lends primitive cadence to his limb movements as he paces the floor like a puma in heat. "He has a natural knack of demonstrating personal power, which in a negotiating situation, is a tremendous asset," noted Igor Kaplan. "People pick up the vibrations of that power subconsciously from the way he moves and listens. It's very subtle, but it works." Black has a highly disquieting impact on most businessmen. A fellow Bank of Commerce director, for example, told me that at one executive committee meeting, during which Argus's financial affairs were being discussed and Black had to step outside, "the boardroom reverberated with Conrad's absence."

When he is thinking out the repercussions of a major business move, Black's face clenches like a fist from the effort of trying to turn his brain into a computer that will assess the downside risks of the proposition he is testing. His concentration is diluted by the occasional gleam of mischief, as if he were a paratrooper colonel in a former African dependency who has hit on the notion of selling TV rights to his takeover of the president's palace during a coup he is planning. Having made a decision, he relaxes into his more customary mode of a middle-weight pugilist gone soft. Six feet tall and pudgy-shouldered, he carries himself as awkwardly as if he were crossing a pond of freshly formed ice. In repose, he makes steeples of his fingers and speculates upon the edicts of the universe. He listens so intently to anyone who doesn't bore him to distraction that the echoes of comprehension are visible on his face. "He is intensely verbal," *Fortune* noted in a profile, "speaking in measured cadences and spinning out long sentences that in the end—on the very brink of disintegration—he somehow manages to salvage."

Black's pomposity can grow tiresome, so that one expects him to describe the Air Canada shuttle between Toronto and

Montreal as "a miracle of heavier-than-air locomotion." He reels in his sentences like dancing swordfish; makes up words (*dowagerish*); hones his insults ("I warn you, this man is an insufferable poltroon"); loves to coin epigrams slightly out of plumb ("Nelson Skalbania would be less of a gambler if he actually *had* $100 million"); and concocts pithy quotes ("Now that we've proven we're no good at playing hockey competitively in this country anymore, takeovers have become the great Canadian sport"). He loves to show off his knowledge. "Andreotti is interesting," he once declared to a roomful of Bay Street regulars who thought he was about to glorify the exploits of some newly arrived Neapolitan chef instead of an Italian prime minister. "Andreotti was possibly the most intelligent head of government in the West. Ironically enough, Italy hasn't been administered with any degree of efficiency or consistency since the early middle Roman Empire—yet he has staged a heroic feat of parliamentarianism."

Not for Conrad any *esprit d'escalier*—the belated *bon mot* that comes to mind as one is descending the stairs after a party. The quip is off his tongue with enviable timing. He is a highly complicated character, perhaps best caught in comparisons with painters and composers. Hippolyte Loiseau, the French essayist, once complained that Mozart was the only person who really understood him. With Conrad, it would take the convoluted and occasionally majestic Gustav Mahler, who suffered from a tormented personality, social isolation and inflexibility of purpose but might have understood Black's neuroses. His mental gymnastics can be best comprehended as a subject appropriate to the pointillism of Georges Seurat. The nineteenth-century French neo-Impressionist imbued his paintings with an inner glow through the use of minute brush strokes, meaningless by themselves but startling in their combination. This aura of multi-dimensional complexity, which Black does little to discourage, is an attempt to create his own brand of immunity. Ready to talk or write on any subject at the drop of a split infinitive, he has dug a deep moat to protect his inner child, who, several of his followers believe, is armed with a flame thrower. As an amateur historian, he knows the importance of creating a vacuum around himself, of generating that quality of remoteness that sets any society's memorable figures apart from their lesser cousins. Through all the speculation about his modes and motives, Conrad remains the prisoner of his perpetual search for redemption—all the while remaining as closed off to feelings as a panicked snail. He profoundly resents the intrusions of the curious and the covetous but is much more troubled by the possibility of being ignored. If only.

———

CONRAD BLACK UNDERSTANDS life as a tangle of ambiguities; he is a lapsed fatalist, convinced that people's destinies—most significantly his own—are always more fascinating than their day-to-day reactions. He subscribes to the exquisitely sad comment by the seventeenth-century French satiric moralist Jean de La Bruyère, who wrote that "life is a tragedy for those who feel and a comedy for those who think." He finds it easy—too easy—to believe in clean slates; atonement by any other name. His natural arrogance is both intellectual and egotistical, tinged by his historian's sense of perspective. But at the top of his daily catechism is his ignorance of what to others appears as a law of nature: that acts have consequences, which require the assumption of responsibility. What makes him so interesting is that he follows the strong existential streak in his nature. It leads him beyond mundane preoccupations to inventions of new challenges and rising to meet them—even if he runs the danger of destroying himself in the process.

A random walk through the mind of Conrad Black is no effortless journey. The Protestant work ethic may be his Holy Grail (in the sense that *achieving* is not a dirty word), but Conrad aims both higher (having at one time nominated himself as the chief animator of Canada's proprietor class) and lower (by observing the entire scene as something of a game that he happens to be better at than any of the other players). That's players, not peers. He has none. Or at least doesn't recognize any.

He has trouble working out any form of understandable motivation for himself, returning always to his pride in not having inherited all his money and his contempt for rich men's sons who consume their resources. "I'm rich and I'm not ashamed of being wealthy," he kept telling me, as if the words were some form of verbal amulet to ward off the plague. "Why should I be? I made all my money fairly."

Most Canadian businessmen are about as introspective as

lion tamers. That minority of thoughtful executives who somehow manage to juggle their ideals and ambitions tend to be
Rhodes-scholar types, affecting upper-class Anglicanism, mid-
Atlantic accents and a strain of transient piety to sustain their
compromised view of life. Conrad Black is different. A conservative to the core of his being, he has what his late Montreal
friend Nick Auf der Maur used to call "this weird little egalitarian
streak. He's insufferable with people he thinks are stupid, dull
or a waste of time. But if somebody's interesting or if he thinks
he can glean some unfathomable mystery of a current trend in
society, he can be quite charming. I introduced him to people in
bars where he'd get the idea he might learn about the workings
of twentieth-century depraved minds or something, and he'd sit
there for hours asking questions like a crown prosecutor, trying
to find out exactly what was up."

At the same time Black has big trouble connecting with
ordinary people in everyday situations—as if he suffered from
psychic jet lag whenever he has to face anyone real. There is in
his bearing Jehovian pride that expresses itself by complicat-
ing the simplest of human exchanges. He suffers from what the
French call *l'orgueil*—an untranslatable quality of the thirst to
play God that implies its possessor is seldom wrong and never
regretful. "I may make mistakes, but at the moment I can't think
of any," Conrad admitted in one of our many interviews. When
a close friend asked Black, then at the height of his infatuation
with French Canada's social renaissance, "If you're so interested
in politics, why don't you run for premier of Quebec?" Conrad

thought it over for a moment. Then he replied, "Quebec's not ready for me. Maybe Spain."

Franco aside, the riposte was an uncharacteristic over-simplification. Black's view of the political process is far more comprehensive than his wisecrack implied. He is one of the few elitists with the wit and intellect to sort his beliefs and preju-dices into some kind of credible philosophical context. "Because intellectuals dominate the power of the word, the conservative philosophy of capitalists has made a very poor showing in the recent history of ideas," he maintains. "Whenever businessmen have tried to defend themselves with words, they have tended to bellow ultra-right clichés like wounded dinosaurs, much to the amusement of the intellectual left. John Stuart Mill labelled the Conservative party in England the 'stupid party'; the truth is that until recently conservative ideas were so poorly articulated that they simply weren't taken seriously." Conrad places himself firmly in the stream of neo-conservatism, alongside Bernard-Henri Lévy, Daniel Bell, Norman Podhoretz, Irving Kristol and their Canadian disciples, such as the indomitable David Frum, who can make readers shudder whenever he is away on assignment and his column space simply carries the foreboding message: David Frum Will Return.

When Kristol spoke in Toronto at an Insurance Bureau of Canada banquet, Black, in his introduction, told the story of the visit to Canada of their friend and fellow traveller, the late William F. Buckley Jr. "He came here to debate with David Lewis, the former leader of our New Democratic Party," Conrad said,

"and when he arrived at Toronto airport, the immigration officer asked, 'What is the purpose of your visit?'

"Buckley countered, 'To de-socialize Canada.'

"With the usual phlegmatic manner of those airport people,
the officer responded not at all to that but moved on to ask what
the duration of the visit would be.

"'Twenty-four hours,' Buckley smoothly replied."

———

CONRAD BLACK'S IDEOLOGICAL roots stretch back to
the stern political doctrines of Great Britain's Whigs—the land-
owning families who held power in eighteenth-century England
under the early Georges, mixing their reliance on individual
enterprise with such touches of reform as the belief in a constitutional monarchy instead of divine-right absolutism. Whiggism
developed in the United States in the early nineteenth century,
uniting some eastern capitalists, southern plantation owners
and pragmatic predecessors of the Republican party. "There is
a bit of the Whig in me," Black admits, "but I tend to be more
conservative than those people, not really believing in their style
of Jeffersonian free thinking. I'm also more of a humanist. I'm
offended at Jefferson, for example, sitting there at Monticello
with all his slaves, agonizing over whether to free them, talking
about how the tree of liberty must be refreshed from time to time
with the blood of patriots and tyrants. There is some non-iden-
tification for me in that, but there's also some truth in it." *Huh?*

During the Liberal ascendancy, when most Canadian tycoons felt that if Ottawa politicians (especially the "soft lefties")could organize it, there would be a bounty on business tycoon's scalps, Conrad's convoluted chatter had a soothing effect—even if few of the Toronto Club regulars privy to his musings had any idea what he was talking about.

Black interrupted his theory spinning with another thought: "Perhaps we're all waiting for a new Karl Marx to emerge from the reading room of the British Museum with the canons of a new order, reconciling the more popular elements of capitalism and socialism." Then he added: "While we await that event, those of us who are preoccupied with both commerce and the humanities may reflect on the curious unevenness of our blessings. We still have the wealthiest and most creative society in the history of the world, but never have relations between the commercial and cultural leadership weighed more heavily. Businessmen tend to think that the government people, elected or otherwise, are either sleazy politicians or officious, intermeddling bureaucrats. The government people tend to regard businessmen as absolute dullards—avaricious boobies advancing forward like a bear to a honey pot, with no interest except gluttony. A mutual reduction of suspicions would be a good thing."

———

BLACK CAN (AND DOES) go on for hours, drawing out analogies, both defending capitalism's achievements and condemning its less attractive by-products. "When I noted several years ago at Christmastime that Walter Cronkite's newscast was sponsored in part by an electric denture-cleaning device, I had a profound conviction that the trajectory of this society simply could not continue," he recalls, then warms to his subject: "We have called upon our entire workforce to maintain traditional bourgeois standards of artisanship, thrift and respect for the work ethic while on the job. And they are encouraged after hours to transform themselves from economic Jekyll to Hyde, becoming profligate and consumptive spenders and swingers, to maintain the system at a breakneck pace of production and self-indulgence."

Although Black likes to parade himself as a Renaissance man, open to the winds of thought from any direction, the character into which he fits most easily is his role model, the late William F. Buckley Jr. For example: "I'm terribly impatient with that New York–Washington group of small-l liberals who fail to recognize the increasing danger to our civilization. By 'civilization' I'm not referring to whether corporate income taxes are 40 percent or 60 percent. I mean that which fundamentally differentiates North American society from others. These people are so full of good intentions, so talented and admirable, yet they have the utmost difficulty in recognizing the danger of our position. To me, the United States before Ronald Reagan represented the most precipitate decline of the relevance of any major country since the fall of France in 1940."

In the spring of 1981, Conrad attended the annual Bilderberg Conference, a private gabfest that usually brings together the free world's most influential citizens, including David Rockefeller and Henry Kissinger. He was gratified to be thanked by Jeane Kirkpatrick, the U.S. ambassador to the United Nations, for his championing of the Reagan administration's foreign policy. "As my last intervention at the conference," he boasted, "I said that I thought Ronald Reagan was going to re-establish the United States as unquestionably the greatest economic and military power in the world, which is what it should be."

Later that year, when Black and his then wife, Shirley, put on an entertainment at the Art Gallery of Ontario for Andy Warhol, who had just completed painting several portraits of Conrad, one of the attending guests was Thomas O. Enders, U.S. assistant secretary of state for inter-American affairs. An old friend of the Blacks from his term as American ambassador to Canada, Enders was at the time masterminding the U.S. response to the military escalation in El Salvador and had been involved with the Cambodian bombings during the Vietnam War. In his brief remarks to the gathering, Conrad complained that it was a pity Enders hadn't taken his advice on how to conduct the war in Southeast Asia. A remark in response to which Gaetana, Enders' outspoken wife, yelled out: "If Tom had, the war would have lasted even longer!" The point was never resolved, but Black had been advocating early mining of Haiphong harbour and a general escalation of hostilities against the North "instead of having all those American draftees slogging around the jungles of South Vietnam."

Black prefers tidiness in human affairs above all else. He yearns for order. The countries he admires run on time. It's the *results* that matter, not the manner in which political power is exercised. That's why his admiration of Napoleon, for example, is expressed not so much in terms of battlefield victories as by recounting the rise in France's health and literacy rates during the Bonaparte regime. Criticism of Maurice Duplessis's autocratic rule is countered by Black's remonstrations about the miles of highway paved and the number of kilowatts of electric generation added to Quebec during his time in office. His short list of political heroes illustrates Black's propensity for seeing history as determined not by mass movements or the struggle of eco-political forces but by wilful acts of eccentric leaders, royal whim and sets of confluent intrigues. He has scant confidence in the perfectibility of man and no faith at all in the perfection of doctrine. But he does hold fast in supporting authoritarian figures who were unafraid to proclaim the grandeur of their dreams: politicians and conquerors who launched themselves on impossible missions and survived.

He has a weakness for grand gestures. "There is something in the belated recognition of greatness that gives me a vicarious pleasure," he confides. "For example, André Malraux writes of going to see Charles de Gaulle at Colombey-les-Deux-Églises when he was in political exile. He had refused his premier's pension and only had his retirement income as a two-star general, which wasn't particularly great. Although de Gaulle liked wine, most of his supply had gone off, and when he opened a bottle, it had turned to vinegar. Being de Gaulle, he betrayed no dismay; he was determined to drink the vinegar and pretend it was palatable. So he said, 'Malraux, you take wine, I believe.'

"Malraux replied, 'Not in your house, *mon général.*'

"Of course, only two years after that, de Gaulle was back in the Élysée Palace and could have any vintage he wanted."

Conrad's admiration for acts of vindication is reflected in the proximity of a large bronze bust of Marshal Ferdinand Foch that sat on the windowsill of his Toronto office. "I've always been impressed with him," explained Black, "not really for his talents as a general but with his determination. As a young student at the Jesuit seminary of Saint-Clément in Metz, he was writing his graduating exams in 1871 when the sound of the German guns announced that Metz had become part of the German Empire. He saw Napoleon III being driven through the town in his carriage, sick, having been defeated at Sedan. It was forty-seven years later, as a French marshal and commander-in-chief of the Allied Forces in the First World War, that Foch re-entered Metz, and on November 11, 1918, that his conditions for an armistice were accepted at Compiègne."

Black truly admires only Mackenzie King among Canadian politicians. "He sincerely believed he was the instrument of divine providence—and people who can talk themselves into such a preposterous notion or slide into such a self-image without at the same time becoming otherworldly in their day-to-day activities are vested with quite powerful self-management." Black bestows considerable credit on Pierre Trudeau as a national leader not afraid to swim against history's currents. At the same time he vigorously condemns the Liberal prime minister's economic policies, though he regarded the use of the War Measures Act in

1970 as his major positive achievement. "The greatest problem with Trudeau as statesman," he maintains, "was not that he was a subversive or arrogant or that he was any of the other things his critics accuse him of. It's that he was so unoriginal. I read everything he ever wrote in his days as editor of *Cité Libre*. It was a mishmash of in-jokes and conceited little asides. Occasionally, there was an elegant phrase but never once anything that was original. Never."

True to his admiration for historical figures who fail to achieve their destinies, Black did write one friendly private letter to Trudeau just after the Liberal leader's electoral defeat:

> Dear Mr. Trudeau:
>
> I am taking the liberty of writing to you to offer a word of encouragement at this extraordinary moment in the history of our country and in the evolution of your own career. My motive is not any presumption that such sentiments are necessary, but my hope is that you will find this a refreshing expression of a widespread sentiment. All Canadians must be grateful to you for what you have achieved for them in the past. And most will be hopeful that, whatever the future may hold, you will still be available, as General de Gaulle said of Georges Pompidou in 1968, "*dans la réserve de la nation.*"

The following excerpt from a letter written by Cardinal Villeneuve to Maurice Duplessis, following the latter's defeat in 1939, may have some applicability in these circumstances:

"Fortunes have been reversed. But that does not change the man you were yesterday, a man with faults but also remarkable qualities of heart and spirit, a foundation of sound ideas, of aptitudes for government, a statesman . . . In spite of the appearances and in spite of the disappointments that could also be added, who knows if the future does not reserve a new power and you will come again with wisdom which will be the proof."

Trudeau, then leader of the Opposition, replied almost immediately:

I have played many roles in my time, but none were as delightfully unexpected as playing Duplessis to your Villeneuve. As his biographer, you are undoubtedly aware that poor Maurice will feel even hotter than his environment when he finds out that words of encouragement sent to him have now been addressed to one of his former tormentors.

In turn, may I encourage you in your recent efforts to lend credibility to the intellectual right. I realize it's an uphill battle, but the reward is worth the struggle. The reward, of course, is that every able conservative who has seriously applied his mind to his philosophy has eventually and inevitably turned into a liberal.

———

DE GAULLE AND NAPOLEON remain two of Conrad's favourites, and he will use any excuse to repeat long passages from their writings and communiqués. But most of his idols are Americans, going back to Abraham Lincoln. "He conducted four battles at once: the war between the states, the war with the radical Congress, the war with his wife, who was a mental case, and the war with his own doubts about himself." Conrad's favourite historical quotation is from one of Lincoln's addresses: "You cannot bring about prosperity by discouraging thrift. You cannot strengthen the weak by weakening the strong. You cannot help the wage-earner by pulling down the wage-payer. You cannot help the poor by destroying the rich. You cannot establish sound security on borrowed money. You cannot build character and courage by taking away man's initiative and independence. You cannot help men permanently by doing for them what they could do for themselves."

Conrad was also inordinately fond of Richard Nixon, more offended by his banality than by his evil. "Nixon's problem was basically psychological and he deserves the compassion due to sick people. He was sleazy, tasteless, and neurotic, but I thought he had one partially redeeming virtue: he had the mind of a foreigner. While he spoke in idealistic terms, he knew that it was all a bunch of bunk. That the world just wanted to steal America's money and use it. I don't find Adolf Hitler a frequent source of quotations, but he had this one truly great line that he uttered in his private train when he was leaving France in July 1940 after his one and only visit to Paris. This was in that movie *The*

Sorrow and the Pity—it's just the announcer saying it, we don't have Hitler's voice for it, and for all I know it may have been invented by these Communist French movie producers. He was sitting in his car while they changed engines when some people on the platform recognized the Führer and started to applaud. He said to his companions: 'Look at them, the French, they're trying to pick my pocket. They don't realize I'm the greatest pickpocket in Europe.' Nixon was a little like that, but in a much more exalted way. He was canalized to purposes that were objectively admirable. His paranoia, I felt, was almost endearing when he summarily ordered Kissinger to submit the entire State Department to lie detector tests."

But his sentimental choice, the only major American political figure he has publicly defended, was former Democrat president Lyndon Baines Johnson. "I felt a real sympathy for him because of the merciless attacks upon him that drove him out of office and because of what I thought to be a tremendously statesmanlike stance that he, as a wealthy white Southerner, took toward civil rights and the issue of poverty in general." Black first encountered Johnson during the 1964 Democratic National Convention at Atlantic City. His friend Peter White (then executive assistant to forestry minister Maurice Sauvé, who belonged to the Canada–United States Interparliamentary Group) had two tickets to the convention's VIP section. Sauvé couldn't leave Ottawa, so White arranged for Black and Brian Stewart, a CBC National News reporter, to go instead. "Conrad went absolutely to the wire with LBJ," Stewart remembered. "It sounds a little histrionic now, but he felt that everything he believed in politically was under assault, and he couldn't enter a discussion anywhere without getting into a screaming match, which happened frequently. Conrad fervently subscribed to the domino theory. He was convinced that the Vietnam war wasn't being accurately reported by the media and that the Americans had a perfectly legitimate right, in fact a duty, to defend Vietnam, the same way they would defend Europe."

On August 25, 1969, a few weeks after Black purchased the *Sherbrooke Daily Record,* Conrad cleared out six columns of advertising to make room for a lengthy accolade he had written marking Johnson's sixty-first birthday. Headlined "A Year after Chicago: Homage to LBJ," the article was a prolonged tirade against the former president's many critics, including Norman Mailer ("the bedraggled warhorse of American blowhardism"); Stewart Alsop ("one of the more torrential snivellers of the American press"); Jesse Unruh ("the mere gross appearance of this man indicates that he has had his front feet in the trough long enough"); and "the cavernously pontifical" Walter Lippmann. Black's obsequious tribute ended with this emotional paragraph: "Johnson's abdication, like that of Cincinnatus, was a classic example of the voluntary surrender of great power, a very dramatic act in history, as in the theatre. All knew that a titan had passed whose like would not be seen again. His talents, his ego, his compassion, determination and capacity for work were, like his services to the nation and his much-caricatured ears, very prominent."

The information officer of the U.S. consulate general in

Montreal sent the eulogy to Johnson, whose long-time crony
Congressman J.J. "Jake" Pickle of Austin, Texas, read it into
the Congressional Record. A year later, Black decided to view
Vietnam for himself and asked Pickle to help facilitate his tour.
The congressman had been so delighted to discover an articulate
supporter of the Southeast Asian War that he brought Black's trip
to the personal attention of William P. Rogers, then U.S. secretary
of state. "When I arrived at the gate of the U.S. embassy in Saigon
and announced my name," Conrad remembered, "the sentry on
duty stood bolt upright as only a Marine can and barked into a
telephone, 'Mr. Black is here!' It was like the meeting of Stanley
and Livingstone. After a few moments, someone came running
down the hall, waving a telegram from the secretary of state, representing me as a personal friend of LBJ's."

The U.S. ambassador arranged for Black to interview Nguyen
Van Thieu, then president of Vietnam, whose awareness of the
circulation and editorial clout of the *Sherbrooke Daily Record* must
have been somewhat sketchy. He chose the occasion to reveal,
for the first time, that he intended to run for re-election, that
he planned to discipline his generals involved in black market
operations and outlined, in some detail, the complicity of the
Kennedy administration in the overthrow of President Ngo Dinh
Diem. "I liked Thieu," Conrad recalled. "He showed me around
the palace. He was obviously a bit of a rascal, but I admired his
courage. My interview turned out to be one of the biggest news
stories of the war." (After being published first in Sherbrooke,
the Thieu story made front-page news in the *New York Times* and

Le Monde in Paris, eventually reaching a worldwide audience.)

Black lived out his Vietnamese tour in Saigon's Caravelle Hotel. "I'd have my dinner on the roof," he recalled. "The Caravelle really had an excellent cuisine. You'd see in the distance planes dropping flares that turned night into day. Then I'd go down to my room and see, *live* by satellite from Dodger Stadium, the latest baseball game. During the day I'd go out to Tan Son, then one of the world's busiest airports, watch six Phantom-5s take off abreast, then be invited to hop on a B-52 and fly out to the Cambodian border or something. It was surrealistic."

"Somewhat to his embarrassment," Brian Stewart says, "Conrad came back to announce that the war was as good as over. *'We've won it,'* he kept saying. What he didn't anticipate was the collapse of American resolve, and that absolutely shook him. He came out of the Vietnam era somewhat battered and certainly exhausted by the whole debate."

———

BLACK'S RELATIONSHIP WITH the press is reminiscent of Jean-Luc Godard's comment about the Gallic temperament: that "the essence of the French character is not to reveal but to withhold." Conrad's sense of friends and enemies within the media is powerful and violently ambivalent. He has enjoyed his high profile, yet every six months or so he would proclaim that he is going permanently underground, refusing to acknowledge even routine press queries. Friends in Montreal remembered a New Year's Eve party where he announced that he was going to become a celebrity—the William F. Buckley Jr. of Canada. Suddenly, Conrad was a force to be reckoned with, becoming one of those quotable people who appeared, as if by magic, on CBC radio and network television panels. Exposed to unwanted press coverage as both subject and object, he has vehemently protested against such attention—yet he deliberately created a public persona of precisely the man he wanted to be, realizing that anonymity and a sense of style were not compatible. Unlike most people, who cross their Hush Puppies and in silent supplication ask themselves, "Who in God's name am I?" Conrad was one of those rare fortunate individuals who, at long last, came to being on good terms with himself. His ego no longer leaked.

Although Black has remained anxious to feed the chimeras of his own legend, he genuinely longed for privacy. Yet even on his first wedding night, reporters were camped outside his bedroom window until four in the morning. Asked, as he frequently is, "Are you *the* Conrad Black?" he would reply, "No. I am *a* Conrad Black." Once, just to get away from it all, the Blacks decided to take a lightning holiday in Hawaii. At every stop along the way, somebody spotted them, but finally they reached the safety of the Royal Hawaiian Hotel. They sprinted happily down to the beach. A split second after they had settled with that first deep sigh of sunny relaxation, a man on the next chaise longue held out a hairy paw and said, "Hi, Conrad." He turned out to be a debenture dealer from Greenshields, hustling Dome preferreds.

Before gaining the Argus and later the Hollinger crown,

Conrad encouraged the beatification of his achievements, testing the arc of his authority, trying to impress his elders. Once safely ensconced in power, he revolted against the notion of having been created by any force except his own brilliance and savagely turned on his former boosters. In a private letter to the editor of the *Globe and Mail*, complaining about an article written by Hugh Anderson in *Report on Business*, Black wrote: "I do express my gratitude to Hugh Anderson for attacking my 'whiz-kid reputation.' This is certainly not my self-image, nor a role I ever aspired to, and is a spontaneous fabrication of the media, including Anderson himself."

While Black has admired a very few individual journalists, he despises their profession. "My experience of the working press," he once declared, "is that they're a very degenerate group. There is a terrible incidence of alcoholism and drug abuse. The mental stability of large elements of the press is more open to question than that of many other comparable groups in society. A number of them are ignorant, lazy, opinionated, intellectually dishonest, and inadequately supervised." Then he got wound up. "The individual journalist, if he has any panache or talent, becomes something of a celebrity. Much of his social life is built up on the press-circuit: bars, hangers-on, media groupies, the stifling and depraved gossip of the degenerate little media community, and the fawning of unfulfilled women, boys, and hucksters. Journalism tends to attract the sort of person who settles whimsically on it as a calling or comes to it after disappointments elsewhere, because of the relative ease of entry to the field. These people, discouraged and purposeless, are easily influenced by their angrier colleagues. It is by inadvertence, inexperience, the investigative nature of the press, the antithetical role of the employee, and the negligence of the employer, and not by any organized subversion, that the press veered away from being a mirror to society, and became a perverse sort of irregular and often disloyal opposition."

Okay. I quit.

————

THE MIND THAT DRIVES him is a remarkable instrument. But it is fuelled by his sense of entitlement, which is at the root of Conrad Black's belief system and the source of his troubles. It governs everything he does, says and writes. He believes himself to be the vanguard of a new social order, superior to everyone else, a breed apart that abides no equals.

It was precisely this attitude that contributed to his convictions and sentencing in Chicago, which at the time this book is going to press, remains under appeal. When he was being sentenced by Judge Amy St. Eve, she declared: "No one is immune from the proper application of law—and that, Mr. Black, includes you." This admonition was meant to be more than just a shot across his elegant bow; it was meant to remind the gracious Lord that he was one of us.

No way, José. On appeals all the way to the United States Supreme Court, Conrad and his lawyers set out to change the law that the jury had been told was enough to find him guilty of fraud: depriving Hollinger and its shareholders of his "honest services." When the highest court agreed that this type of fraud had been used too broadly, it granted Conrad what he had always considered to be his entitlement: another chance to have the lower Court of Appeals set aside his convictions. And with that court's quick decision to release him on bail, he awaits the outcome as a (relatively) free man. While this book goes to press, before the final result is known, what is certain is that Conrad will continue to maintain his complete innocence, as he has done with resolution from the outset. You've got to admire his staying power. My favourite tableaux from Conrad Black's glory days were the games of croquet he played on the manicured lawn of his Toronto mansion with some of his illustrious peers, including Brigadier Richard S. Malone, then publisher of the *Globe and Mail*. It was his only sport, ideally staged on balmy summer evenings by the glow of Chinese lanterns, like a Monet painting, with the women in long lace dresses and the men cosseted in their blazers with their regimental crests, batting away.

When he was flying high, Lord Black became an elitist brand with what he imagined would be an unlimited mandate. His future appeared limitless. He had completed his daring takeover of Argus Corporation, multiplying the $7 million he'd inherited from his family into control over corporate assets worth $4 billion. He qualified on all counts—including membership in the Toronto Club, which has since been withdrawn. He misjudged his country and his times. He acted like an aristocrat, and lived like one, in a society that prided itself on being classless or, as

George Orwell so memorably put it, on belonging to the "lower-upper-middle" class.

The beginning of the end was his appointment, in the autumn of 2001, to Westminster's upper chamber as Lord Black of Crossharbour after he had jettisoned his Canadian citizenship without the slightest twinge of concern. Once encased in his ermine robe (which was real, not dyed rabbit fur, as worn by other, more impecunious lords), he began to act as though he had joined a higher order of humanity. Thus his declaration when climbing aboard one of his private jets: "I'm not prepared to re-enact the French Revolutionary renunciation of the rights of nobility."

That was how he saw himself: as a late-blooming member of an aristocracy in its most self-indulgent incarnation. His best known photograph (apart from the security-camera shots of him removing thirteen boxes of private papers from his offices) was taken on July 1, 2000, when he and Barbara Amiel attended an 18th-century-style ball at Kensington Palace, dressed as the notorious Cardinal Richelieu and the luxury-obsessd Marie Antoinette. According to Jane Fryer, writing in the *Daily Mail,* their choice of historical figures "represented everything that was flamboyant, pompous and arrogant about the press baron and his galmorous wife."

It all came down to his sense of entitlement. Conrad considered himself one of the anointed, superior to the rest of us. He convinced himself that he was immune to the mundane regulations that govern ordinary behaviour, not because he was an outlaw, but because he couldn't be bothered to follow the pedestrian edicts that govern our pedestrian lives. He was governed by a brash, mile-wide streak of righteousness, a glut of self-confidence that transcended run-of-the-mill arrogance. Because he had so much, he felt he should have it all. Within his imperious bearing, there thrived a decided inclination toward avarice that, like Bab's love of luxury, knew no bounds. Such a profound sense of privilege turned out to be as passé as the divine right of kings—or "divine right of things" according to the Amiel version.

Absolute power no longer holds men or causes. Privilege has to be earned; it is no longer granted. American playwright Arthur Miller noted that "an era can be said to end when its basic illusions are exhausted." Conrad Black's sentencing provided precisely that occasion. We should feel grateful to him for turning our smug, self-dealing elite into a rambunctious, globally minded platoon of bottom-line feeders, determined to earn their keep. He will become their poster boy on how not to conduct their business, or their private lives.

Out of his truly spectacular early success, there developed a smugness not only unworthy of his heroes—Napoleon, de Gaulle and Buckley—but of himself. At the end of my final interview for the book I wrote about his first thirty-five years as an earthling, I asked Conrad Black how he felt about what he had done. "Short of death, imprisonment or demonstrable insanity," he replied, cloistered in his ego: "I'd say we were in a pretty good position."

One out of three ain't bad.

—1982, 2010

Sir George Simpson: The Birchbark Napoleon

A BASTARD BY birth and by persuasion, George Simpson dominated the Hudson's Bay Company during its four most crucial decades, when it was expanding its dominion over one-twelfth of the earth's land surface. He was the agent of its inordinate growth, its muscular ethic that overwhelmed friends and foes alike. "To dare and dare again" ought to have been his motto—though his family crest bore the enigmatic inscription *Avis nutrior* ("I am fed by birds"). Birds had nothing to do with it. He was one of the few mercenary adventurers (outside the madhouses) who lived up to his Napoleonic illusions. Except that he didn't carry his right arm bent under his vest, he *was* a bushleague Napoleon who never met his Waterloo.

On reality's scale his triumphs were more commercial than military—though his tactics had touches of both. Simpson triumphed over the more adaptable Nor'Westers, the HBC's only serious competitors, by employing battlefield tactics originally followed by his Corsican idol: that one must never interfere with the enemy while he is in the process of destroying himself, which was exactly what his overextended, undercapitalized rivals were busy doing. A painting of the French emperor decorated the anteroom of Simpson's office. Like his idol, the wilderness autocrat laid claim to uncommon privilege, nurtured by the obsequiousness of his lieutenants in the field, deferring to his certitudes. In height and bearing, he even resembled history's "Little Emperor," except that his dreams of glory were realized, while his role model languished in exile.

Simpson's darting eyes betrayed the canine tensions of a setter constantly on point; his hair, which had the consistency of gun-metal-grey fleece, curled tightly against the back of his neck. John Henry Lefroy, who toured the Canadian Northwest in 1843, noted that Simpson was the toughest-looking hombre he had ever seen, "built upon the Egyptian model. Like one of those short, square massy pillars one sees in an old country church, he is a fellow whom nothing will kill." His legions of critics reviled George Simpson as a malevolent wraith—ruthless, chauvinistic and petty. Yet if the history of countries and great institutions flows from an interplay between character and circumstance, he was the right man in exactly the right place at precisely the right time.

His style of buccaneering capitalism belonged less to an age than to a system. At a time when the HBC's international counterparts—the once-glorious East India Company and similar concerns—were collapsing beneath administrative overloads, Simpson's whip hand was transforming a fur-trading enterprise into an ornament of empire. Its outriders carried the Union Jack (with its identifying HBC initials sewn into the fly) across the North American continent, all the way down to San Francisco and across half the Pacific to Hawaii. While the early patriots of a Canada born in the ancient fiefdoms of the St. Lawrence basin were struggling for responsible government, Simpson became a one-man agent of manifest destiny, surging across the boundless reaches of his domain and claiming its treasures for the London-based Company of Adventurers.

Following four decades of deadly competition with the Nor'Westers, the highly independent traders out of Montreal, Simpson established his firm supremacy by dispatching his most ruthless search-and-destroy teams into the outer reaches of his empire with orders to eliminate putative rivals. The territories south and east of the Columbia River, which Simpson believed might one day be claimed by the United States, were trapped clean in a deliberate scorched-earth tactic, meant to confound the American mountain men. Where encroachment by other activities, such as lumbering in the Ottawa Valley or fishing in the Great Lakes, already existed, the HBC launched itself into these enterprises, absorbing sizable deficits to capture these loss leaders and keep his opponents at bay.

To diversify the Company's holdings, he started the first factory farms on North America's West Coast and even sold ice to Californians. In the 1850s, when San Francisco's population was swollen by the local Gold Rush and ice still had to be shipped around Cape Horn, the HBC leased glaciers in the northern Pacific to American entrepreneurs, who cut and shipped the ice south. It proved such a success for meat preservation that at one time a fleet of six large HBC vessels participated in the trade.

Within the galaxy of his personal universe, the Company meant everything, but Simpson's psyche was more complicated than that. Like some orange-headed magpie with quivering beak and glittery eye, he hoarded private grievances against anyone brave enough to question his iron will. He was a masterly politician, picking his surrogates and underlings with a view to perpetuating the personality feuds that would leave him in place as the one indispensable presence. He played his associates off against one another and, like most charismatic leaders, maintained a luminous distance between himself and lesser associates. He was so determined to retain this aura of mystery that even in 1841, when he was knighted and the editor of Dod's *Peerage, Baronetage and Knightage* requested the usual personal details required for publication, Sir George refused to supply anything beyond his name, position and address.

———

THE SMALL ARTS of popularity found little place in Simpson's business makeup. He was in charge of a wilderness empire under siege by jealous competitors and regarded any form of corporate welfare as something good only for spayed weaklings. His

servants—and few occupied territories have ever been held by
such a thinly spread garrison—were mostly stolid Orkneymen,
Métis on short-term contracts and ambitious but inexperienced apprentice clerks. To parlay such a corporal's guard into
an effective work and occupation force required an iron man.
His audacity, his compulsive work habits and the brute force of
his manner when he was riled left lesser men gasping for forgiveness, but it was seldom forthcoming. He had little patience
with underlings brazen enough to suggest that considerations
other than the maximization of HBC profit (such as the welfare
of the Indians) might govern the conduct of the fur trade. "It
had occurred to me," he wrote to one would-be emancipator, his
quill pen dripping with sarcasm, "that philanthropy is not the
exclusive object of our visits to these Northern regions."

The main reason Simpson aroused so much loathing among
his contemporaries was his obsession with "OEconomy"—his
Draconian version of cost cutting—which was precisely what was
needed to get the business back on track and thus earned him
such high esteem among the Company's London proprietors—if
not among the people actually on the ground. No detail escaped
Simpson's attention. Leaky boats, the proper manner of observing the Sabbath, declining buffalo tongue harvests, the going
rate for Mexican silver dollars, how much mustard should (or
should not) be used at each post, tea rations, even cutlery audits
were dealt with in the minutest fashion, with primitive spoons
and forks expected to last six years. The Natives who represented
the bulk of the HBC's labour force were treated like slaves. "I

have made it my study to examine the nature and character of the Indians and however repugnant it may be to our feelings," Simpson wrote in his private journal, "I am convinced they must be ruled with a rod of iron, to bring and to keep them in a proper state of subordination, and the most certain way to effect this is by letting them feel their dependence upon us. In the woods and Northern barren grounds this measure ought to be pursued rigidly next year if they do not improve, and no credit, not so much as a load of ammunition, given them until they exhibit an inclination to renew their habits of industry." (To impress the Indians, Simpson had a tiny music box attached to his dog's neck in such a way that when it was wound up, music seemed to come from the animal's throat. Generations later, the Carrier tribe was still referring to George Simpson as "the great chief whose dog sings.")

Unlike his principals in London, Simpson was no absent landlord but spent much of his time whizzing around his empire aboard one of his express canoes, manned by a praetorian guard of Iroquois boatmen from the Caughnawaga (Kahnawake) band across the St. Lawrence from Lachine, Quebec. A dozen men paddling at speeds up to sixty strokes a minute could propel the boats, each measuring thirty-three feet, ninety to a hundred miles a day. In 1889 the remains of the *Rob Roy* were discovered at Fort Timiskaming. Measuring seven fathoms (forty-two feet) long, it was authenticated as one of Simpson's personal craft— the largest birchbark canoe ever built.

The governor's travels were legendary. During all but three

of the thirty-nine years he spent in charge of the HBC's fur trade, Simpson ranged across the continent in furiously paced forays, inspecting each post, hectoring discouraged factors, preaching the doctrine of cost efficiency and enjoying every minute of it. He was constantly in motion. He crossed the Rockies at three latitudes, made eight visits to Boston and New York, and three great journeys to forts on the Columbia River in the Oregon Country. His most trying trek was by snowshoe during the winter of 1822–23, when he stomped through deep drifts from Lake Athabasca to Great Slave Lake and back, up the Peace River to Fort Dunvegan and across Lesser Slave Lake to Edmonton House. Simpson loved being on the move, wafting through the melodious forests of the great Northwest, dictating memoranda to his accompanying secretaries and being treated everywhere like a resplendent emperor on an imperial progress. "It is strange," Simpson once wrote to his friend John George McTavish, "that all my ailments vanish as soon as I seat myself in a canoe."

Simpson drove his crews sixteen hours or more a day, determined to demonstrate his own immunity to human weakness and demanding by example that they do the same. "*Levez! Levez! Levez, nos gens!*" he would call out at two or three o'clock in the morning before plunging into some nearby lake or river to flaunt his own *joie de vivre*. After that morning dip and half a dozen hours of hard paddling, he would call a brief halt for breakfast and, three or four hours later, another for a quick lunch, his crewmen munching pemmican while he sat back and allowed his manservants to present him with tasty tidbits and wine. The governor had a habit of dozing off between meals, but his crews were never allowed to relax. While he appeared to be asleep, he would trail the fingers of one hand over the canoe gunwale, testing the cruising speed by noting how high the water splashed up his wrist. The killing pace never let up. One steersman became so exasperated on one of the longer stretches that he picked the governor up by the collar, lifted him over his head and pitched him into the river—then, with immediate remorse, dove in to help him out. Paradoxically, Simpson never had any trouble recruiting crews of men proud to test their endurance.

He set speed records that have never been beaten (or even attempted), and when he ran out of challenges in North America, he embarked on a voyage around the world. He was the first man to circle the earth by what was then called the "overland route"—and was thought to have been a model for the hero of Jules Verne's *Around the World in Eighty Days.*

One reason for his whirling-dervish approach was that Simpson wanted to catch his post managers off guard so he could check up on them. To heighten the patrician impact of his presence at the woebegone little forts, Simpson arrived at each stop with a sequence of punctilious flourishes worthy of a pope presuming worship. The pomp always outdid the circumstance. Simpson's party, which usually included an escorting canoe or two, would put in to shore just before entering a settlement, to give the governor time to don his beaver topper and his paddlers a moment to spruce up in their best shirts. Ready and set, they would sweep towards the fort's tiny log docks at top speed.

Once they were within sight and sound of the HBC fort, the performance would begin. A bugler, plus the occasional bagpiper and the voices of his chanting paddlers, would meld into an impressive orchestration. This was how Chief Trader Archibald McDonald, who accompanied Simpson in his own canoe during the 1828 inspection tour to the Columbia, described the spectacle: "As we wafted along under easy sail, the men with a clean change and mounting new feathers, the Highland bagpipes in the Governor's canoe were echoed by the bugle in mine; then these were laid aside on nearer approach to port, to give free scope to the vocal organs of about eighteen Canadians to chant one of those voyageur airs peculiar to them, and always so perfectly rendered . . . On the signal hill of rock, from a tall Norway Pine shaft, floated the 'Grand Old Flag.' From the 'hollow rocks'—the world of rocks—all around us, awoke the wild echoes, by 'the bugle,' 'set flying.' Then the grand thunder—skirrl of 'the bag pipes,' with their 'Campbell's Are Coming, Hourray! Hourray!' or some such 'music of our mountain land,' loud droned out to the very vault of heaven. And then—as a cadenza of soothing, gladdening, exquisite charm—the deep and soft and so joyously toned voices of those full throated voyageurs, timed with a stroke—so quick—of glittering paddle blade, singing with such heart their 'La Claire Fontaine,' or some such loved air of their native land—our own land, let us say . . . when the Governor's canoe, with its grand high prow rounded, and brightly painted, flashed out of the dark rock 'at the point' into our full view, and gracefully turned into the little 'port' at our feet, the heart seemed to swell with admiration and delight at the sight. Never; never, had anything so grand and splendid, and delightful withal, been seen in those primitive wilds!"

Flags flying, cannon blasting, Simpson's bagpiper leading the way, the governor would step ashore in his theatrical Royal Stuart tartan cloak with collar of soft Genoa velvet. Simpson's insistence on being convoyed by a piper was only partly vanity. What better, what more emotional way to reach the hearts and souls of his men in these lonely huts than with the wail of bagpipes, the mantra of the glens? Simpson's chief piper was Colin Fraser, who arrived in 1827 at York Factory from Kirkton, in Sutherlandshire. To win the £30-a-year job, he was ordered to walk in front of a carriage the twenty miles to the point of embarkation, playing all the way; Fraser was the only one of three candidates who made it.

The bagpipes may have wowed the highlanders, but Simpson's caravan left behind many puzzled Indians. According to one anonymous and quite possibly apocryphal story, a Cree who heard Colin Fraser play at Norway House reported to his chief: "One white man was dressed like a woman, in a skirt of funny color. He had whiskers growing from his belt and fancy leggings. He carried a black swan which had many legs with ribbons tied to them. The swan's body he put under his arm upside down, then he put its head in his mouth and bit it. At the same time he pinched its neck with his fingers and squeezed the body under his arm until it made a terrible noise."

———

SIMPSON'S VENTURE TO THE PACIFIC was especially rushed, covering the 3,261 miles from York Factory to Fort Langley near the mouth of the Fraser in a breathtaking sixty-five days. On that voyage he was accompanied by his "country wife," Margaret, the Mixed Blood sister of his servant, Thomas Taylor. "The commodity has been a great consolation to me" was the chauvinistic tribute to his female companion in a letter he sent from Stuart Lake, along the way.

During these and other excursions, Simpson devoted most of his time to assessing the strengths and weaknesses of his men in the field. He could be occasionally compassionate and frequently cruel, displaying little sympathy for the Company's veterans. In a confidential letter he wrote to the London Committee's Andrew Colvile in 1826, he explained: "Many of our principal Clerks are nearly worn out and I should not consider it good policy to allow them to have commissions as the step from a Chief Tradership to a Chief Factorship I think ought to be gained by important active services which none except such as are in the prime and vigour of Life should be qualified or required to perform. I consider it highly injurious to the general interests to have old worn out men in our councils, they are timid, indolent and helpless and would be of no manner of use in cases of difficulty danger or emergency. Worn out Indian Traders are the most useless helpless class of men I ever knew and the sooner the Company can get rid of them after their days of activity and labor are over the better; but that will always be a difficult matter as they become attached to the Country to the half savage Life they have been accustomed to lead and to their women and Families and will not move unless actually forced away."

Still, Company morale during most of the Little Emperor's reign was high, partly because service with the HBC had become something of a family affair. Youngsters had been following fathers and uncles into the Company for five or more generations. Out of touch with their extended families in Scotland, many of the more isolated traders nurtured a filial relationship with Simpson, seeking him out for advice about their lives, personal as well as corporate. They asked for his help in finding wives, lost children or new postings; they turned their savings over to him for investment and often named him executor of their wills. Loved or hated, he was the great patriarch of the clan. One of Simpson's best friends was John Rowand, the chief at Fort Edmonton who stood even shorter than Simpson but was known as the Big Mountain for good reason, his ample girth being supported by equally outrageous quantities of bombast and bluster. His temper made even Simpson seem a bit of a milquetoast. When several of his servants came down with a serious malady, Rowand accused them of shirking their duty and decreed that "any man who is not dead within three days' illness is not sick at all." His operating philosophy was summed up in the terse credo: "We know only two powers—God and the Company!"

George Simpson's obsessive career left few observers neutral—even in retrospect. Historians praised him for rescuing the HBC from its fragile fiscal status and turning it into an effective instrument of empire. But Alan Cooke, the head of Montreal's

Hochelaga Research Institute, roundly condemned the Little Emperor for his money-grubbing single-mindedness: "Simpson must have been one of the best-hated men in North America. He existed only as a man of business. More than any Indian, he was a slave—a willing slave—of the exploitive machinery of nineteenth-century mercantile capitalism. Although he achieved power, prestige and wealth, his only satisfaction came from work."

Well, not quite.

———

GEORGE SIMPSON'S RELATIONS with women were legendary. Whenever he was referred to as "the father of the fur trade," it was usually with a nudge and a knowing wink. Grant MacEwan, a former lieutenant-governor of Alberta and a popular western Canadian historian, claimed the governor had "fathered seventy children between the Red River and the Rocky Mountains." That was an unlikely if mathematically possible proposition, but he certainly made the most of his bachelorhood.

His sexist and racist references to Indian Country women as "my bits of brown" were the best known and most reviled of his boasts. In a letter to his friend McTavish from Île-à-la-Crosse, where three babies were born during his brief visit, he remarked that "the White Fish diet of the district seems to be favourable to procreation, and had I a good pimp in my suite I might have been inclined to deposit a little of my Spawn . . . ." His lechery, not uncommon for the times, was unabashedly rampant.

In the same letter to McTavish at York Factory, in which he asked him to arrange a "private or separate entrance to my apartments" to make it easier for his nocturnal female companions to come and go, he instructed his friend to "turn off" Betsey Sinclair, the first of his wilderness loves. The daughter of Chief Factor William Sinclair and his Native wife, Margaret Nahoway, she had borne him a child. "Simpson continually violated the custom of the country, creating confusion and anguish. Fur-trade society thought it appropriate, for example, to consider Betsey Sinclair as 'Mrs. Simpson,' but to Simpson she was just a mistress of whom he soon tired," Sylvia Van Kirk, the University of Toronto historian who is a specialist in social aspects of the fur trade, noted. "He never really served an apprenticeship in the country which might have conditioned him to the 'custom of the country' and his attitude coincided with the first missionaries' attacks on country marriages." Once Simpson wanted to be rid of her, his instructions to McTavish were crude and precise: "My Family concerns I leave entirely to your kind management, if you can dispose of the Lady it will be satisfactory as she is an unnecessary and expensive appendage. I see no fun in keeping a Woman, without enjoying her charms which my present rambling life does not enable me to do; but if she is unmarketable I have no wish that she should be a general accommodation shop to all the young bucks at the Factory and in addition to her own chastity a padlock may be useful; Andrew is a neat handed Fellow and having been in China may perhaps know the pattern of those used in that part of the World."

Simpson's longest-lasting country relationship was with Margaret, the daughter of George Taylor, York Factory's sloop master. She accompanied him on his 1828 Pacific adventures. When he left her pregnant on Hudson Bay during another journey, he gave these curt instructions to McTavish: "Pray keep an Eye on the Commodity and if she bring forth anything in proper time and of the right color let them be taken care of but if anything be amiss let the whole be bundled about their business." As well as two sons by Margaret, Simpson also had at least two other simultaneous affairs (and a child each) with Mary Keith, the daughter of Chief Factor James Keith, the other with a Montreal mistress named Ann Foster. "He was utterly ruthless, and introduced the regency-buck approach to women into Western Canada," concluded the fur-trade historian Irene Spry. "His sex-object attitude to women was largely responsible for the breakdown of marriage *à la façon du pays*, which was a humanly decent type of relationship. He created a total dislocation in what had been a perfectly valid type of society."

Unlike the American West, where the so-called squaw men living with Indian women were regarded as inferior, in the Canadian Northwest, country marriages were respectable liaisons, many lasting their partners' lifetimes. The liaisons worked well, even if the women had fewer rights than church-wedded wives of the time. It was Simpson himself who disrupted this cozy arrangement by marrying a white woman and importing her into the Fur Country as his consort. The fact that it was the governor—their role model—who had irrevocably altered the pattern of what had become accepted sexual practice produced cataclysmic consequences. Once the Bay men began to marry in Scotland and England, Indian women, on whose kindness and energy the vast fortunes of the fur trade had largely been built, were relegated to inferior status as either workhorses or mistresses. "The coming of white women to the Indian Country," argued Van Kirk, "brought into disrepute indigenous social customs of the fur trade. Marriage *à la façon du pays* was no longer acceptable, especially with the presence of missionaries intolerant of any deviation. The presence of white women underlined the cultural shortcomings of Mixed-Blood wives, particularly in more settled areas where their native skills were no longer required. Unfortunately, European ladies themselves, by zealously guarding what they considered to be their intrinsically superior status, actively fostered an increasing stratification of fur-trade society."

When Simpson decided to visit England in hopes of finding a suitable bride, he sent his country wife, Margaret Taylor (then with child), to Bas-de-la-Rivière at the mouth of the Winnipeg River, presided over by Chief Factor John Stuart, whose own country wife was Margaret's sister. Simpson told them nothing of his plans, and by the time he received a letter from Stuart telling him that he had a bonny wee son, the governor was within two weeks of marrying his beautiful cousin Frances, twenty-six years his junior.

Back in Canada, Simpson treated Frances as a prized but almost inanimate possession, seldom allowing her to express any will or view of her own. After a term inland, in 1845 she returned to live with him at HBC's headquarters in Lachine near Montreal. She continued to be heartsick for London, enduring her chatelaineship of the Canadian fur trade with well-trained grace but little enthusiasm. Her husband was impatient with the formalities of the times, even with such simple rituals as reciting grace before meals, and at one formal dinner, when Frances insisted he do so, Simpson embarrassed her by abruptly blurting, "Lord have mercy on what is now before us," then digging into the first course.

Their mansion on the north flank of the old Lachine Canal (large enough that it had once been an inn) became the Company's overseas headquarters, although most commerce still flowed in and out of York Factory on Hudson Bay. By moving to Lachine, Simpson for the first time tied the Company into Montreal's commercial mainstream. Here at last he found an outlet for his social aspirations, quickly claiming his place as a key member of the fledgling metropolis's business establishment. To exploit that function to the full, he converted his house into a showplace, permanently exhibiting paintings and objects from the continent's hinterland. Besides the inevitable portrait of Napoleon in his antechamber, the house was filled with a dozen oil portraits from the Indian Country by Paul Kane and other artists, Indian bark boxes with porcupine quill embroidery, ornamental canoe paddles, a model Indian bark tent, buffalo robes and glass cases brimming with stuffed birds.

From a large office overlooking Lake St. Louis on the main

floor of the magnificent residence, Simpson ruled his empire, entertaining visiting dignitaries, dispensing rough justice and, in calm possession of authority, comforting himself with the certainty that his tenure was fulfilling heaven's command.

———

MASTERMINDING THE THIN vanguard of HBC functionaries holding together a territory ten times the size of the Holy Roman Empire, Simpson acted with the lordly hauteur of a man in charge of his private universe. The real source of Simpson's authority flowed from the fact that he was the London Committee's man in North America. He held a tight grip over the HBC's Northern Department from 1821 onwards, and as overseas governor the most important leverage in his struggle for expanded authority was the slowness of the communications system with London— the days of transatlantic cable transmissions still being well in the future, conveniently after his time. As it was, a letter forwarded aboard the Company's spring supply ship to Hudson Bay was delivered in late summer, duly answered, and the reply received in England only by late autumn—to be acted upon the following spring in time for the vessel's return to York Factory, a full year after the original inquiry. By the time this annual cycle had run its course, most operational decisions had already been taken.

One plaintive countervailing voice of protest to Simpson's dictatorial ways was that of Alexander Kennedy Isbister. The articulate son of an HBC clerk and a Cree mother, he had joined the Company and served with distinction at Fort McPherson, then its northernmost outpost. Angered by Simpson's reluctance to promote Mixed Bloods, he resigned. After spending some years at Red River, he enrolled in the University of Aberdeen, was admitted to the bar and eventually became dean of an important British teachers' college. He used his prestigious position to lobby Westminster and the Colonial Office for granting free trade to the Red River Métis, but his speeches, articles and books went unnoticed. His petition remains one of the most eloquent and unanswerable indictments of the Hudson's Bay Company's treatment of the Indian peoples: "When we assert that they are steeped in ignorance, debased in mind, and crushed in spirit, that by the exercise of an illegal claim over the country of their forefathers, they are deprived of the natural rights and privileges of free born men, that they are virtually slaves, as absolutely as the unredeemed negro population of the slave states of America—that by a barbarous and selfish policy, founded on a love of lucre, their affections are alienated from the British name and government, and they themselves shut out from civilization, and debarred from every incentive thereto—that the same heinous system is gradually effacing whole tribes from the soil on which they were born and nurtured, so that a few years hence not one man among them will be left to point out where the bones of his ancestors repose—when we assert all this in honest, simple truth, does it not behoove every Christian man to demand that the British legislature should not continue to incur the fearful responsibility of permitting the extinction of these helpless, forlorn thousands of their fellow creatures, by lending its countenance to a monopoly engendering so huge a mountain of human misery? For the honour of this great country, we pray it will not be; and, sincerely trust that some few voices will respond earnestly, Amen."

In 1838, the British government had renewed the Company's licensed monopoly for a further twenty-one years, and during the next three years, Queen Victoria had rewarded HBC governor John Pelly with a baronetcy and a knighthood and its overseas monarch, George Simpson, with a knighthood—ostensibly for their support of Arctic exploration.

It was an auspicious moment. The young queen was restoring the popular splendour of the monarchy, and although there is no firsthand record of Simpson's visit to Buckingham Palace, it would have been a grand occasion. The past triumphs of Lord Nelson and the Duke of Wellington, followed by its magnanimous treatment of France, had made England the pre-eminent leader among nations; the Royal Navy patrolled three oceans, ready to sink heretics at a moment's notice. The empire was already being touted as an instrument of Christian destiny, and burgeoning London was the arbiter of world commerce and culture. It was a splendid time to be a member of the British gentry, and Simpson had just been initiated into its golden circle. He might merely be the viceroy of an empty land, but he was still a worthy field marshal in the imperial obsession of anglicizing the outer reaches of what was condescendingly defined as "the civilized world."

The Hudson's Bay Company was in a similar state of euphoria. Its Rupert's Land monopoly had been successfully extended in every direction; no significant rivals had replaced the Nor'Westers; American settlers had not yet captured the Oregon Country; the monetary returns of the Company's operations had never been higher; its governor and his committeemen had Britain's leading politicians in their pockets; and even if changing fashions were depressing the price of beaver hats, the Company's commercial prospects were sound. Sir George was being accorded most of the credit for this halcyon state of affairs. His freshly minted knighthood permanently altered Simpson's outlook. Gone was the wilderness administrator; the governor now ranked himself an international diplomat and market-setting financier.

———

BY THE 1850S, Sir George Simpson must have been aware, however reluctant he may have been to admit it, that his brand of absolute power could no longer hold men or causes. Now that he was in his mid-sixties, the coils of wrath having retreated deep inside him, he assumed the mantle of the fur trade's elder statesman and turned his attention to profitable investments on his own account.

With free trade a reality not only at Red River but spreading like a flash fire through the Company's once insulated territories, the HBC's days of dominance were clearly numbered. Yet its daily operations ticked on as methodically as before. As in the past, the Company treated a shift in its commercial environment as a circumstance to be carefully co-opted, not as a reason for any sudden switch in strategies.

Simpson still sallied forth on his annual inspection tours, but they had evolved into royal processions, staged more for show than any specific purpose. His declining energies were concentrated on building up his private portfolio in Montreal's expanding banks, railway companies, canal construction firms, shipping lines and other enterprises. A shrewd assessor of each business proposition's risk-reward ratio, Simpson purchased (from the estate of Sir Alexander Mackenzie) some of the most desirable land in the centre of Montreal (between what are now Dorchester and Sherbrooke streets) and subdivided it into building lots; he was first a director of the Bank of British North America and was later associated with the Bank of Montreal. He became part of the syndicate that built the original Beauharnois Canal, invested heavily in the commercial boat operations that dominated the Ottawa River, was one of the founders of the Montreal Mining Company set up to explore Lake Superior's north shore and was a co-sponsor of the railway line between Montreal and Lachine that was expanded to the U.S. border and eventually bought out by the Grand Trunk. He also purchased a partnership in the enterprises of Hugh Allan, the shipping magnate who was Montreal's wealthiest businessman at the time.

Although Simpson's name appeared on the prospectus of nearly every important new Montreal business venture, his major concern remained conduct of the HBC's overseas operations. That no longer meant dashing from one wilderness outpost to the next, trying to catch some hapless chief trader with an incomplete inventory tally. Instead, it required intense lobbying in both London and Montreal to keep the politicians aware of why the Company and its royal charter still ought to be accorded such extraordinary privileges.

One of his problems was that the fur trade itself, at least in beaver hats, had declined precipitately from the instant Prince Albert, Queen Victoria's consort, had appeared at a public function in 1854, wearing a silk topper. That switch was disruptive enough, but what was really at stake was the continued existence of the Hudson's Bay Company as a continent-spanning monopoly.

The main problem Canada's politicians had in dealing with the HBC was that they were not daring enough to confiscate its immense land holdings nor did they have the necessary funds to buy them. Their solution was to fight the Company on the legally slippery ground that its charter was no longer valid and that, as heirs of the French who had originally claimed most of its real estate, they had full rights to all the territory west of Lake of the Woods. George Brown, the influential editor of the reformist Toronto *Globe*, was still championing his version of manifest destiny, which meant acquiring Rupert's Land from the HBC. Brown was now able to rally not only his own Clear Grit supporters, but some of the most articulate Quebec politicians in his crusade.

The HBC's London Committee could be of only limited assistance in helping to avert British public opinion from swinging against the Company, not so much for any specific Canadian reasons but because it had so clearly become an anachronism. The East India Company was in the process of being wound up, the Royal African Company was long gone and the originating justification for these and other royally chartered enterprises— to encourage exploration of unknown continents by rewarding groups of investors in such ventures with trading monopolies— had become irrelevant. The HBC was under attack in the British House of Commons by the influential social reformer (and future prime minister) William Ewart Gladstone, who despised monopolies in any form. "In England," wrote Jan Morris in her monumental history of the period, "the trend of empire was against the Company. The radical imperialists wanted all of Canada open to settlement. The evangelists wanted every valley exalted, the financial community resented the tight-lipped and privileged manner of the Company." In Select Committee hearings to investigate the case for renewing the HBC's trading monopoly, several hostile witnesses—including A.K. Isbister, the chief British advocate for the people of Red River, and Richard Blanshard, the first governor of Vancouver Island—condemned the Company as a barrier to enlightenment and civilization, stressing its obnoxious monopoly and tyrannical ways. Unlike previous witnesses who had praised the HBC as a universally benevolent force, these critics were specific, showing with actual examples why the lack of competition meant the loss of freedom for the 158,000 inhabitants (11,000 of them whites and Mixed Bloods) of the HBC's licensed territories.

On February 26 and again on March 2, 1857, the Westminster politicians appeared in full regalia, puffed up with self-importance as they welcomed to the stand the witness whose testimony they believed would decisively sway their verdict. As he stepped tentatively into that gilded committee room, Sir George Simpson looked all of his biblical span of threescore and ten years. He felt uncomfortable in his surroundings. His rectitude had always been taken for granted, but here were these politicians in their dandy vestments, none of whom would last an hour hiking up a stiff portage, asking *him* to account for his actions—to justify what he considered to be the Company's natural privileges. He had never felt himself accountable to anyone except the HBC's proprietors, and he was not about to indulge these popinjays with his confidence. Yet there was nothing for it but to keep his temper in check as he resigned himself to answering what he expected would be silly little questions. As it turned out, the questions were chillingly sensible, and, for the first time, Simpson must have felt publicly humiliated by his performance. When asked whether he was familiar with the characteristics of the Pacific Coast, Simpson answered confidently: "Yes. I have gone along the coast from Puget's Sound to the Russian principal establishment at Sitka."

"Do you believe that coast to be altogether unfit for colonization?"

"I believe it to be quite unfit for colonization."

This was a careless assertion for Simpson to make, since previous testimony had already confirmed that the HBC's Fort Langley, near the mouth of the Fraser—which Simpson had just described as worthless—was enjoying great success as a Company farm. Sir George Simpson recovered quickly from his parliamentary ordeal, but the serious illnesses that had periodically plagued him now came on more frequently and with debilitating consequences. Waves of fatigue left him so weak he could hardly dress without help. Doctors kept leeching him, but his pulse remained abnormally slow. He was liable to bouts of fainting and occasional seizures. He had suffered two mild apoplectic strokes in 1851 and two years later was devastated by the terminal illness of his beloved Frances; her delicate health had broken after the birth of their second son in 1850.

The governor could still work up the energy for his annual visits inland, but as one of his former comrades-in-arms, Edward Ermatinger, remarked: "Our old Chief, Sir George . . . tottering under the infirmities of age, has seen his best days. His light canoe, with choice of men, and of women too, can no longer administer to his gratification."

In the early summer of 1858, feeling a bit more chipper, Simpson briefly visited the Council meeting at Norway House and, after some ill-tempered remarks, retreated the way he had come.

BEFORE THE FOLLOWING season's inland journey, he penned a confidential letter to the London Committee. Suffering from periods of near-total blindness, he had shrunk into himself, and his clothes hung loosely on his once imposing frame. "In February next, I shall have completed forty years Service with the Hudson's Bay Company," he wrote. "During that very long period I have never been off duty for a week at a time, nor have I ever allowed family ties and personal convenience to come in competition with the claims I considered the Company to have on me . . . It is high time, however, I rested from incessant labour. Moreover, I am unwilling to hold an appointment, when I cannot discharge its duties to my own satisfaction. I shall therefore make way for some younger man, who I trust may serve the Company as zealously and conscientiously as I have done." Before receiving a reply, he set off westward on his final inspection tour, but when he reached St. Paul, he was too ill to continue and returned to Lachine.

Slowed by the strain of his years and the sibilant rain falling hard on the granite blocks of the Lachine Canal, Sir George Simpson reflected on how alone he had become. Somehow it didn't seem fair that everyone—family, friends and foes—had abandoned him. Like a latter-day King Lear, raging against his own mortality, he dragged himself painfully across the land he had once ruled.

Rather than staying at Lachine, he spent much of his time on nearby Dorval Island, where he had purchased a large summer home. One of his few remaining pleasures was to attend

Sunday services at St. Stephen's Anglican Church, so that he could stomp out as noisily as possible whenever he disagreed with the sermon.

At this point his ordered life was enlivened by a distinguished visitor: the Prince of Wales, the future Edward VII but then an awkward eighteen-year-old, who was on his way to be the officiating dignitary at the opening of the Victoria Bridge spanning the St. Lawrence. Simpson decided to give him a treat and called out his Iroquois paddlers from Caughnawaga one last time. Having put in a lifetime's apprenticeship at playing the *grand seigneur,* Simpson scurried around for weeks beforehand, making certain that details of the magnificent tableau he intended for the travelling prince would be exactly right.

On August 29, 1860, His Royal Highness inspected a military parade on the Champ de Mars in a thunderstorm, then at noon was driven to Hudson's Bay House at Lachine and welcomed under eight triumphal arches made of pine boughs. As the sun burst from behind the clouds, the royal entourage left their carriages and set out in two barges belonging to the frigate HMS *Valorous* (anchored downstream from the rapids in Montreal Harbour) towards the wharf at Dorval Island, a quarter of a mile away.

Near the foot of the island, Simpson had assembled a flotilla of a dozen birchbark voyageur canoes, their HBC flags whipped by the summer wind. Each was manned by twelve Iroquois in full regalia of red flannel shirts, blue trousers and round caps decorated with dyed feathers pretending to be ostrich plumes.

As soon as the prince's barge pushed off, the canoes darted out to meet him. Chanting *voyageur* songs, the paddlers allowed the royal party to pass among them. Then, suddenly wheeling around in perfect formation, the colourful convoy escorted the prince to his landing place, where Sir George was waiting.

At four-thirty, the party embarked in the Indians' canoes, the prince in one and Simpson in another. They wheeled about perfectly in line and crossed to Caughnawaga, where the Iroquois paddlers showed off their passengers to the people of the village, more than two thousand of them watching along the St. Lawrence's shore. With twilight painting the scene a golden amber, Simpson and his prince were paddled back to Lachine, where they parted.

That day in the sun with the future king had been Sir George Simpson's last goodbye. Only two days later, still flushed with the exhilaration of the royal occasion, the governor was stricken with apoplexy. On the morning of September 6, his attending physician, Dr. William Sutherland from Montreal, came into his sick room to hear Simpson say: "Well, doctor, this is the last scene of all . . ."

"Would you wish any particular inscription be put on your tombstone?" asked the doctor.

"That," shot back the dying governor, evacuating his last breath, "that is the business of my executor, not yours . . ."

The Caughnawaga *voyageurs*, chanting wild, doleful dirges, crossed the river to escort the cortège from Sir George's house to the landing, where a special train was waiting to carry Simpson's body to Montreal. He was buried beside Frances under a simple headstone.

The saddest legacy of this magnificent, if ill-tempered birch-bark Napoleon was that those who felt most diminished by his passing were his enemies.

—1987

The World According to Garth

THAT'S NOT THE Garth Drabinsky I know, I thought to myself, watching his features twisted in agony as the humbled impresario stumbled out of the Toronto courtroom, where he had just been convicted of fraud, forgery and systematically manipulating his balance sheets. A self-made man who worshipped his creator, he had become a hunted animal, his eyes darting to find sanctuary. But the jig was up, and no number of Greenspans could save him.

I knew the troubled Garth Drabinsky best when he was on the make, carving out his remarkable career in Toronto's hothouse entertainment industry. We had the occasional drink at Bemelmans, then a fashionable Bloor Street bar that featured the cool musings of Gato Barbieri, the gritty Coltrane-style free jazz tenor sax player from Argentina, who was Garth's favourite.

This was in 1977, when he was twenty-seven and still lacked the self-confidence to reveal that his middle name was Howard.

Drabinsky was—and is—a novelist's dream, a Duddy Kravitz turned theatrical entrepreneur, brought down by his unquenchable ego and a runaway sense of entitlement. His life was more operetta than opera and his manner of speech, an imitation of Damon Runyon with a Bronx lilt. His personality was evenly balanced: a chip on each shoulder—the first chip was his childhood polio, which left him with a gimpy leg and a bruised ego; the second chip was his sensitivity about being Jewish, which he treated less as a religion than as his calling card, daring anyone to hate him for it.

By the time we met, Drabinsky had already written a book on entertainment law, published two monthly movie magazines and produced one bad film, *The Disappearance*, with David Hemmings. I remember him handing me, unasked, his CV that catalogued every detail of his young life, including his club memberships, which had only one entry: the Cambridge Club. (This was supposed to sound vaguely British and decidedly academic, but the Cambridge was in fact a downtown fitness club that any male who loved to sweat and had the annual fee could join.)

I wasn't at all surprised about the trial's revelations that Drabinsky's expense account topped more than $200,000 per month, including his chauffeur-driven Cadillac, which he described as "my Jew Canoe." Talking to him even that long ago, I realized that Drabinsky's thirst for legitimacy could never be quenched. Paul Anka's powerful ditty "My Way" was written for Frank Sinatra, but it really ought to be the national anthem of The World According to Garth. That was why I found his criminal convictions so surprising. His conduct didn't square with his almost desperate longing for respect, which had been his dominant quest since he survived puberty.

Maybe he was in too much of a rush to do anything right. One acquaintance told me Garth was in such a hurry to succeed that "he could go through the twenty-four-hour flu in eight hours." Moses Znaimer, who shared Drabinsky's ambitions but not his accounting methods, once confessed, "Garth is the only guy who makes me feel avuncular." The most telling Freudian slip was made by Peter Gzowski, then the dominant voice of CBC Radio, at the end of one of his *Morningside* interviews: "And that was Darth Grabinsky," he blurted out before correcting himself.

The title of Drabinsky's 1995 autobiography, *Closer to the Sun*, which cost him more than $200,000 in ghostwriter's fees, said it all. The mythological tale of Icarus, the son of Daedalus, who was determined to fly and soared to the heavens but plunged into the sea when the sun melted his wax wings, was the perfect metaphor for Garth's troubles. Typically, he told an interviewer at the time: "The bastard just gave up too soon—he should've gotten himself another set of wings and taken off again."

There was a story making the rounds about the socialite at a party who had sidled up to Garth, kissed him on the cheek and coyly asked: "How is the biggest entertainment name in the city?"

"You mean the *country*," Drabinsky acidly corrected her, probably meaning the world, or at least the continent.

Neither participant in that long-ago conversation imagined that Garth's name would some day light up Broadway and make all of us sing; but neither could we credit the prospect that he would end up facing seven years in jail. But that's where it's at, gut-wise, for Garth-baby at the moment.

—2009

Sir Herbert Holt: The Tycoon Who Tried to Buy Canada

THE REMARKABLE ECONOMIC power of Sir Herbert Holt isolated him as a financial monarch in an age when the success of a man was judged by his millions and the rich inhaled the smoke of Cuban cigars wrapped in hundred-dollar bills to savour wealth's heady aroma. He was the only businessman in Canadian history to match the influence of a Rockefeller, a Carnegie or a Ford. Yet he lived in self-imposed solitude that catered to no exceptions. He fostered his image as an unknown quantity, feeding the mystery of his existence; had no intimates and few diversions. He wove brilliant and uncommonly intricate financial webs, remaining within a seldom-punctured cocoon of anonymity. No other robber baron left so meagre a trail, and none was so universally resented.

Holt did not, as his enemies often charged, control the fiscal policy of Canada. But he approached that stature closer than any other Canadian before or since. In the forty years before he died, on September 28, 1941, three hundred companies on four continents swelled under the yoke of his genius. Holt's empire of ownership included banks, mountains of ore, fur shops, hotels, streetcar systems, railroads, forests, flour mills, shipyards, theatres, life-insurance firms and utilities in proportions so sovereign that he owned or controlled most of the economy— including Holt Renfrew, the only firm that bore his surname but was actually founded by a Quebec City fur trader named John H. Holt, who died in 1915.

Canada in 1928 had paper money and coinage in circulation worth $300 million. Holt in the same year was shepherding corporate assets with a value of $3 billion—that was three thousand million.

Holt's financial sleight-of-hand branded him so decisively as a money mogul that many Canadians, even in his lifetime, ignored his more practical achievements. He had been the engineer in charge of punching the Canadian Pacific Railway through the sliding-earth passes of the Rocky Mountains. At the start of the First World War, he designed the railroad transportation network which supplied ammunition to halt the Kaiser's decisive thrust across France. During the sombre beginnings of the Second World War, he quietly donated to England a full squadron of Spitfires, which played a decisive role in the Battle of Britain.

When members of the 1934 House of Commons Committee on Banking and Commerce angrily insisted that Holt reveal the exact number and size of his corporate affiliations, he calmly replied: "I cannot tell you. I have never kept any record." When the size of his empire was finally revealed—those twenty-seven major businesses he owned or controlled, plus his three hundred directorships—it was such a staggering total that it was almost comical. (Leaving out weekends, he would have had to attend more than one board meeting per day). They were not toy enterprises, ranging from the giant Montreal Light, Heat & Power Consolidated, which he founded, to a key railroad through the Peruvian Andes that he had surveyed on mule back. Montrealers in the late 1920s complained, with justification: "We get up in the morning and switch on one of Holt's lights, cook breakfast on Holt's gas, smoke one of Holt's cigarettes, read the morning news printed on Holt's paper, ride to work on one of Holt's streetcars, sit in an office heated by Holt's coal, then at night go to a film in one of Holt's theatres." That was a severely reduced list of how much he influenced peoples' lives, but it made the point. There was no way for Holt's contemporaries to escape the influence of his holdings, yet no one knew anything about him. In the days of multi-millionaire mystery men, Holt was the Canadian equivalent of Sir Basil Zaharoff, the secretive Greek who turned himself into the greatest armaments salesman in history (mainly by selling arms to one side in a conflict, then selling even more arms to the other side) and Montagu Norman, the tradition-shattering Bank of England governor. On the eve of the Depression, Holt was

about to become the head of the world's largest corporation—
Hydro-Electric Securities Limited, a utilities holding combine.
He was also well along with his plan to merge Canada's primary
steel producers into one giant monopoly under his direction. His
mills were turning out 10 percent of the world's newsprint.

DURING THE TWENTY-SIX YEARS of his presidency, he
multiplied the Royal Bank of Canada's assets fifteenfold. Before
it was expropriated by the Quebec government for $112 million
in 1944, his Montreal Light, Heat & Power Consolidated became
the world's largest privately owned utility.

Holt's economic legacy included the original commercial
seigneuries out of which have grown such key Canadian firms
as the Consolidated Paper Corporation, the Dominion Textile
Company, Canada Cement and the Dominion Steel & Coal
Corporation. The mention of Holt's name could impart stock
market fortunes their breath. When shareholders of Brazilian
Traction, Light & Power panicked during the 1925 revolution
in São Paulo, rumours were leaked to the floor of the Montreal
Stock Exchange that Holt was becoming a company director.
The sell-off stopped, although the revolution continued and
Holt never did join Brazilian's board.

Holt was not a business administrator. He promoted his fortune by refining the sleight-of-hand involved in the acquisition
of corporate control through the trading and re-trading of stock.

His spectacular instinct for gaining control of potentially profitable situations gained him international stature. "Sir Herbert is the business brain of Canada," wrote London's *Daily Express* in a 1926 editorial. "He holds a position in the commercial and industrial life of the Dominion, for which it is impossible to find any parallel. He is certainly a more important figure in the Canadian world than the Prime Minister is in that of Great Britain."

To his less successful rivals, to the leaders of the burgeoning union movement, and to left-of-the-middle politicians, Holt was a symbol of the business aristocracy that exploited labour and was blamed for the country's economic difficulties. Holt believed devoutly that business was a dog-eat-dog proposition, and he did not propose to be eaten. He fought publicity with the fervour of a hot gospeller besting the devil. When he subscribed to charity, which was not often, it was on the condition that the source of the funds not be revealed. Montreal wags of the day claimed that when some of Holt's blood was used in a transfusion for one of his grandchildren, the youngster froze to death.

During the 1931 strike of the Canadian Union of Linemen & Helpers against his power companies, Holt's life was threatened so often that Montreal papers had his obituary set and waiting in their composing rooms. But Holt refused to give up his morning habit of walking to work. He marched through St. James Street enclosed in a square formed by four guards with cocked rifles. A year earlier he had ducked under his mahogany desk barely in time to avoid the bullets of a deranged stockbroker, unhappy with one of his Holt investments.

HOLT HAD NONE of the bankerish characteristics associated
with his type. Three inches over six feet, he walked with the heavy
gait of a tugboat skipper, flexing his knees to compensate for the
roll of an imagined ship. His face resembled nothing so much
as a scrubbed and smoothly polished Irish potato punctured by
pinched, garter-blue eyes. The broad, crew-cut head bulged as
if straining to hold in the turmoil of its contents. His rain-grey
suits and stiff white collars, with their encircling funereal neck-
ties, gave him the awkward air of a staunch Presbyterian minister.
He had an irrational hatred of barbers.

"Sir Herbert," according to R.O. Sweezey, a Montreal investor who often fought with him, "was a ruthless, lonesome old cuss
with no friends, but fundamentally sound and honest." Though
he shied away from publicity, Holt wanted it said of him that he
had been a power. "He was quite determined to get on in the
world," remembered his son, Herbert P. Holt, a retired British
Army officer. "Probably his two chief characteristics were a passion for efficiency and a love of work for its own sake."

Holt's closest associate was Sévère Godin, who was his private
secretary for thirty-seven years and later became one of French
Canada's richest businessmen. "Sir Herbert," Godin told me in
Holt's former office, "wanted everyone to think that he was a
man of steel. Actually, he was lonely and extremely shy."

At odd moments Holt's solitude melted the brutality of his
business manner. During the seesaw negotiations which even-

tually resulted in the formation of the huge Canada Power & Paper Corporation, he took time out to show the young Rowan Coleman (later director of placement at McGill University) how to knot a necktie properly. (After a week of interviewing his contemporaries, trying to humanize the man, that was the only example I could discover.)

Holt's private life was prudishly Spartan. Pleasures were entered into reluctantly, rather than being used to counterpoint the frets of office. "Most tired businessmen," he would tell his luncheon companions at the Mount Royal Club, "get tired because of the things they do *after* business hours." He tried golf but stomped off the green, arguing about the number of strokes he had taken. He slept an invariable seven hours, never drank, seldom smoked. After dinner he often went for a walk along the south side of Sherbrooke Street. Alone and unrecognized, he watched the games at the Westmount Lawn Bowling Club as his chief diversion. Montreal society's gossip highlight of 1931 was an account—more highly coloured at each telling—of the first time Holt played bridge in the Mount Royal Club. At the end of a lost rubber, Holt socked his dull partner in the jaw. The game continued without explanation or apology. But next day a club member appeared carrying a shotgun, explaining that he feared he might be asked to play with Sir Herbert. The incident was not uncharacteristic of Holt's temperament. Once, in Chicago, he rushed to the defence of a woman being held up by two armed men. He slugged one of the bandits so hard that he was nearly booked on a manslaughter charge. During the building of the

CPR, he flattened two intoxicated section hands, fumblingly trying to murder him, by cracking their heads together.

When he was seventy-six, he took a mineral-bath cure at Karlsbad in Czechoslovakia. In two days he became bored with the chatter of old men, climbed a nearby mountain, slipped near the summit and tumbled down a cliff, partly paralyzing his right side. Two years later he suddenly joined the Montreal Light Aeroplane Club and learned to fly, though he did not buy an aircraft. He had no holiday home until 1935. Then he built a small, frescoed mansion on Hog Island in the Bahamas, where he spent most of his last five winters.

Holt's three-storey stone house on Stanley Street in Montreal impressed its visitors as being more of a mosque than a rich man's sanctuary. The large entrance hall was backed by a floor-to-ceiling fireplace with set-in family crests. A drab dining area led into the main drawing room. Though always spotless, it conveyed the musty mood of a first-class railway carriage. Fourteen bedrooms and seven bathrooms were spread through the top two floors.

Lady Holt, the quietly dignified daughter of a Sherbrooke industrialist, filled many cupboards with her china collection, later willed to the Montreal Museum of Fine Arts. Among the home's distinguished but never advertised guests was the Duke of Windsor, who stayed briefly with Holt during his 1927 Canadian tour. Sir Herbert did not give up his master bedroom for the royal visitor.

———

JUST AFTER EIGHT every weekday morning, Holt walked the mile and a half from his house, past the Craig Street pawnshops, to his third-floor office in the Montreal Power building. He was chauffeured to directors' meetings in his 1912 Rolls-Royce and saw no reason to trade it in for a newer model. Holt's office manners were those of a compulsive housewife. He worked behind a desk as big as a ping-pong table in a puritanically unadorned, forty-foot-long room. Objections from subordinates were cut off with stiff finality. "You," he would say, "have had a bad brainstorm." Holt spent most of each day dictating to Godin, at a staccato pace of two hundred words a minute. He accepted invitations to business luncheons on the condition that he would not be asked to speak. According to his son, he detested publicity in any form: "There are no family records bearing on his career. My father was born in an age when life was taken seriously and he retained this outlook up to the time of his death."

Holt's contemporaries could understand him no better than the historians. He did not live according to the mores of the society in which his wealth placed him. It was a time when rich Montrealers looked to the late Victorian and Edwardian days for inspiration. A man was judged by how he disposed of his cherry pits. By far the most idle of Canada's idle rich was Elwood Hosmer, the son of Charles Rudolph Hosmer, president of Ogilvie Flour Mills. Elwood spent most of his days drinking gin and smoking cigars in a lobby chair at the Ritz-Carlton Hotel, often answering nature's calls in the pot of a nearby palm tree. His routine was climaxed daily at 6 p.m., when Elwood—his chair surrounded

by the accumulated droppings of his day's smoking—would pass
out, half covered by the funny papers that were his favourite
reading. Bellboys would carry him outside, where a chauffeured
limousine took him for the two-block drive home. This timetable
was seriously disrupted only once. Elwood decided he wanted
to fly the Atlantic. The attempt ended with his aircraft crashing
a few minutes after takeoff, and he soon was back in the more
stable Ritz-Carlton armchair.

It was also an age of conspicuous consumption in which Holt
did not wish to share. Sir Henry Pellat, who made most of his
fortune bringing hydro power from Niagara Falls, built himself
Casa Loma in Toronto. It has ninety-eight rooms, fifteen marble-
floored bathrooms, twenty-three fireplaces and a kitchen oven
big enough to roast simultaneously three oxen. Melba McMartin,
the daughter of the prospector who helped grubstake the discovery of the Hollinger gold mine, bought a sixty-four-carat
diamond the size of a man's thumb joint. Her cousin Jack used
to march into Montreal bars and with his walking stick smash
every bottle behind the counter. Weary bartenders let him enjoy
himself because they knew they could charge him a flat $1,000
fee per performance. Despite such antics, the McMartin fortune
proved to be amazingly durable. When Melba's brother Duncan
was an RCAF instructor near Calgary during the Second World
War, the pay packet failed to arrive one Friday and he wrote out
a cheque to cover the station's payroll.

———

HOLT COULD EASILY have outdone any of the country's richest spenders. Instead, he furiously continued to build up his fortune without demonstrating to the world either its extent or his personal feelings. Although he headed the Royal Bank of Canada for nearly three decades and his portrait adorned the bank's $5, $10, $20 and $100 bills, his files in the Royal's morgue contained merely the copies of his speeches to annual meetings. The only personal data Holt ever passed for publication was the antiseptic description of himself in the Canadian *Who's Who* as "Civil Engineer and Capitalist." In 1938 Frederick Griffin of the *Toronto Star* wrote Holt for an appointment, promising a favourable story. "I am," Holt replied, "certain that anything favourable you might write about me would only give the Communistic yellow press another opportunity to vilify and lie about me; consequently, I think it better to continue my past policy of not appearing in the press." Concluded the *Star* in an editorial, "Sir Herbert is quite nice to newspaper reporters, as long as they don't come near him. He does not believe in charity and has little faith in hope."

When one well-known Montreal writer was commissioned to prepare a profile of the financier, he was received in Holt's office and told: "As long as you print nothing libelous, I suppose I cannot prevent you. But at least I won't aid or abet you." The project was dropped.

One of the few newspapermen permitted to spend an afternoon with Holt was the financial editor of the *Times* of London, who visited Montreal in 1914. "I had seen the archbishop, who

wanted to pick me out a French-Canadian wife, and Sir William
Van Horne, the builder of the CPR who kept me five hours talking about painting and philosophy," he wrote. "But this man
Holt seemed to inhabit a world absolutely foreign. He sat behind
a desk at the end of a long office, so that everybody coming to
talk to him was inspected *en route*. He spoke like a high priest,
and convinced me I should never like to be his private secretary."

Holt's few public predictions were frosted with an almost
divine pessimism. J.H. Gundy, the Toronto financier who was
one of his closest associates, once told a friend, "If I had to eat
lunch with Sir Herbert every day, I would be the greatest pes-
simist in Canada." In 1934 Holt predicted another crash and
warned his company officers to sell their stocks. He continually
advocated amalgamation of the CNR and CPR as the only alternative to national bankruptcy. Holt was a lukewarm Anglican.
His politics were conservative. "But," a colleague remarked, "Sir
Herbert really understood nothing about politics except how to
manage Cabinet ministers." A more useful public-service request
came from the British government soon after the outbreak of
World War I. The War Office asked Holt to apply his railroading experience in planning the war-zone French railways. For
two months he stalked around the trenches, studying the army's
matériel requirements. Then he outlined an emergency transportation system. It was mainly responsible for providing the Allies
with enough ammunition to halt the Kaiser's initial attacks. The
1915 honours list of George V rewarded him with a knighthood.

Holt was an enemy of paternalism in any form. He believed

that Canada offered every man the opportunity for financial independence and that charity was bad because it kept people from working. His gift to the machine-gun battery organized by Sir Clifford Sifton in 1914 consisted of a little cash and the recommendation of a young recruit, who, wrote Holt, "owns a first-class motorcycle which he is willing to place at the service of the Empire." But he could be generous. In 1910 he financed the Typhoid Emergency Hospital in Montreal. When Dr. E.A. Garrow, a Montreal surgeon, successfully operated on him, Holt overpaid his modest bill, took over the management of the doctor's investments and made him a millionaire.

Holt had little time or patience for community projects. In 1916, however, he became chairman of the Federal Plan Commission set up to redesign Ottawa and Hull into a properly impressive capital. His 160-page report suggested the rearrangement of Ottawa's railway lines much as it was later implemented by the National Capital Commission. He also recommended a dramatic alternative. This would have eliminated level crossings by burying the railroads in an east-west crosstown tunnel. Holt's report predicted a 1950 Ottawa population of two hundred and fifty thousand—within fifteen thousand of the actual count.

———

THAT HOLT WAS able to find such a gainful asylum in the mazy orbits of high finance was due in part to his tough business indoctrination in Canada's early railway construction camps.

Born in King's County, Ireland, he landed in this country during the 1875 depression—a freckled, nineteen-year-old civil engineer, freshly graduated from Trinity College in Dublin. His first job, surveying the Toronto Islands for waterworks installations, brought him in contact with James Ross, later one of the CPR's builders and an early Canadian coal baron. Ross hired Holt to be assistant engineer for the laying of a crude lumbering line called the Victoria Railway, running from Lindsay, Ontario, north into the Haliburton bush. Two years later Ross picked him as his superintendent of construction for the Credit Valley Railway, later part of the CPR's main Montreal-Windsor connection. The road's credit was at first so poor that part of Holt's job was to collect the fares at Parkdale, the Toronto terminus, take the money to a nearby yard and buy enough coal for each journey.

While he was building the Credit Valley, Holt awarded his tie contracts to William Mackenzie, a schoolteacher turned lumberman, later co-builder of the Canadian Northern Railway with Donald Mann. Holt at this time was living with his brother and sister in a Toronto boarding–house and saving twenty-five dollars out of his thirty-five-dollar pay each month. In 1883, when Ross was awarded the major contract for CPR construction west of Winnipeg, he took Holt with him as his chief engineer. A year later Holt resigned to form his own construction firm. His first contract was for grading near the mouth of the Kicking Horse River. On a surveying expedition from the head of the Kicking Horse Pass to the Columbia River, his horse shied and knocked him down a cliff. He somersaulted on top of a dead tree caught in the canyon's wall, almost thirty feet below the trail, and was pulled up, just in time, with a lariat secured across his chest.

When Holt's construction gangs reached the Selkirk Range, the CPR temporarily ran out of funds. The gambling house bosses at nearby Beavermouth, deprived of their income, fanned the men into a strike mood. Holt armed his clerks with his available weapons—nine Winchesters and six revolvers—threw a log across the trail from Beavermouth and waited, six-shooter drawn. The army of strikers, many of them carrying rifles, marched toward Holt's barricade. "The first man who crosses that log, I shoot," Holt warned. "We have guns enough to take care of the 150 of you. Now you know." Not a man moved.

In the last eighteen years of the nineteenth century, Holt became one of Canada's most active railway builders. With Mackenzie, Ross and Mann, he threw 550 miles of track across the Prairies (from Macleod to Edmonton and from Regina to Prince Albert); he built most of the CPR links through the Rockies and the Selkirks; helped design, and was in charge of constructing, many of the pioneer lines in New Brunswick, eastern Quebec and Maine. A railroad stop near the summit of Kicking Horse Pass, where for a time he made his headquarters, now known as Lake Louise Station, was originally called Holt City.

Provision was made for Holt to be in the front row during the driving of the last CPR spike at Craigellachie, B.C., on November 7, 1885. But when he was asked where he stood during the ceremony, he said: "I wasn't there, I was too busy." He couldn't attend because he was repairing the still shifting rails west of Revelstoke, to ensure the safe passage of the inaugural train. Mackenzie and Mann, both later knighted, went on to build the ill-fated Canadian Northern, while Ross undertook the rehabilitation of Toronto's horse-car transportation system. Holt permanently deserted the contractor's car in 1901 and moved to Montreal.

———

THE CITY WAS at that time served by eighteen small gas and electricity firms distributing energy with lottery-like inefficiency. Holt became the largest shareholder in the Montreal Gas Company, founded by leading citizens in 1848, and merged it with the Royal Electric Company to form Montreal Light, Heat & Power Consolidated. During the next twenty-three years, he methodically swapped stock in his company for the shares of his competitors, crushing those who wouldn't sell. By 1924 he had a monopoly of the energy distribution on Montreal Island and controlled the city's tramways system.

Herb Holt, the railroad builder, had become Sir Herbert Holt, the financier. Stockbrokers marvelled at his intuitive market touches. Each share in Montreal Light, Heat & Power Consolidated, originally worth $100, had by 1925 multiplied in value to $1,140. Royal Electric stockholders who had paid $15 dollars for their shares in 1896 owned, by 1925, M.L.H. & P. Consolidated stock worth $185. Most Canadian corporate quarrels are settled in a broadloomed hush, between the walnut panelling of boardrooms. Holt provided a dramatic exception by challenging Sir Adam Beck, the founder and chairman of the Ontario Hydro-Electric Power Commission, to a strange public duel. Beck had told a reporter that Holt's stock manipulations had forced the price of Montreal electricity from $42 to $75 per horsepower. Holt exploded. He offered $10,000 to any charity named by Beck if he could prove his charges. "The challenge isn't worth the time required to pick it up," Beck lamely replied.

In 1924 Lord Atholstan, the founder and publisher of the *Montreal Star*, ran a series of well-documented articles revealing the details of how Holt had dangerously watered the Montreal Light, Heat & Power stock structure. Values of the shares tumbled thirty-nine points. Frantic investors clamoured for Holt to make a statement. He refused to defend his company. Instead, he quietly ordered his brokers to buy up the depreciated stock. As values gradually recovered, Holt's calculated silence netted him more than a million dollars' profit. Holt extended his power empire to the international level in 1926 by joining the board of SIDRO, a Belgian holding trust with effective control over fifty utilities, including the huge Mexican Light & Power and Barcelona Traction, Light & Power. The president of SIDRO was the Belgian capitalist Captain Alfred Loewenstein, one of the world's least-known, yet most influential, businessmen. In 1928 Loewenstein wanted to amalgamate his holdings with Holt's properties into a trust called Hydro-Electric Securities Limited. In terms of its controlled assets, it would have been the world's biggest corporation. Holt agreed, with one provision: that he would become the merger's president.

To settle the preliminaries, Holt sent Godin to Loewenstein's New York hotel room. The talks started badly. The European financier travelled with a staff of forty and wanted at least a dozen assistants to witness the negotiations. Holt's man insisted on privacy. Godin finally sketched out the anatomy of the world's largest company while squatting on the ledge of Loewenstein's bathtub. The wet, cornered Belgian agreed to Holt's presidency while soaping his armpits.

The ambitious arrangement ended abruptly on July 28, 1928, when Loewenstein leaped into the English Channel during a private flight from London to Brussels. His secretaries testified at the inquest that he had opened an exit instead of the wash-room door by mistake. But many were of the opinion that it had been suicide; air pressure would have made the difference in doors obvious. Others believed that he had never been on the plane but had entered a Catholic monastery. The London press reported he had run off with a Yugoslav beauty.

Holt eventually became the dominating influence in sixty-five power companies, including the municipal systems of Monterrey in northern Mexico; Baltimore; Calgary; Fort William; Sydney, N.S.; the Okanagan Valley; and most of Quebec. In 1919 he financed the Andean National Corporation, which snaked a 350-mile pipeline across the Republic of Colombia for Tropical Oil.

Holt had meanwhile become president of the Royal Bank of Canada, which then had 100 branches and assets of about $50 million. He captained the Royal for twenty-six years. In that time assets increased to $750 million and the number of branches rocketed to 688. He brought his instinct for merger to the Royal's presidency and bought out the Union Bank of Halifax, the Colonial Bank of London's branches in the West Indies, the Traders Bank, the Quebec Bank and the Northern Crown Bank. "Holt did more to build this bank than anyone else," said Sydney Dobson, for a time the Royal's president under Holt's chairmanship. "He had a strong character and because of his stature was able to influence business to the bank." Just before Holt died, the Royal outgrew the Bank of Montreal, fulfilling one of his great ambitions. It later became the world's seventh-largest bank.

———

HOLT'S BANKING CONNECTION cost him the presidency of the Canadian Pacific Railway. He had been a CPR director and member of the executive committee since 1911. He was nominated for president in 1918, but that would have meant a switch of the railroad's banking account to the Royal from the Bank of Montreal, and the latter had enough representatives on the board to kill the appointment. Not all of Holt's interests were in huge corporations. He was one of the syndicate of rich Montrealers who invested $2 million in 1913 to build the Ritz-Carlton Hotel, intended as a refined roost for important visitors. He also was the key promoter of Famous Players Corporation, organized in 1920 to establish the first major chain of Canadian moving picture theatres. In 1929, just after talkies were introduced, the 153

Famous Players theatres attracted thirty-two million Canadians. The country's population was then just over ten million. Holt himself seldom saw a movie.

To provide his paper mills with unlimited pulpwood, Holt bought the Island of Anticosti, a virgin, whale-shaped stand of fifteen million cords of timber at the mouth of the St. Lawrence River. Discovered by Jacques Cartier in 1535, the island was originally purchased by Henri Menier, a French chocolate manufacturer, who bought it for $125,000 in 1895, built a *château* at Port Menier and stocked his retreat with fish, beaver, deer, caribou and moose. Holt's Anticosti Corporation took over the island for $6.5 million, not including fishing rights on the Jupiter River, a famous salmon stream. Holt sent in three thousand lumberjacks and built five ships to bring the wood to his mills. Because of the high initial investment, Anticosti timber cost ten dollars more per cord than any other Canadian pulpwood. The shareholders of Anticosti bitterly referred to their investment as the "Ain't-It-Costly Corporation." In 1934 they realized three dollars on an average original per-share price of ninety-four dollars.

As the Depression of the thirties cut world demand for newsprint, the shares of Canada Power & Paper plummeted from a 1929 high of ten dollars to a 1931 low of one dollar. The entire industry suffered, but Canada Power & Paper was hit hardest. Its isolated timber limits could not be economically coordinated with its scattering of mills, and the dead weight of the extensive carrying charges and its bloated capitalization nearly tumbled the company into bankruptcy. Shareholders rioted at annual meetings, demanding withdrawal of their original companies from the floundering dinosaur.

Into this hysterical financial jamboree, Holt injected salvation. Canada Power & Paper would, he promised, absorb Abitibi Power & Paper, the St. Lawrence Corporation and the Backus-Brooks Canadian interests, making it a $500 million enterprise controlling the production of a quarter of the world's newsprint. The move would have left only two major Canadian pulp and paper companies outside Holt's grasp. But it was too late. No new recruits were willing to become part of Holt's elephantine venture. His vision of a pulp and paper empire was snuffed out on October 31, 1931, when the Canada Power & Paper Corporation was replaced by the Consolidated Paper Corporation. Shareholders received one Consolidated share for ten in the old company. Consolidated eventually became Canada's third-largest paper maker, but it didn't recover from its debt-ridden birth sufficiently to pay dividends until March 1946.

The 1929 crash destroyed any notion of Holt's immunity to financial flops but left his personal fortune only slightly dinted. His position was at no time in jeopardy. According to Sydney Dobson, the former Royal Bank president: "Sir Herbert got out of the market in time. He never played on margin."

"Whatever may have been the result of the crash," recalled Holt's son, "I noted no change in my family's way of living." Holt's personal funds provided a lifebuoy of solvency for many associates during the Depression. One company he didn't help was a well-known but badly overextended Montreal investment firm. When one of its partners was told that Sir Herbert had instructed the Royal Bank to no longer carry his company, he barged into his office and tried to shoot Holt. His bullets missed. But the man, thinking that he had committed murder, went home, locked his garage doors, started his car and sat behind the steering wheel until he expired.

Holt's own death at eighty-five, on September 28, 1941, came from the shock of having stepped into an overheated bath. "More than anyone else," wrote London's *Daily Express*, "Sir Herbert made Canada great in peace and powerful to defend her greatness in war." Eight carloads of flowers followed Holt's coffin out of St. George's Anglican Church. But even in death, he presented Montreal society with a dilemma. Senator Lorne Webster, one of Canada's great business princes with a pleasant disposition, had died five hours before Holt and was being buried an hour later at Dominion Douglas United Church. Most of the mourners decided to attend Webster's funeral.

Holt received his public elegy that afternoon. During the International League baseball game at Montreal's Delorimier Stadium, the bottom of the fifth inning was interrupted by the rude blast of a loudspeaker announcing: "Sir Herbert Holt is dead!"

The crowd hushed, whispered—then cheered.

—1959

The Murder of Harry Oakes: Why Nobody Cried

IF ACHIEVEMENT COULD tame a man's peremptory grip
of his ambition, Sir Harry Oakes would have lived happily, died
quietly and been revered by his world. Instead, he spent the
potentially most productive period of his life booting his millions
about, and when he was hacked to death in one of the century's
most gruesome murders, only his family mourned.

Oakes spent twenty-five years ransacking the rind of four
continents in his furious hunt for gold and finally found a quarter-
billion-dollar lode on the south shore of Kirkland Lake in northern Ontario. It brought him the largest fortune ever garnered by
an individual from Canadian mining.

He was the only prospector in Canadian history to stake and
bring into dividend-paying production a major shaft without sur-
rendering financial control. During his lifetime, his Lake Shore
Mine became "the richest half mile in the world." The stock that

he had peddled for 32 ½ cents rocketed to $62.50 while he still held an estimated million shares.

Oakes could easily have fathered a Canadian mining complex of unprecedented scope. But instead he spent much of his fortune in the blunt pursuit of pleasure. A short (5' 6 1 ½"), belligerent barrel of a man, he had a nose shaped like a half-empty toothpaste tube and eyes that appeared to shift in an instant from a man's expression to probe the motives behind it. He was incapable of a belly laugh, hated to listen, but would lecture authoritatively on every subject in almost grammatical English. Having had to outrun rabbits for his daily diet during most of his life, he regarded society's manners as rules meant to be broken by those who wished to maintain their self-respect. He would spit seeds from his hothouse grapes across the table at dinner guests. If a dowager began to twitter at him about "his early days," he would shuffle away, whistling to himself.

Ten-cent poker was his limit. When he was still a prospector, he was known among Kirkland Lake bootleggers as "One-Treat Harry"; he bought more than one drink for no man but gladly guzzled all that others would buy. Once wealthy, he indulged in a carousel of extravagances. He owned mansions in Niagara Falls, Bar Harbor, London, Sussex, Palm Beach and Nassau, and built himself a nine-hole golf course and a fancy *château* in Kirkland Lake, overlooking the tailings dump of his mine; he stopped his engineers from sinking a new Lake Shore shaft near his grounds because he said it would ruin his game.

He was the most niggardly philanthropist among the rich

Canadians of his time. His gifts to Kirkland Lake consisted of a church site, free skates, toboggans and Books of Knowledge for local school children and a $75,000 skating rink. When he was being conducted to the rink's opening ceremonies, a hobo asked him for a dollar. Oakes cut him down with an oath. "Why," a companion demanded, "if you are about to give away seventy-five thousand dollars, didn't you give a dollar bill to a poor misfit who probably needs it?" Oakes replied, "The rink is for the kids; men can look after themselves."

"What Harry Oakes might have done, and what he did for Kirkland Lake, which gave him its wealth, are as far apart as the poles," the *Rouyn-Noranda Press* stated in an editorial after his death. (On the other hand, Kirkland Lake did not exist when Oakes first arrived in northern Ontario.) Spurred by the silver riches of Cobalt, discovered in 1903 during the building of the Temiskaming & Northern Ontario Railway, prospectors had followed the old Troyes Trail to find the region's first gold in narrow, high-grade veinlets fingering through the greenish dolomite on the eastern shores of Larder Lake. Twenty-six miles west of Larder, at Swastika, more ore was dug up and the first tiny processing mill was built. But the Kirkland Lake district between Larder and Swastika was ignored by the rush of prospectors, more interested in the significant Hollinger and Dome strikes farther to the north.

Oakes heard only distant and distorted reports of the Canadian gold finds while living on his flax farm in New Zealand. He had put $30,000 from a small gold strike he made in Australia into the agricultural venture to help grubstake his future gold hunting on a grander scale. When he lost his entire investment, he returned to North America.

––––––––

THE FIRST-BORN SON of a CPR civil engineer living at Sangerville, Maine, Oakes had started his obsessive pursuit of gold in 1896 following his graduation with a liberal arts degree from Bowdoin College. After an unhappy stint selling for the Carter Ink Company, he was bitten by the Klondike madness then sweeping the U.S. and Canada. He arrived in the Yukon during the spring of 1898 and almost immediately walked out to the less crowded but also promising gold finds of Alaska. With a Swedish partner, he soon discovered a gleaming quartz vein sprinkled with free-gold showings the size of peas in an inaccessible branch of the Kuskokwim River. He rounded up twenty miners to dig the bonanza, but it turned out to be only a shallow pocket with narrow streaks of ore worth about $6,000. The party floated out of the bush on a raft—the miners were paid off and satisfied, the partners were bankrupt. Their next venture was even less successful. They built a skiff to explore the Alaska coast but were blown across the Bering Strait to Russia. They were captured by a band of Cossacks, escaped under rifle fire and permanently abandoned their northern exploration.

For the next thirteen years, Oakes roamed the world for gold, tapping likely-looking rocks in the Philippines, Australia,

West Africa, the Belgian Congo, South Africa, Mexico and Death Valley in California. Sometimes he scratched out enough ore to buy food, but more often he had to earn his grubstakes by farming, surveying or lumbering. When he arrived at Swastika in June 1911, he was thirty-six, still hunting and still hungry. His total assets were a knapsack with prospecting tools and $2.65 in cash.

Some historians claim that the Temiskaming & Northern Ontario railroad conductor picked Oakes's destination by kicking him off the train at Swastika because he couldn't pay the full fare to the Porcupine country. Others say that he got off the train voluntarily because he had heard about some unclaimed gold properties from a drunk in a Toronto Chinese restaurant. The prospectors who knew him insist that Oakes met a fellow sourdough on the train and got off when he did to help kill a bottle of his companion's Scotch. Oakes himself maintained that his trip was a scientific prospecting venture, based on government reports about the area and a conversation with Gilbert LaBine at Haileybury.

"On July 4, 1910, I met Oakes in a Haileybury hotel," LaBine recalled. "I remember the date, because it was the night of the Johnson-Jeffries fight. I told him about an area west of Swastika and advised him against going into the Porcupine, which was by then entirely staked over. I went with him to buy a small grubstake, and next day accompanied him on the train as far as Swastika. There he disembarked and started prospecting."

Among the few prospectors who had not already left Swastika for the Porcupine by the time Oakes arrived was Bill Wright, a

Boer War veteran who had been a butcher in Lincolnshire before immigrating to Canada. His first job was painting the mill at the Mining Corporation of Canada property in Cobalt. Then he began prospecting with Ed Hargreaves, his brother-in-law. They located their first ground on the fringe of the stakings east of Swastika near an unnamed lake, later called after Winnie Kirkland, a pretty clerk with the provincial Department of Lands & Forests. These claims eventually became the great Wright-Hargreaves Mines Limited, which started production in 1921 and eventually paid out more than $60 million in dividends. In 1936, with part of the income from his quarter share in the mine, Wright bought two Toronto papers, the *Mail & Empire* and the *Globe*, and merged them into the *Globe and Mail.* Hargreaves sold out his share in the property for $3,000.

The Tough brothers—George, Tom, Rob and Jack—who held the contract for cutting a road from Swastika to Larder, had heard about the Wright-Hargreaves strike and decided to stake nearby. On the evening of January 6, 1912, they were out-fitting themselves for the trek into the bush at Jimmy Doige's general store in Swastika when they met Oakes. He told them that some land originally staked by the Burrows brothers in 1907 was coming free later that night. The claims had been recorded, some trenches had been dug and a Cobalt bartender had even organized a syndicate to mine the properties, but the tempta-tions of Porcupine had left them unworked for more than five years, throwing them open for re-staking. Oakes could not profit from his knowledge because he didn't have enough cash for the new recording fees. He offered to take the Toughs to the area in return for a partnership.

Eight inches of freshly fallen snow slowed the seven-mile walk to the abandoned diggings. Oakes guided the party through the drifts with a lantern, wearing five pairs of variously patched trousers to ward off the bone-chilling fifty-five-below wind. The Tough brothers and Oakes had just finished their re-staking and were sipping tea when Bill Wright appeared, also eager to repossess the pits. He staked, instead, the adjoining western property. It was developed into the Sylvanite Gold Mine, whose five shafts eventually yielded gold ore worth more than $55 million.

Three days later George Tough pulled up a patch of moss under the snow and found a heavily mineralized vein. The ore was packed by canoe and portage to Swastika, where assays showed average values of $457 a ton, with some chunks running as high as $700. To get capital, the Toughs and Oakes had to bring in Clem Foster from Haileybury, a backer of some Cobalt mines. Foster sold the stock in England, but the deal ended in litigation. Many years later Oakes was awarded $200,000 damages by the courts. He avenged himself on Foster by having the judgment reprinted and distributed throughout the mining industry.

————

BY 1916 GOLD WORTH A HUNDRED thousand dollars was being hauled by bucket out of the Tough-Oakes shaft each month. But the veins turned out to be narrow—a fault cut most of the gold off at three hundred feet. The shaft eventually was sunk to nine-teen hundred feet, but values became so poor that the property was abandoned in 1928. It was dewatered and worked by Toburn Gold Mines Limited in 1931, but after another $3 million worth of gold had been extracted, the company gave up its charter.

Although Oakes had finally found the gold he had so long sought, he quickly realized that this was not the bonanza-sized discovery that could satisfy his quest. He continued prospect-ing during the summer of 1912. One Wednesday afternoon in July, he spotted a spatter of gold on some rocks dipping into south Kirkland Lake. He staked two claims. Wright immediately grabbed the two water lots next to Oakes, but in his hurry he overstaked one of the claims by seven acres. Arthur Cockeram, another prospector, noticed the mistake and formed a syndi-cate to acquire the excess land. When Oakes incorporated his Lake Shore Mines Limited in 1914, he gave Wright two hundred thousand shares in the company for his two claims and paid Cockeram and his partners $30,000 plus fifty thousand shares for their seven-acre triangle. Beneath this wedge rested two-thirds of Lake Shore's gold, including the richest ore ever found in Canada.

Oakes had only $30 in his pocket when he walked into Matheson to record his Lake Shore stake. He began with hand steels to dig into the little lakeside gold streak. Values were spotty, but the mineralization persisted. By the summer of 1913, Oakes's shaft was down a hundred feet. The ore had been lugged up an inclined ladder in an old barrel. He had spent the little

money he had received up to that time from the Tough-Oakes
property and had tried to sell his fledgling mine to Charley
Denison of Cobalt for $80,000. But Denison, agreeing with the
many engineers who had inspected the workings, declared them
worthless. Even Jimmy Doige, the Swastika merchant, preferred
to give Oakes outright credit, rather than trade Lake Shore
notes for grub. Oakes's brother, a Maine lumber dealer, and his
sister, a government stenographer in Washington, helped him
to the limit of their funds. "If Lake Shore," Oakes later complained, "had possessed as rich surface ore as the Tough-Oakes,
I would never have had to go to the public for money." But a few
hundred feet of rock still separated Oakes from the fabulously
rich Lake Shore ore body.

Few Canadians outside the mining business realized how
long the odds were of a mineral strike becoming a dividend-
paying mine. Between 1904 and 1933, for instance, only 1.56
percent of the mining companies incorporated in Ontario
reached production.

Oakes finally decided in 1914 that his solo battle to make
Lake Shore a mine was hopeless. He formed a company with
1,500,000 shares of one dollar par value and offered them for
public subscription at 40 cents. The *Globe* and *Saturday Night*
refused to accept his ads. Lake Shore, they decided, smelled like
a wildcat. Only the *Northern Miner* would run a small announce-
ment. A few shares were sold, but by 1917 Oakes was bankrupt
again. He had spent $82,000 on development work; his immedi-
ate liabilities totalled $34,000.

With his last funds, he rented a private railway car to bring into Kirkland a group of Buffalo businessmen. He bought them a roast beef dinner, poured their whisky strong, then offered them half a million treasury shares of Lake Shore at 34 cents. The beauty of the lake, gilded by the light of the harvest moon, did the rest. With the stub of a pencil, Oakes wrote out the sales agreements, dated August 6, 1917, on a piece of brown wrapping paper. The Buffalo financiers who held onto their shares eventually realized a return of 130 times their investment in dividends alone.

Oakes used the newly acquired $150,000 to put up a primitive mill. It chugged along for a year with minimum results, but its presence pushed the stock to 39 cents. A lateral cut that Oakes had run north from a drift under the lake in March 1918 hit the north vein that turned out to be the mine's main mineral break. It ran across the lakeshore, sometimes a hundred feet wide, its values testing up to a spectacular $1,200 a ton. By the end of 1918, the little mill had turned out gold worth half a million dollars.

Every new stope that followed revealed more fully the magnificent anatomy of the Lake Shore deposit. The mine's production topped the output of the great Hollinger Consolidated in March of 1929. Lake Shore became the biggest producer in North America and the sixth-largest gold mine in the world. The mine's dividend rate eventually reached 300 percent a year— Oakes could have earned his staking fee in two minutes. The stock hit its peak of $62.50 in 1936. Oakes hired professionals to run the mine and spent most of the time landscaping his Kirkland Lake property.

To feed its hungry 2,500-ton-a-day mill, the Lake Shore's four shafts were extended continually farther into the earth. The No. 4 shaft reached 8,177 feet—the deepest gold-working horizon on the continent. Production had to be reduced in November 1939, owing to the many rock bursts at extreme depths. The mine prospered without interruption during Oakes's lifetime, but by 1957 it was again in financial difficulties. Despite government subsidies, profit for the first quarter of the year amounted to only $629. After having distributed dividends of more than $100 million, the company halted its operations in 1957.

————

THE MEN WHO worked with Oakes claimed that wealth changed his character only by accentuating its ugly streaks. The enormous drive and tough physical labour he had put into the creation of Lake Shore now lacked outlet. His fortune established, he lost all interest in mining. He took a trip around the world, then bought Buffalo utility magnate Walter Schoellkopf's mansion on the escarpment overlooking Niagara Falls. He renamed it Oak Hall and spent half a million dollars putting in a five-hole golf course, a swimming pool with underwater coloured lights and an artificial hill built up by steam shovels, to afford him a view in an otherwise flat country. (So that he would not tire of his panorama, Oakes had this hillock moved three times to different corners of his estate.)

The main door of Oak Hall was carved of black oak, four inches thick. The old-fashioned square knocker thudded through into the living room—a tennis-court-sized hall sixty feet long and thirty feet wide. The entire downstairs was lined in English oak, including some of the original panels from Cardinal Wolsey's room at Hampton Court. Thirteenth-century columns enclosed a huge, granite fireplace. The room's furniture was placed around a large table on which the treaty ending the Boxer Rebellion had been signed. Oakes also purchased the entire "Red Parlour" suite of the Queen's Hotel in Toronto, where Sir John A. Macdonald had often sat with his cabinet.

On another round-the-world cruise in 1922, Oakes met Eunice McIntyre, the daughter of an Australian civil servant. They were married that June. The bride was twenty-four; he was forty-eight. Back in Niagara Falls, Oakes began to remake the city on a grand scale. He charted a plan for moving all factories away from the river banks so that the shores could become parkland and personally purchased the Ohio Brass plant across the street so that its smoke would not cloud his vision of the Falls. Oakes did not have the true instinct of philanthropy. He treated most of his gifts as investments. But in 1937 he subscribed half a million dollars to the St. George's Hospital in London, an institution openly aided by the Royal Family. Two years later the king's honours list included a baronetcy for him.

His efforts in Canada to become a senator were equally costly but less successful. He donated many hundreds of thousands of dollars to the Liberals for their 1930 campaign and had already bought a large Rockcliffe mansion for his senatorial residence. But R.B. Bennett's Conservative victory squashed his political career. Oakes complained at every opportunity that he paid more taxes on his personal income than any other Canadian. He estimated his 1933 tax assessment at $3 million. One night in 1934, while travelling from his *château* at Kirkland to his mansion at Niagara, he decided to quit Canada for the tax-free West Indies. He resigned from the Lake Shore and never again set foot on Canadian soil. The 1935 annual report of the Lake Shore did not even mention his name. Oak Hall was later converted into a home for the chronically ill; its grounds became a public park.

"This is what came to me that night I bid Canada goodbye," Oakes later told Gregory Clark of the *Toronto Star*. "If I died the succession duties would leave my family in the red, not the blue. True, I found the pot of gold at the end of the rainbow, and I found it in Canada. But I was paying out 80 percent of the gold I'd found in taxes. Man don't work for that."

For his self-imposed exile, he decided on the Bahamas and bought from the American actress Maxine Elliott, for half a million dollars in cash, a twenty-bedroom, pink-plaster house near Nassau on New Providence Island. He quickly became one of the island's most talked-about characters, sometimes parading around the estate in planter's white whipcord trousers and a beige sombrero but turning up just as often among the island's road-building gangs in a dirty sweatshirt. He worked full shifts and was so convincing in his role that a compassionate American tourist once tipped him a shilling.

He directed successful raids on Palm Beach real estate, bought the three-hundred-room British Colonial, Nassau's largest hotel and spent half a million dollars redecorating it to match the colour of his wife's favourite sweater. Oakes's main gift to the island consisted of omnibuses for the natives. But instead of allowing them free rides, he established a charge of a penny for three-mile journeys.

————

SIR HARRY WAS bludgeoned to death sometime after midnight on July 8, 1943. He was sixty-eight. The killer had struck him brutally four times behind the left ear with a miner's hand pick, then burned insecticide over his body, concentrating the flame around the eyes. The corpse had been sprinkled with feathers dug out of the mattress. When it was discovered, they were still being blown gently over the mutilated corpse by the bedroom fan. The only man accused of the murder at the time was Alfred de Marigny, the thirty-seven-year-old playboy who had married eighteen-year-old Nancy, Oakes's eldest daughter, a year before. His trial, which lasted twenty-two days and ended in acquittal, pushed much of the war news off the front pages. Those who knew Oakes were not shocked by the news of his slaying, only by its timing. They wondered how Sir Harry, considering his legion of enemies, had been able to survive as long as he did.

Oakes's personal estate amounted to $14,686,000. A cache of gold bars rumoured to be his was found on nearby Eleuthera

Island. The will divided his money among the family. Nancy had her marriage to de Marigny annulled, opened a Nassau night-club called the Hong Kong Room and married again. Oakes's murder was not followed by the sugary editorials which custom-arily mark the deaths of wealthy Canadians. A few commented kindly about his perseverance in bringing the Lake Shore into production, but many resented his lack of gratitude to the coun-try which had given him his wealth. Shortly before his murder, one of the Lake Shore Mines's former directors, who was visiting Nassau, asked Oakes: "Harry, what do you consider to have been your greatest error?"

"I made a mistake about that name," Oakes growled. "I should've called it Oakes Consolidated."

—1959

Peter Nygard and His Twenty-Five Best Naked Friends

HIS EYES DART like bouncing lottery balls.

Anything might come up. A mixture of vanity and fun, Peter Nygard is showing me his new home. Fun House? Villa? Mansion? Palace? Coliseum? Pleasure Dome? Playboy Pad?

What do you call a structure that spreads over four acres, its habitable area covering one hundred thousand square feet? How do you describe a residence that requires guests to drive electric cars to their bedrooms, located somewhere in its suburban extremities? In Nygard's case, what you call this architectural monstrosity is a temple. It's a place to worship his outsize personality; a shrine to his remarkable success as one of Canada's largest manufacturers of ladies' quality garments; a cathedral for a man whose appetite for women and in-your-face architecture knows no bounds.

Nygard takes me on tour. His athletic, six-foot, three-inch

body is crammed into a pink silk shirt, a pair of fashionable short pants and label running shoes. He watches for my reaction as I stumble around his acreage, at first trying hard not to laugh but gradually realizing that while a dwelling this size is strictly looney tunes, it is bold in concept and stunning in execution. Located on the western tip of New Providence Island in the Bahamas, on a cay that Nygard has named after himself, the building is a lavish labour of love that has taken him a decade of planning and work, plus an estimated $12 million to put together.

"Is this," I ask, exhausted from hiking across the living room, "is this the world's largest house?"

"No," he reluctantly acknowledges. "Buckingham Palace will always be bigger." *Right.*

"Actually," Nygard goes on, "it's sort of wrong to call my place a house. It's more like a resort."

Actually, the place sort of gallops to infinity; it's a series of inter-connected pods that house his entourage and fourteen guests, plus professional-size tennis, volleyball and basketball courts that can be transformed into covered runways for fashion shows. The dominant motif is sensual curves and secret places from which to watch a sunset, hear the ocean, and make love. There are bending roadways everywhere to carry the narrow-gauge electric cars that interconnect the sprawling structure's outlying regions. (I can visualize some exhausted guest, roused from deep slumber by a call of nature, complaining, "Damn it. Now I gotta drive to the goddamn bathroom. I better step on it.")

"I'm trying to go back to nature," Nygard insists. "It's as if

Robinson Crusoe had found a huge shipwreck and built himself
a home."

Well, not exactly. As far as I remember, Robinson Crusoe's
wilderness bedroom didn't have a mirrored ceiling, which
Nygard proudly shows me when I inspect his bedroom in a
cozy, double-storey tree house, furnished like a Fifth Avenue
Penthouse, accessible only by cable car. I also doubt whether
Crusoe availed himself, as Nygard does, of an exquisitely carved
stone sauna built for twenty-five of his best naked friends.

But I quibble.

Much like Crusoe's island, Nygard Cay is self-sufficient,
producing its own electricity, fresh water and soil. (The soil is
refined from palm leaves, which when mixed with water, become
a fertilizing agent, so that the once-arid cay is green and lush.)
Nygard loves rock gardens, but nature's available boulders are
the wrong shape and size. That's why he has a "rock factory,"
which uses intense heat to mix real stones with fibreglass and
iron-reinforcement rods to create rocks of specific bulk and con-
tours. Nygard has thrown up massive cliffs with overhangs made
out of this moulded substance and claims it has the strength to
hold up eighty-storey skyscrapers. The miniature, fifty-foot-high
Matterhorn he built has special significance. "I had this girlfriend once who liked mountain climbing," he confides, "and so
I said, 'I'll build you a mountain.' She left me, but I thought the
mountain was a good idea anyway. It had a huge thirty-five-foot-
deep lagoon underneath it, so you could dive into a cave where
there was a little discotheque and a wet bar."

The entire peninsula has been turned into a bird sanctuary, with free-flying peacocks, parrots, flamingos and other photogenic species. "I'll have a skywalk above their nesting space," Nygard rhapsodizes, "so that at sunset we can play classical music and watch the birds preening underneath." He also promised to turn part of his property into a retirement home for aging circus animals and already has his eyes on a couple of white Bengal tigers.

When I ask him who built his tropical dream, he becomes surprisingly defensive. "I'm the best bloody crane operator on site, lifting those seven-thousand-pound palm trees," he boasts. "I run the biggest crane here." Then he grows very quiet. "When we first came over from Finland in 1952, I was ten," he recalls, "and our family lived in a converted coal bin in Deloraine, a small town in the southwest corner of Manitoba." Nygard pauses, and for a moment the mask slips. "I didn't have a crane when I was a little boy," he confesses, sounding very much like a little boy. "I didn't have a choo-choo train or a tree house either. But I've got a *big* crane now."

An official resident of the Bahamas since 1975, Nygard divides his time among luxury pads in Winnipeg and Toronto, his Caribbean extravaganza and another gigantic tranquility base he has built out of two seaside condos at Marina Del Rey, near Los Angeles. A curious mixture of macho posturing and artistic posturing, Nygard is built as solidly as a wrestler, with wavy blond, Samson-like hair. His creations—whether they're $799 cocktail dresses or $12 million houses—are endowed by his superb

Finnish sense of colour and design. Inordinately vain about his appearance, he panics when I want to take his snapshot. "I don't look good in pink," he shouts over his shoulder as he rushes away to change. He reappears in a blue tunic that makes him look like a Scandinavian sea dog, straight out of *Gentleman's Quarterly*. (At his annual reception for fashion buyers, Nygard usually rents an elephant or camel and paints it white.) Scattered among his various *pieds-à-terre* are five Excaliburs. The $70,000 automobiles (fibreglass reproductions of Adolf Hitler's 1920s Mercedes SSK roadster) are carefully colour coordinated with Nygard's wardrobe and the dominant colour of his various domiciles. "The cars have to suit the clothes I wear," he patiently explains, "because I'm in the fashion business." (The hues of his current Excalibur fleet include fawn brown, silver, burgundy, white and beige.) He can afford to finance these and other luxuries out of the double-digit millions he nets as majority owner of a $350-million-plus international empire that employs 2,500 people and ranks in the top ten of North America's most profitable fashion houses.

Nygard sold his Morgan 51 sloop that he used to moor in the Bahamas but maintains his status as an Olympic-class sailor by keeping a sailboat at each of his locations. Starting out in twenty-two-foot Tempests on the Lake of the Woods, he won the Manitoba championship, eventually became a North American gold medallist and was ranked as the world's fifth-best Tempest racer.

WHILE GROWING UP in Winnipeg, he married his girlfriend Helena Jaworski and later Carol Knight, one of his in-house models, and purchased the former Gilbert Eaton mansion on the city's Wellington Crescent as his matrimonial home with Carol, but never moved in. "All of a sudden," he says, "it became a struggle as to which society I would belong to. I've never subscribed to the Establishment's rules and regulations. I don't really know what they are and haven't bothered to learn. I find them kind of boring." At the time, Carol complained to a friend that before he proposed, Peter wanted it clearly understood she would get only 6 percent of his time. There were no children from that misalliance, but Nygard has had at least two daughters and two sons by other women. He claims that another marriage is not part of his life plan. "Fortunately," he confesses, "at a very young age, I got totally in tune with myself. My mind and my body are very much in harmony. I've got complete freedom. I don't want to be married and be running around for other women. My whole attitude is that I really can't tell a person that I'll live with her happily ever after. But I really go out and spoil my women. I create an environment where they prefer my company. I say, 'I'm going to make it difficult for the next guy to top this.' I hardly ever break up with them anymore. I just have more of them. I'm not jealous. And that's because of my sense of security. There's a certain air of excitement I create because I'm always on the move."

He has squired glamorous women such as Elke Sommer, Jaclyn Smith, Jane Kennedy, Joan Collins, supermodel Iman, Cybill Shepherd, Maud Adams and AnneMarie Pohtamo and a Miss Universe or three; squads of blonde knockouts seem always to be in reserve. To an outsider, they appear to be more of a menagerie than love objects, props for his extravagances. "Some are better friends than others," he acknowledges with one of those looks that implies everything or nothing. One of Nygard's Winnipeg acquaintances who made a casual study of his female companions was lost in admiration for the functional criteria he applied to his choices: "For example, when Peter was training for the sailing Olympics in boats that required frequent hiking—which means hanging far out over the edge of the gun-wale, squirming around with all the weight you can muster—he was always taking out girls with legs six feet long and big bottoms. I don't know how he does it." The Winnipeg lawyer Alan Sweatman recalls, "I remember Peter racing his catamaran. He always had a lot of women and picked them for whatever the other activity was, but he had a girl on this thing with legs right up to her ears and a round hard bottom. The idea was, he'd put her out in a trapeze and Christ, there was all that weight out there. I don't think he ever saw her face! He had a luxury boat that followed him, so that at night he'd have caviar and . . . He is quite a guy."

———

WHEN PETER'S FAMILY emigrated from Finland, they started a bakery, and young Peter was on the go almost as soon as he got into long pants. At twelve he was already subcontracting four newspaper-delivery routes, selling them to immigrants who wanted their sons earning pocket money but didn't know how to go about it. He would lend money to his sister Liisa, then charge her interest in the form of claiming half the candy she bought with it. Summers he worked as a carnival age-and-weight guesser, lifeguard and supermarket stock boy. He studied business administration at the University of North Dakota and went back to Winnipeg where he became a management trainee at Eaton's and listed his name with a firm of corporate head hunters. He happened to be in bed with the then–Miss Sweden when the telephone call came notifying him that Nathan Jacob, a local clothing manufacturer, was looking for a sales manager. Over the next seven years, he bought out the firm, altered its merchandising patterns and expanded east and south. "Luck," he philosophizes, "is the crossroads of opportunity and preparation." He changed the company's name from Jacob Fashions to Tan Jay and completely reoriented its product line. "Everybody was telling me that half the market was under twenty-five and that to survive you had to sell to that sector. I cleverly figured out that if half the population was under twenty-five, the other half must be over twenty-five and that they probably weren't being properly catered to. I jumped into an industry that was ripe for change."

Peter Nygard is a movable zoo. He achieved spectacular success in the most competitive of industries, and he did it his way. A hedonistic workaholic, he gives free rein to all his senses while minting millions in the process. If the compulsion to flaunt his wealth annoys his peers, that's just too bad. He has a tree house with a mirrored ceiling—and they don't

—1981

My Adventures in Bronfman Country

FOLLOWING PUBLICATION OF *The Canadian Establishment*
in 1975, I began researching another volume, meant to feature
the Jewish community. The notion of Jewish power had always
intrigued me. Although they wielded tremendous collective influence, individually their wounded eyes and hyper egos reflected
profound vulnerability, their feeling of being at hazard with the
society that surrounded them. Theirs was a kind of cousinhood,
men and women who still regarded survival as a contest, and in
self-defence, formed the most vital and effective Establishment
of them all. I watched their elders attend election campaign rallies, sipping their flat ginger ale, nodding like wise old turtles,
as some hapless politicians tried to explain why his government
hadn't done more for Israel lately. Some of their best friends
might be WASPS, but they acted as if their next supper might be
their last. And I knew how they felt.

As I probed deeper into their curious power structure, my lines of inquiry inevitably led to various branches of the Bronfmans, Montreal's distilling dynasty that had become, as I later described them in the subtitle of my book, with only a pinch of hyperbole: the Rothschilds of the New World. When I interviewed Sam's son, Charles Bronfman, who was in charge of the Canadian branch, I quickly realized that this remarkable tribe deserved a context of its own.

Even among that small group of pre-eminent families who dominated world commerce, the Bronfmans were unique. By devoting a separate volume to them, I could draw a clinical portrait of how international power was exercised, diffused, hoarded and camouflaged, all within the cloak of a fiercely proud (and constantly feuding) Jewish family that rose from being peddlers of firewood and frozen whitefish in Brandon, Manitoba, to selling some of the best vintage liquor, worth $2 billion a year, all in one generation. My initial session with Charles, who was such a proud son that he had seven pictures of his father, Sam, decorating his office, also made it very clear that the family was not about to share the secrets of its origins.

The Canadian author Terence Robertson had written a commissioned biography of Sam Bronfman in 1970 but took his own life after completing a rough draft of the manuscript. When the publisher McClelland & Stewart sued Mutual Life to collect the $100,000 on Robertson's life, Roderick Goodman of the *Toronto Star* editorial department testified that the author had telephoned him from his New York hotel room to report that he had

"found out things they don't want me to write about." Graham
Caney, another *Star* editor, testified that Robertson had told him
his life had been threatened and that "we would know who was
doing the threatening but that he would do the job himself."
While he was still on the telephone, Caney had the call traced
and alerted the New York Police Department. Detectives burst
into Terence Robertson's hotel room just minutes before he
died of self-administered barbiturate poisoning. That was not a
promising start for the *non-commissioned* book I intended to write.

There was another problem. I was editor of *Maclean's* at the
time, and Seagram (the main Bronfman company) were our
lead advertisers. Lloyd Hodgkinson, the magazine's publisher,
stood squarely behind me, providing I made damn sure I got
everything right. That was the attitude of Jack McClelland as
well, because his company was shaky enough without having to
entertain a hefty libel suit. He placed his faith in Doug Laidlaw,
a top libel lawyer, who warned me that before I published any
controversial material, he would examine me in his office as if I
were a witness in a court of law.

———

THE MYSTERY THAT had been deliberately created to shroud
the Bronfmans' early careers as bootleggers in the Prairie provinces (mostly selling booze into the U.S. during the Prohibition
period) was not simple to dispel. Fortunately, the Royal Canadian
Mounted Police came to my rescue. Cliff Harvison had been a

young corporal in Manitoba and Saskatchewan, constantly on their tail, finally arresting the four brothers on criminal conspiracy charges in 1934, leading Sam out of his office in handcuffs. He eventually rose to become commissioner of the RCMP but kept his Bronfman records. When his widow, Doris, heard I was doing the book, she gave me his files.

In a rented car I spent part of a summer visiting the dusty one-elevator towns nestled into Saskatchewan's bleak southeast corner, along the North Dakota boundary: Oxbow, Bienfait, Carnduff and Torquay, among others. I haunted the retirement homes on their outskirts and finally managed to track down several of the surviving drivers who had been behind the wheels of the hyped-up Studebakers.

Stripped down with reinforced springs and upholstery removed, they could carry forty cases of whisky, worth $2,000. Once across the border, they eluded American federal agents by disappearing into clouds of dust stirred up by thirty-foot chains dragged behind these speeding boozemobiles. At night miniature searchlights mounted on rear windows would direct fierce beams into the eyes of police pursuers. Now in their nodding eighties, they remembered vividly how they used to "run the booze for the Bronfmans" and shared their memories with me. Among them was Ken John, a hale and articulate retired Estevan accountant who, in 1922, had been in Bienfait the night Paul Matoff, Sam Bronfman's brother-in-law and operator of one of Saskatchewan's busiest "boozoriums," was killed by the blast from a sawed-off shotgun poked through the railway station window. These and others were first-hand sources who had never been tapped before. (They also broke the secret of the formula used to make the early batches of the Bronfman hooch: the sixty-five-overproof white alcohol was reduced to its required bottling strength by being mixed with water; then a bit of real Scotch was added plus a dash of burnt sugar (caramel) for coloring and sulphuric acid for aging. When the caramel ran out, iodine was used, and after that, some of the distilling crew just spat their chewing tobacco remnants into the vat.)

MY OTHER ADVANTAGE was that the Bronfmans had been *Canadian* bootleggers. Unlike their American counterparts, who settled arguments with gang warfare, being otherwise law-abiding citizens, Sam and his brothers went to court. I spent many a day in dusty archives, reading up on their many legal challenges and eventually was able to piece together what had really happened. As supporting documentation, I managed to winnow a bootleg copy of the unpublished diary of Harry Bronfman, Sam's older brother, detailing his days in the liquor trade, which even the other family members hadn't seen.

In the three years it took to complete *The Bronfman Dynasty*, I interviewed a dozen Bronfmans, several dozen of their critics, competitors and friends, plus the usual retinue of hangers-on, camp followers and the whisky priests that a fiscal galaxy of this magnitude inevitably attracted.

The group profile that emerged was of restless men in Gucci loafers, still in search of themselves. The warring members of this unusual and impassioned tribe lived behind the tightest curtain of privacy money could buy. It was my toughest assignment. Away from the glare of public concern and attention—through tier upon tier of private holding subsidiaries listed only in the offices of the many lawyers they retained on full-time standby— the Bronfmans had amassed assets worth more than $7 billion, which in 1978 was one of the largest capital pools remaining in the non-Arab world.

———

FOR ALL HIS BUSINESS ACUMEN and boundless success, Sam was never able to fit harmoniously into the society that enriched him and that he himself enriched, having become a generous philanthropist in his later years. A Russian by background, a Canadian by adoption, a Texan by temperament and an upper-class Englishman by aspiration, he was not the easiest man to please.

Haunted by his past, too full of passion to hide his feelings, Sam spent the final three decades of his life in a tumultuous struggle to join the Canadian Establishment. He never made it. He longed to be named a governor of McGill University, elected a member of Montreal's Mount Royal Club, appointed a director of the Bank of Montreal and summoned to the Senate of Canada. As these distinctions kept eluding him, he began to retreat into himself, defining his life more by its exclusions than by his remarkable commercial achievements.

Except for their fear of publicity, the Bronfmans demonstrate little compunction about enjoying their money—although some members of the family's fourth generation were raised in a very different tradition. To teach his children the value of money, Gerald Bronfman (son of Harry) gave his teenage daughters a weekly cash allowance of thirty-seven and a half cents. He accomplished this by paying out thirty-eight cents one week and thirty-seven the next week. Their affections often wore boxing gloves. In the early morning hours of May 30, 1970, when a squad of radical Quebec separatists threw four sticks of dynamite into the foyer of Peter Bronfman's house, it was front-page news in Montreal. But the only comment that Sam's wife, Saidye, made about it next time they met was "Why *you?*" implying that he was hardly an important enough member of the clan to have been singled out for special treatment.

Mr. Sam was not an impressive-looking man—five feet five, with a paunch and thin mats of hair—but the expressive eyes, flickering out at the world, gave off precise barometric readings of the weathers of his soul. They could change in an instant from a look of Arctic fury to the delighted sparkle of a child's first glimpse of Santa Claus. His staff treated him like a killer whale. Whenever he appeared, they scattered like pilot fish darting behind protective barriers with unreasoning fright. Any given group of Seagram executives attending a meeting in his office would be constantly shifting about, each man craning to keep the boss in direct sight, monitoring thoughts and words, trying to guess what Mr. Sam wanted them to think and comment. He alone could say and do exactly as he pleased, treating his underlings with the faintly forgiving air of an Albert Schweitzer among the incurables. He made Frank Marshall, who was director of export sales during the early 1950s, so nervous that the executive arranged his schedule to be away from Montreal whenever Sam was in town. In case Bronfman should return unexpectedly, Marshall kept a packed suitcase in his office so that he could immediately drive to Dorval Airport, where he'd buy a ticket to one of Seagram's world operations. The system worked fine for a while because overseas sales were booming, but eventually Bronfman realized that he hardly ever saw his export manager, and the word went out: "Find Marshall. Mr. Sam wants to see him."

The hunted man kept moving around the globe for a few more months, but Mr. Sam's sixtieth birthday party was coming up, and that was an obligatory occasion for head office executives. The staff had mounted an elaborate film presentation, complete with sound track, depicting highlights of Seagram's sales campaigns during the past year. Sam was sitting in the front row at the ballroom of the Windsor Hotel, laughing as he watched scenes of slightly tipsy Egyptian army officers toasting one another with Crown Royal on the terrace of Shepheard's Hotel in Cairo. This was followed by a long shot of a Bedouin riding a camel toward the Pyramids, a bottle tucked into his burnoose. The camel approached the camera. Sam suddenly sat up, peering at its swaying rider. The focus was much tighter now, and the "Bedouin," it became clear, was none other than Frank Marshall in long night-shirt with a fez on his head, brandishing a bottle of V.O.

Sam leaped out of his chair. Pointing excitedly to the image of his errant export manager, bellowed at the screen, "There's the son of a bitch! That's where he's been spending his time! Riding a goddamn camel!"

Once Bronfman had calmed down a little, Marshall, who had slunk into the hall after the lights were turned out, came up behind him, tapped him lightly on the shoulder and plead-ingly whispered, "That film was taken on a Sunday, Mr. Sam." The reply went unrecorded.

———————

THE SENIOR BRONFMAN felt that elevation to the Canadian Senate would crown his name with the mark of legitimacy, a sure sign of acceptance into the upper strata of his country's society. Having set his sights, he decided to buy his way into the upper cham-ber. His chief agent in these transactions was Maxwell Henderson, who later served as Canada's auditor general. Ever the methodical accountant, Henderson not only kept records of all the donations, but to Sam's amazement, obtained signed receipts for the bribes as they were changing hands. At one point Bronfman became so frustrated that he confronted C.D. Howe with a direct threat: if he wasn't made a senator, he would cut off all contributions to the Liberal party. The great C.D. fixed Bronfman with a steely gaze through the foliage of his magnificent eyebrows, smiled a sweet smile and said: "It doesn't matter, Sam. We'll just raise the excise tax on liquor another 10 percent and get it that way." Then he gently asked the distiller to leave his office.

Sam Bronfman's problem was that he never learned to appreciate the subtlety of the process in which he was involved. Any number of senators had purchased their appointment by contributing to party coffers. But while senatorships might be for sale, they could not appear to have been purchased. Worst of all, when Sam briefly tried to lobby on his own behalf by joining the Ottawa cocktail circuit, he found himself the object of some unwanted attention. Wherever he appeared, Clifford Harvison, then the RCMP's assistant commissioner, who had once arrested him, would noiselessly join any group of people that included the distiller and stand there quizzically staring at him. When Bronfman moved on, Harvison would follow and repeat the treatment.

Sam Bronfman and a caucus of his senior executives were conferring in Seagram's boardroom on the morning of July 28, 1955, when his secretary brought in the bad news that David Croll had been appointed Canada's first Jewish senator. Henderson remembered Sam exploding, parading about the room in a kind of military mourner's slow march, wailing, "I'm the king of the Jews! It should have been mine . . . I bought it! I paid for it! Those treacherous bastards did me in!"

As publication of *The Bronfman Dynasty* approached, in the summer of 1978, I started to receive warnings from Leo Kolber, who was the non-Bronfman Bronfman, so close to the family that

Sam treated him as a son, while Leo worshipped him as a father. He brought to the table a shrewd, street-smart understanding of Canadian society, and the family used him to do some of the things they preferred not to have done with their names attached to them, such as stopping my book. He was a tough cookie but fair and surprisingly shy in public, though he was always honest and had a sense of humour about himself.

"We're too smart to try and stop publication or withhold our advertising from *Maclean's,*" Kolber told me in a way that made me realize these options were on the table; then he suggested I show him the manuscript, so that he and Charles could read it in a locked room. When I politely refused, he invited me to a Harry Belafonte concert and a private party with the star afterwards. On another, less hospitable occasion, he took me aside and whispered: "You better bloody well be kind to us in your book, or I'll cut your balls off." When I pointed out that all my writings were objective, he shot back: "I didn't say objective; I said kind."

Except for one copy that had gone off to the Book of the Month Club, which wanted the book as a main selection, Jack McClelland kept the manuscript and galleys in a company safe because we feared an injunction. But on the evening of August 25, I received a call from a mutual friend, informing me that Charles had received a copy "from an unsolicited source" (how were we to know that the Bronfmans were silent partners in the Book of the Month Club?) and was furious. He informed my friend: "McClelland and Newman may make a lot of money on the book, but they'll spend the rest of their lives in court."

The two of us were invited to meet with the two of them at their private office (graced by a gorgeous Joyce Wieland tapestry) on the fifty-fifth floor of the main TD Tower, which everyone thought only had fifty-four floors. We met for seven hours, seated around a small, rectangular table in the middle of the room, like negotiators for the ceasefire line between North and South Korea. I was nervous because there was one central issue. I had originally gone to them with the idea that they would be part of my book on the Jewish Establishment, which indeed was my intention. But I had become so intrigued that their story turned into the entire book. I hadn't told them, because I didn't want to scare them away, though I would have thought that to have me hanging around their homes and offices for three years might have provided a clue.

They began the conversation by stating that they had a list of seven hundred errors, and what the hell were we going to do about it. I said that I was interested in accuracy and that if I had indeed made errors of fact, as opposed to interpretation, I would be glad to correct them.

The bulk of the "errors" were trivial, such as never having mentioned that Mr. Sam had chubby cheeks, not "leathery folds," in his face and that when I described a party at Leo Kolber's Montreal house, which was so huge that his neighbours thought it was an elementary school, I had been inaccurate in pointing out that during the goings-on, his bedroom had accommodated sixty of his friends and a six-piece band. "It was only a three-piece band," Kolber insisted. He and Charles accused me of downplaying Mr. Sam's pivotal role in the support of Israel and his truly impressive philanthropic activities. What it came down to was Charles's emotional outburst that he didn't recognize his loving father in my portrait. To that I pleaded guilty, gently pointing out that he was not *my* father and that I could only write about him as a successful businessman. He replied that if we were fair-minded people concerned with our integrity, we would not publish such a book and that if we delayed it six months, they would supply us with enough information to turn it into a balanced piece of work. He accused me of hating his father, though I had never met him (he died in 1971) but confirmed my story about his trying to buy a Canadian senatorship.

———

WE WERE GETTING NOWHERE. At the end of his mournful soliloquy, Charles sat back grieving, and Leo took over. At one point he leaned over and threatened McClelland, "Jack, if you publish this goddamn book, we'll buy out your company!" Jack, whose firm was going through one of its many comatose financial phases, jumped up as if shot from a cannon and almost leaping over the table, with a relieved smile on his face, exclaimed: "Leo! Leo! Would you really do that?"

"That was pretty well the end of the conversation," McClelland noted in his memo to himself about the meeting. "There were no threats except by implication, but it was clear that the issue had been the subject of a family conclave. And it is also clear that they are going to do everything they can to destroy the book."

We did make the factual corrections they had requested, but the tone and bulk of the book remained inviolate. After publication, Charles's brother Edgar labelled my effort "a cheap collection of gossip-column trivia, anecdotes, caricatures and amateur psychologizing." And, of course, historian Michael Bliss chimed in on schedule, with his usual sting of venom, calling it "part Harlequin romance, part encyclopedia . . . a wretched, trashy book." My faith in Canadian book reviewers was further devalued when Larry Zolf turned down a request by *Saturday Night* magazine to review it. I thought he would have been the ideal choice because he was from Manitoba, where many of the incidents I described had occurred, and would know how difficult it had been for me to document them. When I met him at a party later and asked him why he had rejected the assignment, he looked unusually indignant. "I couldn't review your book," he said, as if he were pointing out a self-evident truth. "I liked it." Others hailed the volume as "a masterpiece of investigative journalism" and stuff like that. Meanwhile, in the stores, *The Bronfman Dynasty* was outselling *The Happy Hooker*, with eighty thousand copies sold in the first three weeks.

Surprisingly, my best reception was in the United States, where the book (re-titled *King of the Castle*) went into three printings, got on the bestseller lists and received a big boost by being chosen as a main selection of the Fortune Book Club. Robert Sherrill, White House correspondent for the *Nation*, wrote in his *Washington Post* review: "Newman has been so devastatingly, cruelly fair as to portray the Bronfmans in the very fashion, I'm sure, they see themselves. I call that a masterful knife job. If I were trying to stir up a nice Trotskyish revolution, *King of the Castle* would be my chief ammunition."

I was interviewed by Mike Wallace and Gene Shalit of NBC's then top-rated *The Today Show*, among others, and always had the same problem. Inevitably, I was asked the names of the Bronfman brands of liquor. There were six hundred, but I had memorized a short list that included Wolfschmidt vodka. Unfortunately, this brand became lodged in my mind as Wolfshit vodka, and try as I might, I would always call it that. Canadian interviewers corrected me, but in the U.S., I could visualize them thinking, "Who knows? Maybe that's what they use up there in Canada." I was never asked to explain the formula.

The Bronfmans never did try to destroy my book, though one of their subordinates launched a harassment-type lawsuit that cost me half my royalties. Instead, in typical Bronfman style, they had a book written for them. Michael R. Marrus, a respected university professor, took on their commission and followed their editorial advice. It was a good book, but it left out most of the juicy bits.

THERE WAS ONE final coda to my Bronfman story. Two distinguished filmmakers, Fil Fraser of Calgary and John McGreevey of Toronto, optioned the book, laid out real money and even cast Mr. Sam (either Dustin Hoffman or Saul Rubinek), with a fine script by Charles Israel. But the cameras never rolled. Most of the production funds came from Calgary, and they mysteriously dried up after Leo Kolber had swept through town paying friendly visits to the misguided financiers.

I remain firmly convinced it was just a coincidence.

Never has a gene pool dried up with more dire consequences. In 1994, when Edgar Bronfman Jr., then thirty-nine, succeeded his father as head of Seagram, the Canadian-based liquor empire—then still the world's largest—his first major decision was to sell its $11.7 billion stake in E.I. du Pont de Nemours and Co., the stunningly profitable giant U.S. chemical conglomerate.

He used the funds to go on a wild buying spree, trading stock in the world's leading chemical company for pop culture by snapping up moviemaker MCA Inc. and PolyGram, the continent's biggest record label. Outgoing PolyGram CEO Alain Levy's parting advice to young Edgar was to caution him that the music business "is more dangerous than astrology." By then the lapsed du Pont investment would have fetched $28 billion, but at least the family still held 120 million shares of Seagram stock, worth $7 billion.

Young Edgar soon took care of that. He sold controlling interest in the family firm to Vivendi SA, the upstart French media empire, headed by a hyper egomaniac named Jean-Marie Messier. Against all sensible odds, Bronfman opted to take Vivendi shares instead of cash for the Seagram share.

That gamble turned sour as Vivendi stock, dragged down by a debt load of US$30 billion, went into free fall, reducing the value of the Bronfman holdings by three-quarters. One of Canada's most enduring fortunes vanished from contention. Charles, its chief Canadian heir, was down to his last billion. (Ironically, while Vivendi tried desperately to stay afloat by selling off its remaining assets, du Pont's 2001 profits jumped 88 percent.)

Meanwhile, Vivendi, the Paris-based investment firm to which the young Bronfman had tied the family's financial destiny, was found by a Manhattan federal court jury to have misled its own investors fifty-seven times between 2000 and 2002. At the same time, Edgar Jr. was charged with improperly using inside knowledge to ditch his shares.

Most dynasties die hard. The once mighty Bronfman Dynasty frittered away its legacy in record time when the family placed its trust in the hands of a Hollywood-crazed neophyte.

—2004, 2010

Victor Rice: How to Fire Fifty-Two Thousand Workers

OF THE MANY business executives who gave Canadian capitalism a bad name, one individual stood out above all the others:
Victor Rice. The head of Canada's most renowned manufacturing
company, Massey-Harris, he persuaded two levels of government
to finance its resurrection and, as soon as it had recovered,
moved the firm to the United States and abrogated the loan.
Adding insult to insult, he chose Buffalo as its new operating
headquarters.

During almost two decades as head of Massey, Rice seemed to
spend all his time firing the people who had made Massey great,
causing untold havoc in the process. On the opening day of the
1986 Blue Jays season, when he walked into Toronto's Exhibition
Stadium and looked around at the fifty-two thousand spectators,
he told a friend: "I suddenly for one fleeting second had this
unhappy thought that everyone in the stadium worked for us . . .

Just that morning our total of laid-off employees had reached fifty-two thousand."

The unwritten rules that have traditionally held in check even the most avaricious of business leaders were broken in the convulsions that shook Massey and finally saw it depart from the country. Rice's actions seemed so reprehensible partly because of Massey's distinguished history. Founded in 1847 by Daniel Massey in Newcastle, Ontario, it had originally supplied the farmers of Durham County with sap-boiling kettles. After amalgamating with A. Harris, Son & Co. in 1891, Massey burgeoned into a major conglomerate, turning out bicycles, windmills, home freezers, milking machines, stoves, kerosene engines and washers, plus its line of agricultural machines of a quality unsurpassed anywhere in the world. During the opening of the Canadian West, a Massey marching band would lead parades of newly delivered tractors and harvesters down the main streets of rural communities. The company treated its beaming customers to dinner and a free concert.

Massey's reputation spread overseas when its harvester won a grand prize at the 1867 Paris International Exposition. Operations were extended into the United States with the purchase of the Johnston Harvester Company of Batavia, New York, in 1910. The introduction of the self-propelled combine, developed mainly at its Argentina branch, revolutionized harvesting methods. Sir Edmund Hillary used its tractors on his historic overland expedition to the South Pole, and Massey purchased the prestigious F. Perkins Ltd. of Peterborough, England, the world's largest manufacturer of premium diesel engines. At its height the company employed sixty-five thousand people in 120 countries.

After the Second World War, Massey slipped under the effective control of Argus Corp., the Toronto capital pool first headed by E.P. Taylor and later by Bud McDougald (and, later still, by Conrad Black). It endowed the Argus partners with the international prestige and aristocratic connections they so craved. Massey's London office overlooked the exclusive Claridge's Hotel, where the firm maintained an ostentatious permanent suite for its chairman; nearby was a carpeted garage housing the two Rolls-Royces and a Daimler, maintained by Massey for its visitors from Canada. (The larger of the Rollses was decorated in royal colours and, to McDougald's panting delight, was borrowed by the queen for ceremonial occasions.)

———

MASSEY'S MANAGEMENT had grown slack by the mid-1970s, having been taken over by Al Thornbrough, an American lightweight who commuted to Toronto for three days a week from his beach home in Boca Raton, Florida, yet claimed Canada's highest corporate salary. The company's problems were both structural and managerial. Its growth and diversification had been grounded in opportunism instead of long-range planning. When Massey moved into the United States, it lost the Canadian market without ever winning over much new American territory. That would have required development of a hundred-horsepower tractor, which the company bungled. With the notable exception of the self-propelled combine, Massey had never really been an innovator, due to lack of research. The crisis first came to the public's attention on March 10, 1978, when Thornbrough announced to the company's annual meeting a first-quarter loss of $38.8 million, temporary plant shutdowns and the liquidation of several manufacturing facilities. Argus had been taken over by Conrad Black, who moved into Massey offices on August 16, 1978, settled into the chairman's quarters and proclaimed: "Logically, Massey should probably have gone bust years before, but some things defy all laws of economics and nature—like bumblebees." Within weeks of Black's takeover, Massey announced the largest annual loss suffered by any Canadian corporation up to that point: $257 million in U.S. dollars. Black kicked Thornbrough upstairs and named his friend Victor Rice as president.

The son of a London chimney sweep, Rice was an impatient man, characterized by quick, rabbit-like gestures with his hands and nose. He seemed so bent on his own path that he appeared seldom to consider how his actions might ruin the lives of others. He replaced fifteen of Massey's twenty-one vice-presidents, closed seven plants and even saved $30,000 through banning inter-office memos with executives' names printed on them. Black and Rice enjoyed teasing Massey's surviving vice-presidents about their grandiloquent titles, especially such designations as vice-president in charge of Africa and so on. At one point Rice proclaimed himself president of the world, and the only way

Black could top him was by anointing himself interplanetary chairman.

Rice canvassed international lending institutions and eventually produced new loans of $580 million from 212 banks, but nothing worked. The cost of servicing Massey's swollen bank debts increased beyond endurance. At the time, the Canadian Imperial Bank of Commerce's Massey obligation was the largest unsecured commercial loan in the world, and the bank eventually had to take a $100 million writeoff.

By the fall of 1980, the company's credit was so overstretched that its bank obligations could no longer be managed. After relentlessly lobbying Ottawa and Queen's Park, Rice persuaded the two governments to provide him with $200 million, which, by his own admission, saved the company.

Black resigned as Massey chairman on October 2, 1980, and less than two months later, he quietly wrote down the value of Argus's investment in Massey to zero (which at its height had been worth $32 million) and later donated the all-but-worthless stock to Massey's pension fund. "I am amazed," he declared as only he could, "by the number of so-called financial experts who are luxuriating in the view that I am some sort of punch-drunk prizefighter on the ropes. Well, screw them."

By the end of 1982, Massey was reporting a $413 million loss, its Australian operation was in receivership and most of its dealerships were in trouble. (Not to worry, that disastrous year, Rice arranged for a pay packet of $554,000—a 40 percent boost from the year before, when Massey had lost only $240 million.)

Meanwhile, Rice had mounted a $715 million refinancing effort, which wasn't quite enough to shore up the company. The $200 million government cash infusion was renegotiated with some stringent conditions, among them that Massey's headquarters would have to remain in Canada and that it would have to maintain or create at least 1,500 jobs here through to May 1993 or pay back $30,000 for each work place not maintained. Rice appeared to accept these conditions, but he had a deadlier scenario in mind.

In May of 1986, Rice divided Massey into two new companies: Varity, which took over the healthy operating assets, and Massey Combines Corporation, into which he folded ownership of the money-losing manufacturing operation at Brantford, Ontario, which employed 1,500 people and was charged with servicing the $200 million government loan, as well as the responsibility for pension and medical benefits of five thousand of Massey's laid-off and retired workers.

――――――

WITH SUCH HEAVY BURDENS, the Combines company inevitably went bankrupt and Rice walked away from the firm's obligations, including the $27 million owed to three thousand pensioners who had spent their lives working for the original Massey. That same month Varity reported profits of $50 million. To twist the knife, Rice bid on the machinery at the bankruptcy auction of the Combines' plant equipment, purchased it for next to nothing and had it shipped off to Varity's new American plant at Des Moines, Iowa. "It's the crookedest deal ever perpetrated on the Canadian public," proclaimed the *Financial Times of Canada*. The arrangement also broke the terms of Rice's agreement for government aid, which had obliged him to maintain manufacturing facilities in Canada and to export the company's technology and machinery out of the country only with Ottawa's approval.

The one cloud remaining in Rice's life was the high taxes he had to pay out of his huge pay packet. He was being paid $1.2 million annually and held stock options worth more than $4 million, as well as a golden parachute that would pay out at least $5 million. But, as he complained to *Financial Post* editor Diane Francis, "when marginal rates hit fifty per cent, something happens in a country. It's at that point that a person begins to cheat." That, apparently was the trigger point. Rice's reaction was to move the whole company, which at that point had sales of $3.5 billion, into the United States. He chose as its state of incorporation the tax haven of Delaware and located its operating headquarters inside a luxurious mansion in suburban Buffalo.

———

THE CANADIAN GOVERNMENT'S conditions for having saved Massey had been violated once again, but when a justifiably disgruntled shareholder at the company's 1990 annual meeting asked Rice whether he felt any moral obligation to keep Massey in Canada, the answer was a blunt: "Not at all." (Only two Massey directors, Hal Jackman, who later became lieutenant-governor of Ontario, and Lynton "Red" Wilson, the BCE Inc. chairman, resigned from the Massey board in protest. Ironically, the patriotic Wilson was eventually replaced on the Varity board by Robert Gates, the former head of the Central Intelligence Agency.) The only reason Rice gave for Varity's intended move to the United States was that he hoped it would help increase the value of its stock. That may not be unconnected to the fact that, along with other Varity executives, Rice used a $7.5 million internal loan to acquire more than 2.3 million company shares. That was on top of his $1 million salary, guaranteed $250,000 annual pension and special "golden parachute" arrangements. The Buffalo move was also handy geographically, because Varity's new mansion headquarters were within comfortable commuting distance (by chauffeured Jaguar, of course) from Rice's magnificent heritage home at Niagara-on-the Lake, Ontario. Such grandeur was taken for granted by the Varity chairman.

———

WHEN CONRAD BLACK initially captured Argus in 1978, he moved in as saviour of Massey for twenty-five months and cleaned house. "There are few genuinely great companies in Canada. Massey is one of them. As such, it is worthy of prodigious effort," he grandiosely declared. "Only a 20 percent prime rate or complete collapse of the North American agricultural market could sink Massey now." That, of course, was precisely what happened, and soon afterwards Massey was in default on most of its bank covenants.

———

RICE'S SNORTY PRESUMPTION that he could do anything he wanted, even when dealing with money that belonged to Canadian taxpayers or Massey pensioners, went beyond acceptable levels of corporate arrogance. Canada's fairly aggressive brand of capitalism doesn't forbid very much, but it does demand that the private sector follow common legalities. According to that standard, Massey should have either made it on its own or been forced into receivership. Instead, Victor Rice used a dubious ploy to get his company into the black, thumbed his nose at his benefactors and jumped ship.

But then, not everybody gets to lay off fifty-two thousand workers and to skip out on a $200 million obligation. At least he felt slightly queasy about it, if only for a ghostly day at the ballpark. If that's the new ethic of capitalism, let's go back to the jungle.

—1990, 1995

How Robert Campeau Caught the Biggest Fish

THE REVOLUTIONARY DECADE of 1985 to 1995 was marked by the disintegration of some of the country's largest business empires. In each case their animators, among them Robert Campeau, Paul Reichmann, Bernard Lamarre and Reuben Cohen, went against the Canadian grain by dreaming too big and thinking too small. They established world-class business empires on shifting foundations of high-risk, leveraged debt and came to grief, corporately and personally, retiring from the field as case histories of rise, decline and fall. In the process they not only damaged themselves, but cost their employees their livelihood, as well as devastating their shareholders and suppliers. Their ego-driven extravagances dramatically validated the rules of capitalism. Instead of countering the market theory that high risk carried high rewards, the lesson of their performance was that the greater an entrepreneur's ambition and flamboyance, the greater the chances of failure.

The most openly grasping and irrationally ostentatious of these high flyers was Robert Campeau, the one-time Sudbury house builder who wangled about $11 billion in loans from Wall Street's astute merchant bankers to purchase two of America's largest department store chains, Allied and Federated. It was an astronomical sum, but then Campeau seldom used cash or collateral of his own when he could get the money on spit and a promise. Neither was Campeau's ambition deterred by the thought of borrowing far more than he could ever repay; Campeau wanted to make deals that would go down in history. They went down, all right.

He presided over North America's largest and most sensational retail bankruptcy and had the distinction of becoming a symbol of the stock market crash of October 13, 1987. Most postmortems agreed that Campeau's erratic behaviour had been a chief trigger of the crash—not just of his stock but the entire exchange. Campeau's inability to meet his debt obligations created a climate of doubt in the junk-bond market that detonated what was then the most serious share-price correction since the Great Crash of 1929. As the *Wall Street Journal* noted: "The shaky junk-bond market received its biggest jolt from Campeau Corp. which created its U.S. retailing empire with junk financing." Campeau soon was into a cash squeeze that caused him to be tardy on his interest payments and to put the prestigious Bloomingdale's department store chain up for sale.

THE JITTERS SET off by the collapse of Campeau's securities, described by the *Financial Post* as "the junkiest of junk," set off a panic about the debt load threatening to sink Campeau's empire. Few national treasuries can afford to carry burdens the size of Campeau's debt. If he had been a country, he would have qualified for Third World developing-nation status, which in the prevailing climate, might have prompted the World Bank to come calling with debt forgiveness and the offer of emergency loans. Instead, Campeau watched helplessly as the value of his company's stock, four decades in the making, plummeted from a high of $30.38 a share to 22 cents. "Thus did an age of excess unravel," wrote Carol Loomis in *Fortune* magazine, "with Robert Campeau as the catalyst and also the symbol of excess carried to its dumbest, most egregious limits. The Campeau drama had no rival for absurdity as it proceeded and for shattering effects as it ended. The overarching wonder of this affair is that so many supposedly shrewd lenders forked over so much money to a man whose instability would probably keep him from being hired as a Bloomingdale's sales clerk."

It was unlikely that anyone with Campeau's psychological profile and financial record could, in fact, have been hired to perform any job, however menial, if it required even the most rudimentary stability and sense of responsibility. Prior to his berserk shopping spree for U.S. department stores, Campeau had suffered three major nervous breakdowns: the first time, during most of 1970, after he temporarily lost control of his company to Paul Desmarais; secondly, in 1980, when he was prevented from taking over Royal Trust; and thirdly, in 1985, when he grew so depressed over his business dealings that he could not force himself to get up in the morning. He was able to work regularly only by appointing his psychiatrist, Dr. Alan Mann, to the Campeau Corp. board of directors, where the therapist could monitor his star patient first-hand.

Even in those moments when he was suspended in mid-arc between mania and melancholy, he hardly qualified as an average, clean-cut, board of trade "leader of tomorrow." The private devils haunting him may well have made Campeau one of the most competitive humans ever to stalk the planet. On a holiday jaunt one summer to a private fishing camp in northern Ontario with a few friends and his son Robert Jr., the group made a fun wager to see who could snag the longest fish. When they compared their catches at the end of the day, Robert Jr. had won. Not for long. His father stomped on his fish until it was longer, albeit grotesquely squashed, to claim victory—over his son! What a grotesque triumph. He refused even to lose his race with age. He had regular injections of sheep brains, supposed to guarantee eternal youth; Campeau at first wore a toupée, then had a follicle-by-follicle hair transplant; his teeth were capped; his face had been lifted so often that his beard had curly hairs and his neck skin had been stretched tight as a tenor timpani; he went through painful Rolfing rituals and swam daily in the private pools attached to his three residences, but not in the usual chlorine-treated water. The pools were equipped with special ozone systems to eliminate impurities; the water was drinkable.

His family quarrels became legendary. When Campeau, then a millionaire many times over, sold his Ottawa house to his daughter, the transfer was held up for months because he insisted the basement washer and dryer hadn't been part of the deal. Campeau's family troubles became public when he sued his son Jacques and his daughter, Rachelle, to retain voting rights over the family trust he had set up in 1961 as a tax-avoidance measure. Father and son did not talk for seven years, and Campeau refused to meet Jacques's wife or visit his granddaughter. Campeau himself was still married to his childhood sweetheart, Clauda Leroux, when he set up a separate residence with Ilse Luebbert, his German-born mistress, who bore him three children and later became his second wife. "A great woman," a friend described her, "provided, of course, you're into Valkyries."

———

ROBERT CAMPEAU'S ORIGINAL climb had been as legendary as his eventual fall. One of fourteen children of a Sudbury blacksmith and auto mechanic, Campeau quit school in grade 8 and, finding himself too young to get work, used his dead brother's baptismal papers to falsify his age and get a job at Inco. He built houses in his spare time, married his childhood sweetheart and moved to Ottawa, where he became a successful developer. Campeau's most spectacular brush with legitimacy had been his aborted 1980 attempt to buy control of Royal Trust, then run by a crusty Montreal-based Anglo retainer who went under the humble monicker Lieutenant-Colonel (Ret.) Kenneth Alan White, C.D. "You may think that money talks," White warned Campeau, "but I don't like you, and I'm going to call up my friends and lock up 50 percent of the stock before you can turn around."

————

IN AN UNPRECEDENTED show of solidarity, the mavens of Canada's Establishment, led by Toronto-Dominion Bank Chairman Dick Thomson, Noranda President Alf Powis and the Reichmann family, slapped together an overnight syndicate that bought $200 million of Royal Trust shares at $4 *below* the Campeau offer—enough to hold the intruder at bay. The movement to save Royal Trust, which was based on a personal dislike of Campeau, rather than his fiscal weakness, grew so strong that being part of it became a status symbol. Don Love, a millionaire Edmonton developer, for example, counted his entry into the Establishment's inner core from the day he was invited to participate in the anti-Campeau crusade. For their questionable tactics, White and John Scholes, one of his senior executives, had their trading privileges revoked by the Ontario Securities Commission. No matter: the Sudbury interloper had been routed.

Campeau went back to real estate promotions, but he neither forgot nor forgave the massive slight he had suffered. "If the Royal Trust tactics had been used in the United States," Campeau blustered, "those people who breached security laws would have gone to jail, and the others would have paid large fines." The man's obsessive desire to grasp legitimacy from the business elite he envied prompted him to take on the entire business community. Typically, he refused to play by their rules. "They're stodgy, ridiculous and anyway, their power is dwindling," he once told me. Consumed with proving himself in their jaundiced eyes, he transferred his acquisitive itch to larger targets south of the border, just to show them he could play with the big boys.

————

CAMPEAU'S FIRST MAJOR thrust into the United States was his $4.9 billion takeover in 1986 of Allied Stores, America's fourth-largest department store chain. Its outlets included such well-known units as Bonwit Teller, and its revenues, at an annual $5.7 billion, were twenty-seven times larger than Campeau Corp.'s. He paid (or, rather, borrowed) $2.4 billion for the initial key block of Allied shares that he purchased from the Los Angeles brokerage firm Jefferies & Co., until then the largest single block ever sold on any U.S. stock exchange. Campeau and his company contributed a measly 4 percent holding in Allied, which was purchased with borrowed money. That amazing deal created so much debt that Campeau had to jettison some of Allied's best assets, including the fashionable Ann Taylor division and Brooks Brothers, the respected New York City men's wear store, which he sold to Britain's Marks & Spencer for $925 million.

Still, had he held on to Allied's remaining assets and had he managed them carefully, the purchase would have been a brilliant move, yielding him a potential net profit of $500 million.

Instead, Campeau plunged into even deeper undertows of debt. Seventeen months later, he paid an inflated $8.2 billion for Federated, the country's oldest chain of department stores, which included such giants as Bloomingdale's, Abraham & Strauss, Berdines, Sterns, Jordan Marsh and The Bon. He grossly overpaid for these bragging rights. Campeau's original offer of $59.70 per share (a total of $5.4 billion, closer to Federated's real value) was run up to $90.70 per share when management enlisted competing bidders to stave off the Campeau terror. Not only did Campeau pay too much; he had to mortgage most of his valuable real estate to meet interest payments that came close to $1 billion a year. He tried his old trick of hiving off Federated's money-making assets to keep ahead of the bailiffs and even put Bloomingdale's, that daycare centre for the New York rich, on the block. "It took the special genius of Robert Campeau to figure out how to bankrupt more than 250 profitable department stores," sniffed the *New York Times.* The more earthy *Daily News* attacked him for devaluing his investments so quickly that no buyer stepped forward to claim Bloomingdale's. "Bloomie's woes," the tabloid editorialized, "are as if Kim Basinger had announced she needed a date and no one responded."

As a result of Campeau's wild gambles, the bonds of both Federated and Allied were placed in Moody's B-3 category— which was just one step above their "anticipating bankruptcy" rating. The two companies lost $367.5 million in the first six months of 1989, and by January of 1990, the Allied-Federated combo was forced to seek Chapter 11 protection under the U.S. bankruptcy code. Campeau had promised Allied bond holders that he would not use junk financing for the Federated purchase.

His endless asset shuffles, his sleight-of-hand borrowing from one source against another and his inability to settle in and actually operate any one of the many companies he acquired—or at least to put competent managers in place and not interfere with their decisions—shook the foundations of the junk-bond market. That was no mean feat in a market populated almost entirely by corporate vultures feeding on paper carrion. After all that sweat and tension, after mortgaging his soul to prove to Canada's elite that he could slap a bigger deal on the table than they could even imagine, Campeau enjoyed only one moment of triumph. That was his house-warming of September 1984 or, to be more precise, his mansion-warming. Campeau invited the glitterati of Toronto's Establishment to his new $8 million house at 64 The Bridle Path, in the city's fashionable northern reaches. He and Ilse had designed the twenty-five-thousand-square-foot home in mock French *château* style, complete with a burled-wood-panelled library that boasted the complete leather-bound works of Honoré de Balzac. The entrance hall, which was three storeys tall, was roomy enough to contain a standard suburban bungalow. It featured floors of Italian marble and a glass dome from which was suspended a tiered crystal chandelier, suitable for swinging from. The house had an expansive granite patio that concealed a roomy shockproof bunker, stocked with canned food and its own forty-five-day air supply, designed to serve as a sanctuary from terrorist or nuclear attack. "It could resist a bad whack and radiation," claimed the mansion's architect. Its indoor swimming pool was covered by a retractable floor and could, at the touch of a button, be transformed from spa to ballroom.

————

TERMINALLY GAUCHE, even in this moment of triumph, Campeau and Ilse insisted on holding court in the hangar-like reception hall, directing the guests firmly back out into the garden before food was served. This created at least one practical problem, resolved by allowing women visitors to use a downstairs hall bathroom. But the men, including Campeau's bankers, found themselves using a device few had ever christened before—the porta-potties scattered about Campeau's lawn—an experience which couldn't have escaped their memories when reviewing their host's credit rating. (Black was the only member of the Toronto business elite who paid serious attention to Campeau—apart from some bankers who nervously held his paper—by appointing him to the board of his main holding company, Hollinger Inc.)

The guests had come not out of respect or even amiability but out of curiosity. Campeau's Gonzo tactics made them shiver with scarcely disguised disgust, but they also knew that Bob and Ilse and their Versailles-on-the-Don had to be seen to be believed.

They were treated accordingly. Apart from the fact that they had been shunted into the garden, their discomfort increased when they saw the place cards on the wooden tables where dinner was to be served. It was as if someone had deliberately set out to embarrass each guest, placing him or her next to the invitee they liked the least or were suing the most. Which was exactly what happened. Campeau had asked Rosemary "Posy" Chisolm Feick, the doyenne of Toronto's beautiful people, to help him with the guest list and seating arrangements. The mischievous Posy knew a potentially dull party when she smelled one, so she thought it might be fun to generate a little excitement—and perhaps even a little reconciliation—by placing the worst of friends at the same tables. At first, the gambit fizzled and the dinner conversation was as glum and terse as the chatter at a Benedictine monastery; later, the guests, trapped beside their least favourite people, began to talk, and some even settled old scores.

As the guests munched wild mushrooms dipped in raspberry vinegar, followed by roast suckling pig with avocado paste, they were serenaded by Paul Anka, "a close personal friend" of Campeau, paid handsomely for the appearance, who just happened to drop in with his entire Las Vegas show band. He sang—what else?—"My Way." In Anka's version, the last verse went:

All Canada loves Bob Campeau,
This Taj Mahal he calls a château,

Is he extraordinaire? Bet your derrière,
But he did it . . . HIS WAAAAY!

———

THERE WAS A BITTER-SWEET quality about Robert Campeau's demise, a fall not from grace, because he had so little, but from contention as a serious player, which was the worst punishment of all. It was the classic tragedy of self-delusion; his career became a metaphor for the excesses of the 1980s. "Even though he cannot escape responsibility for the wreckage he left behind," wrote Arthur Johnson in a devastating profile of Campeau in the *Globe and Mail*'s *Report on Business*, "Campeau was also a product of the times. Never before and perhaps never again will the ambitions of a Robert Campeau coincide with the flood tides of such easy money on Wall Street. It wasn't just a flawed character that brought him down. It was a flawed system."

It was indeed. What made Campeau's gamble possible was the fact that by the mid-1980s, Wall Street had turned into a casino using junk bonds for chips, and the "house" always won the richest pots. High-powered lawyers, bankers, consultants and money-letter writers pocketed $250 million in fees for assembling the Frankenstein's monster of Campeau's deals. If even one of them had possessed the decency to reject his fat fees and explain to him why the properties he was buying could never carry the gargantuan debt load they accumulated, he might have saved himself. But Campeau was flying so high at the time that he would have been impervious to advice, however sensible and well meant.

Edward De Bartolo, an American shopping centre tycoon out of Youngstown, Ohio, and Paul Reichmann moved in to rescue his tottering empire, but their price was high. De Bartolo snagged some of Federated's best shopping centre properties and the Reichmann loans totalled $510 million, secured by drastically reducing Campeau's ownership of his own firm. In the process, Campeau lost control of Toronto's Scotia Plaza, his most valuable remaining asset. Meanwhile, Montreal's Banque Nationale came looking for repayment of the $150 million loan it had foolishly made to Campeau to buy shares in his own company—the shares themselves, which were rapidly becoming worthless, being the loan's main collateral. (Campeau's lead banker was Cedric Ritchie of Scotia Bank, whose 1993 pay packet totalled $2.6 million, the year's highest compensation for any Canadian bank chairman. Presumably, the bank's investment in its top executive had been justified by Ritchie's ability to size up a good credit risk, which meant that the abstracted department chain buyer with a debt ratio similar to that of postwar Bosnia had met Ritchie's standards.)

Saddled with the burden of having to pay the cost of their own acquisitions, Allied and Federated declared bankruptcy in January of 1990. Campeau found himself facing claims of $8.2 billion, including settlement packages for 6,500 laid-off Federated employees, as well as threats from an angry horde of fifty thousand suppliers shortchanged on delivered goods and banks screaming to get their loans repaid. That chaotic scene was followed by three consecutive blows to his ego: he learned that Campeau Corp. was about to be drastically restructured, leaving him without any corporate assets; the Bank of Montreal suddenly called an outstanding $30 million personal loan; and, asked to testify before a U.S. bondholders' committee in New York, Campeau was deterred by forty-three lawyers, ready to challenge his every word. Instead of facing them, he sent a doctor's certificate, pleading yet another nervous breakdown.

———

HE MADE ONE last curtain call, at Campeau Corp.'s annual meeting on July 30, 1990, where he announced that he was discharging his bankruptcy and everything was looking up. This must have seemed dubious even to the most optimistic shareholders, since the company's stock price had dropped in the previous year from $22.25 to 85 cents a share, and it had reported a loss of $1.74 billion (the second-highest in Canadian history). The loss included a $958 million writedown, the amount Campeau had overpaid for control of Federated. He told the shareholders whose investments he had ruined that he shared their pain. "My family and I understand how you feel," he lamented—then, waving a V-for-victory sign at the cameras, he was gone.

But not forgotten—and not really gone either. Campeau had moved large quantities of cash to the tax haven of Liechtenstein in central Europe and used it to build a $10 million castle on the southern shore of Lake Attersee at St. Gilgen, near Salzburg, Austria. The cost of the magnificent structure escalated many times over because of Campeau's insistence that an Olympic-size swimming pool be built on its enclosed roof, so he could enjoy a scenic view through cathedral windows while taking his morning dip. This latest extravagance was unwittingly financed by Campeau's ill-starred shareholders, since most of the money had come from a Campeau Corp. loan backed by the Bank of Nova Scotia. It seemed the ultimate insult.

Stanley Hartt, Ottawa's former deputy minister of finance, who became one of the private sector's most imaginative and most intelligent animators, took over the pitiful remains of the Campeau empire in the fall of 1990 and nursed the much-reduced company into the black. He sued Campeau to recover $10 million in wages and another $1.3 million and for the return of corporate artwork, cars and a communications system still in his possession. Another suit, undertaken in Liechtenstein, demanded the payback of $4.6 million that Campeau had used to acquire the 15.5 acres of land upon which he'd built his storybook castle. The case was lost because it turned out that Campeau had not bought the land outright, but instead had acquired it through a trust arrangement known as a *Stiftung*, which owned the property. (A *Stiftung* is an investment vehicle used mainly by those who want to hide the source of their funds. It cannot be touched under Liechtenstein's strict secrecy laws.) Campeau promptly countersued his former company for $100 million, claiming damages for the "high-handed and callous way" he had been treated and other such mischievous nonsense.

Like a latter-day Sampson in his own biblical epic, Robert Campeau tried to pull everything and everyone down around him. But he no longer had the power to hurt anyone except himself. I have often thought about Campeau after his tumultuous demise, but my impressions have faded with time. I am left with a mental image of him astride the ramparts of his Austrian castle, his Valkyrian consort, armed with shield and spear, at his side. Campeau seems to be bellowing something.

But nobody is listening.

—1995

Nelson Skalbania: Not a Poor Country in the Balkans

IT WAS ONE of those crazy events that caught the essence of the wilder shores of West Coast capitalism, its circus mentality and the gambling ethic on which it is based.

Herb Capozzi, majority owner of the Whitecaps soccer team and a playboy-entrepreneur whose idea of throwing a good party was to helicopter a side of beef for a barbecue and a string quartet to play Mozart for a bash at the top of Grouse Mountain's best ski run, was out to prove his prowess as a racquetball player. How better to establish his credentials than to challenge Nelson Skalbania to a public match?

Skalbania had recently donated $275,000 to the Vancouver YMCA for two extra courts, with the stipulation that they be available exclusively to him at 5 p.m. daily for the rest of his life. To Skalbania it was the only sensible way to eliminate worry about reservations for his daily workouts, but Capozzi felt that the gesture had somehow threatened his unofficial status as godfather of Vancouver's middle-aged jocks. So the two men agreed to the match and, just to make things interesting, bet $5,000 each on the outcome, with the loser after two sets holding a double-or-nothing option on a third.

A dazzle of the city's beautiful people gathered behind the court's glass walls to watch, cheering their favourites, exchanging $30,000 in bets. There were pompon girls, a Dixieland band, official handlers done up in togas throwing bunches of grapes to the crowd, while a gloomy Doberman slouched around in a T-shirt proclaiming, "SKALBANIA IS A POOR COUNTRY IN THE BALKANS." Striding through the rowdy assembly were the lean young lionesses of the Vancouver jet set, zipped up in their Frye boots and raw silk tunics, barely covering their bronzed bodies without the tan lines. The men eyed each other and each other's women, boasting about their cross-court tennis slams, watching Nelson slowly psyching out Capozzi.

The players had split the first two sets, but Skalbania had slowed the third set down to a walk, and Herb (playing in his WOPS ARE TOPS sweatshirt) finally packed it in at 21–18. "I bet on Capozzi to win," bitched one of the pretty young things. "I should have bet on him to survive." The match, which took place in the summer of 1979, became important in the annals of the Vancouver scene, its details growing more lurid with each retelling.

The sequel is less well known.

Capozzi, who had been a pro football lineman in the 1950s

with the Montreal Alouettes and Calgary Stampeders, was determined to get revenge. Recently separated, he was living with a spunky beauty named Ellen Brown. Capozzi is not exactly a retiring type (asked about monogamy, he replied: "I think it's a wonderful wood but I wouldn't want a whole house made of it"), but Ellen's nerve took his breath away.

At the time, nobody knew anything about Capozzi's lady's outstanding tennis prowess. So one sunny afternoon about a year after their racquetball match, Capozzi casually suggested that Nelson have "a friendly hit with Ellen" on the tennis court.

She waxed him, 6–2, 6–3.

Smiling her sweet smile, she walked up to the net and said, "Hope I didn't embarrass you, Nelson."

Skalbania graciously replied, "Fuck off," and walked away.

(Not at his best when he's losing, Skalbania found out somewhat later that one of the few people who knew about Ellen's tennis game was his new wife, Eleni. She had secretly bet $500 on Ms. Brown to beat her husband.)

———

NELSON MATHEW SKALBANIA is one of those rhinestones in the rough whose glitter has added a new dimension to what was once the staid Canadian Establishment. He belongs to a unique category that could well have been invented to commemorate his macho lifestyle and financial derring-do: he is Canada's first full-fledged Bonzo capitalist.

The world is his windowsill.

It took his purchase of half a dozen sports franchises in 1980 and 1981 to make him well known, but Skalbania established a record of sorts as Canada's most successful real estate speculator, playing the market as he would some giant Monopoly game, spinning profits out of his uncanny skill of flipping half a billion dollars' worth of properties a year. "I sell probably 70 percent of everything I buy before each deal is closed," he told me. "I don't know of any better return on equity. It's called infinity, or close to it."

This isn't business, it's gambling—and the riddle most of British Columbia's money movers who knew the man best kept asking was, "What's the capital of Skalbania?" Guesses ranged from "very little" to "about $70 million." The true answer depended on the day of the week—or, more precisely, on the time of day.

His friends and rivals watched Skalbania with the fascination accorded a tipsy guest of honour lurching dangerously near the balcony edge at a penthouse cocktail party. But there was no question about his ability to make up the money he lost in the many deals that went sour. "Nelson can make a million bucks any day of the week he wants to go to work," said Canarim chief, Peter Brown, who became one of Skalbania's active partners in the acquisition of the Alouette football team.

It was the saving grace of his recuperative abilities that drove Skalbania to ever greater risks. He once lost $70,000 in four minutes at a Las Vegas gaming table and played off a $150,000 land deal with Peter Pocklington, the Edmonton entrepreneur, on a

backgammon board. "He scares the hell out of me," says Bob
Carter, the Vancouver-based oilman, and no mean crap shooter
himself, who has done several deals with Skalbania. "We hire the
same lawyers, and one of them told me, 'God, Carter, we used
to think *you* shot from the hip. But this guy Skalbania never puts
the gun away.'"

Most real estate speculators are little more than puffed-up
used-car salesmen. Their technique consists of knowing how to
give potential buyers *the significant look*, the meaningful elbow
squeeze and, occasionally, the old kissaroo. They usually give
themselves away by going into a state of apprehended hyperven-
tilation at the crucial moment of a deal, then expiring from an
overdose of non sequiturs.

Nelson Skalbania was different.

He looks as if he played the title role in a road company of
Jesus Christ, Superstar, with messianic beard, beseeching eyes and
the inner calm of a spaced-out yoga adept. There's something
very theatrical about the man. He expresses himself in drawn-
out mock sighs, the habitual gambler in him hostage to another,
more rational self. He seems filled with cinematic sorrow that
more people don't understand or appreciate him, the Polack
from Wilkie, Saskatchewan, who's out there turning bucks by
the million. His ego is permanently in traction because he can't
shake either his background or the social stigma that marks real
estate speculators. "Certainly, I have a social conscience," he will
confess without being asked. "I only fired one guy in my entire
career, and I fired him twice."

He is a committed fitness freak, inordinately proud that at forty-three he weighs the same (162 pounds) as he did when he was seventeen. He jogs every day, logging at least fifty miles a week, and when the Vancouver Canucks were having a bad season, he bet the team members "any amount" that he could beat them around the Stanley Park seawall. Though the Canuck players average about twenty years younger, not one took up the challenge. He has climbed mountains in Switzerland and has run the original marathon course in Greece. ("I took my lawyer and accountant along, promising to pay their expenses if they completed the twenty-six-mile course. Both the bastards beat me.")

Skalbania lives up to his billing. He is almost always late for appointments, building up an aura of suspense and apprehension. Then he appears, walking on the balls of his feet like a ballet dancer, dressed in his inevitable jeans. The cadence of his speech is reminiscent of an IRA gunrunner's silky blarney, conjuring up fantasies to tickle desire and promote greed.

Inside his small circle of fellow deal makers (who have nicknamed him "Denny"), he is treated as a cult figure, with each of his "flips" being endlessly analyzed and reconstructed. "We call him the Polish Godfather," says Bill Sherban, a Vancouver insurance broker who is an old friend. "The Italians make you an offer you can't refuse; the Poles make you an offer you can't understand."

———

ONE REASON FOR Skalbania's success is that he harbours
no doubts about his motivation. He is not in business to build
an empire, to help preserve the capitalist system, to enjoy the
fun of the chase or anything silly or pretentious like that. He's
in it for the money. "I want to taste it, spend it now," he insists.
"The cars, the boats and the houses I've purchased I could never
afford when I bought them. So the more I buy, the harder I have
to work."

The roster of Skalbania's possessions is daunting. He is always
searching for new ways to impress himself. At one time he owned
simultaneously a pair of Mercedes 450 SLs and four Rolls-Royces
(two Corniches, a Silver Cloud and the 1928 Phaeton convertible
used in filming *The Great Gatsby*); a $2.7 million de Havilland-125
jet that he bought from Chunky Woodward; and four hundred
or so pieces of art, including half a dozen Rodins, Renoirs,
Riopelles and ten canvases by, as he described him, "what's-his-
name—A.Y. Jackson."

———

JUST BEFORE ALLENDE'S overthrow, a Chilean friend of
Skalbania telephoned him from Santiago to negotiate special
deals with some private collectors about to flee their homeland.
Nelson jetted down three times with bundles of American dollars and purchased twenty-five canvases, ranging from Monets
to Picassos. Nineteen turned out to be fakes, but the profit he
made on one Jacob van Ruisdael masterpiece more than made

up for his losses. For a while he was into the art game, opening the Galerie Royale on Vancouver's South Granville Street.
He logged two hundred thousand miles in his jet, visiting the
important salesrooms, and put together a stock of 240 pieces
worth $1.7 million, including Russian icons, English watercol-
ours and French Impressionists. (The highest-ticket item was
Berthe Morisot's *Vieux Chemin à Auvers*.) "The good pieces sold
quickly, and we were left mainly with the junk," he recalls, "so we
had to keep buying the good stuff for others to collect, and I had
to keep pumping in dollars to maintain the bad stuff. I ended
up selling the business and the building to Ken Heffel." (Heffel
paid more than $6 million to George F. Clark of BSC Alloys for
his Group of Seven and Emily Carr collection and resold the
canvases to Peter Pocklington in Edmonton and—through Peter
White—to Conrad Black in Toronto.)

His craziest purchase was the 506-ton diesel yacht *Chimon*,
originally built as the *Maid Marian* for the British bicycle tycoon
Sir Harold Bowden, a latter-day high sheriff of Nottinghamshire.
Later a floating pleasure palace for the Vietnamese playboy-
emperor Bao Dai, it was eventually bought by John David Eaton
for $625,000. The 173-foot ship carries eight tenders and has
a permanent crew of fifteen. But except for one brief summer
cruise in the Mediterranean, Skalbania spent exactly three days
aboard his ship. In addition to the original purchase price of
$665,000 he invested a further $1.5 million, converting it to his
specifications. After that, the *Chimon* swung at its moorings in
Corpus Christi, Texas, an extravagant, unused toy.

———

SKALBANIA'S LIFESTYLE VARIES with his marital state. He was married to Audrey, his high school sweetheart, for nearly twenty years. In the summer of 1979, when he asked for a divorce, he handed her a list of his assets and allowed her to choose whatever she wanted to keep. "She took the things with clear titles and positive cash flows that didn't require feeding or work to maintain," he recalls without a trace of bitterness. "I ended up with things like the jet, the ship and development properties." He claims that his former wife eventually got nearly three-quarters of everything he owned, including his condominiums in Maui, Puerto Vallarta and San Francisco, as well as the $1.5 million house where they'd lived on Vancouver's Belmont Avenue. It may well have been the largest divorce settlement in Canadian history. Skalbania's only residual regret is that it cost him $150,000 in legal fees "just for me to give my stuff away."

The reason for the divorce was a strong-willed, blonde, Greek beauty with scimitar cheekbones called Eleni Marinakis. At the time they met she was married to a Vancouver lawyer. When he threatened to sue for divorce, Eleni hired a young "hostess" to attend some of the many swinging parties he was throwing after his wife's departure. The hostess's reports persuaded Eleni to countersue, but her husband wouldn't drop the case. Finally, some of the other guests at the parties, including many of Vancouver's more prominent business personalities who didn't want to get caught in any public crossfire, persuaded him to settle on Eleni's terms. (The stormy affair was somewhat complicated by the presence of Laverne Marion Sadler, who said she had been Skalbania's "de facto wife and business partner" during the last eleven years of his first marriage, enjoying "a long and intimate business and social relationship." Skalbania denied the allegation but settled Sadler's claim for $500,000 plus three oil paintings by Endre Szász worth $500,000. She promptly purchased a Jensen Interceptor.)

Skalbania is candid discussing Eleni's temper with his friends. He's learned to live with negative publicity, but she hasn't, and he admits she has tossed him out of the house twice because of quotes attributed to him about their marriage. They're an attractive couple, but they scrap about how to bring up their combined family. She is still basic Greek, believing kids should make their own way, and gets enraged when he wants to give them Mercedeses for their birthdays. Nelson stoutly maintains that "kids shouldn't have to stand on their own two feet. They should be allowed to start on their parents' shoulders."

A dramatic and capable lady, Eleni wanted something to do, so Nelson bought her the Devonshire Hotel, later flipping it for the more prestigious Hotel Georgia next door, which he purchased from a group of Chinese investors for $13.5 million. She has become the Georgia's full-time manager, rekindling some of its faded glory. She insists she is the true owner of the Georgia, but it was Edgar Kaiser Jr. who signed the note for the $5 million she needed, as a favour to Nelson. Skalbania is proud of his new wife but frustrated because she won't let him flip her hotel. He has tried to sell it eight times and has already turned down an offer of $30 million.

After the breakup of his first marriage, Skalbania bought thirty-three of Vancouver's most valuable residential acres on Southwest Marine Drive. Here stood three mansions that had once belonged to some of Vancouver's best-known families: the Reifels (liquor exports), the Farrells (B.C. Telephone) and the Malkins (wholesale groceries). The house on the old Malkin property, which had been totally renovated in the French Regency style by Chunky Woodward in the 1960s, quickly became the victim of Eleni's penchant for Greek villas. Though worth an estimated million dollars, it was torn down (eight bathrooms, mirrored reception hall, swimming pool and all) with this bene- diction, pronounced to Moira Farrow of the *Vancouver Sun* by the ever-bashful Nelson: "Whether or not I knock down a house is about as important as what colour pants I put on."

The $4 million megahouse the Skalbanias have built is sev- enteen thousand square feet of Mediterranean cosiness that includes an indoor racquetball court with a glass viewing wall opening into the living room, which has a grandstand.

It was not always so.

———

AFTER MOVING WEST from Wilkie in 1943, the Skalbanias settled in the gritty east end of Vancouver. Nelson's father was an apprentice carpenter "who went to work with his tools in a cornflakes box." The family was so poor that Nelson had to stay home from school on washdays because he had only one pair of pants, and when his mother contracted tuberculosis, his younger brother was sent to a foster home. "My older brother Richard and I were at home alone," Nelson recalls. "The two of us, six and seven years old, used to get up with Father and cook breakfast. Father would give us twenty-five cents every day to buy dinner. After school we would clean the house, then walk downtown across the Cambie Street Bridge and do the family shopping at Woodward's, where food prices were low. We had the option of taking a bus back. But that cost a nickel, and we always did something else with it. I don't know of many guys who, at the age of six, could come home and wash their clothes, scrub the floor, and cook family meals, simple as they were." He remembers eating boiled rice every night for the first ten years of his life.

The adversities of his youth are reflected in a surviving fragment of a poem called "Futility" that young Nelson wrote in high school, describing life as being ". . . dead to purpose after a brief remembered existence." But he studied hard and was fortunate enough to come under the personal tutelage of a history teacher named Walter Moult, who coached him for a university scholarship. He worked his way through a Civil Engineering degree at the University of British Columbia and later won a scholarship to the California Institute of Technology, graduating with a Master's degree in earthquake engineering. He returned to Vancouver in 1964 to become junior partner in McKenzie and Snowball, an engineering firm that designed and certified high-rise apartments. It was there that he first came into contact with real estate developers who knew how to use other people's money to make themselves rich—meanwhile sidestepping Skalbania's modest invoices for earthquake advice.

He persuaded five banks to lend him $5,000 each and, with his engineering partners, bought an eleven-suite apartment building for $74,000, turning a modest $2,000 profit within twelve months. "I literally worked fourteen, fifteen hours a day," he recalls, "chasing jobs to build up the engineering practice, designing like hell, working my ass off, and in a successful year, we would clear $25,000 each. Then I discovered I could option a piece of land or a building for $5,000 or so, resell it before I needed to raise the money and make a hundred thousand. Perhaps working as a structural engineer was the nice thing to do in the community, and my mother and father could understand what I was up to. But it wouldn't help me buy a Rolls, own a jet or travel all over Europe."

He recruited a group of Vancouver doctors, dentists and teachers, who put together $150,000 and built a 107-suite apartment building near Stanley Park. Skalbania flipped it while the cranes were still on the site, doubling his partners' investment. He went public briefly through a company called United Provincial Investments ("I found out that people go public for only two reasons: they're either broke or they're stupid") but spent most of his time and energy perfecting the flipping technique. "The main key," he confesses, "has been doing my deals in an inflationary rising market, so that even when I make a mistake, it's been erased in six months. Also, I've stuck to buying properties in growth areas and leveraged the hell out of them. If I'd tried it in Saint John or Winnipeg, I'd have died with my mistakes."

The speed of Skalbania's flips can be breathtaking. "I'll never forget coming from a hockey meeting with Skalbania and arriving in Toronto on the same plane," recalls Johnny F. Bassett, the Toronto entrepreneur. "He had this briefcase with him, and we stopped somewhere on the way into town. I asked Nelson, 'Where the hell are you going? We've got a meeting at Carling's and they're waiting for us.'

"He said, 'I'll just be a minute.'

"He came out in about seven minutes, and I asked him what he'd done.

"'Just bought a piece of property,' he said.

"A few minutes later, Skalbania stops the cab again, and when I wanted to know where he was going now, he replied, 'I'll be back in a minute.'

"He came back out, and I asked what he'd done.

"'Just sold it,' he said and told me he'd made a million bucks. The poor cab driver—I don't think he'll ever get over it.

"I like Nelson. He does things in a hurry, and his word is his bond—except for one thing. I won his jet from him one night in a gin game, flying back from somewhere. He never delivered."

THE TRAIL OF Skalbania's herd of holdings leads back to an untidy office at Cardero and Alberni streets, just up from the Bayshore Inn. "The first thing you see on the building," wrote Sean Rossiter in *Saturday Night*, "is a large crest, filling most of a ground floor window, around which are block letters CONSULADO GENERAL DE PERU. Your instinct is to double-check the address. The address is correct. 'Of course,' you say to yourself, 'Nelson's bought Peru.'"

Not quite. He does pride himself, though, on being Peruvian vice-consul for B.C., Alberta and the Northwest Territories—no mean feat for an individual who speaks not a word of Spanish and has been in Peru for only three brief fuel stops. The largely honorary title allows him to travel on a diplomatic passport, carry diplomatic licence plates and attend monthly consular briefings. He admits that he'd feel more comfortable representing "some Caribbean island, but Peru happened to be the only country available."

Apart from a huge Peruvian flag, his office decorations are a Rodin sculpture of George Bernard Shaw, a magnificent Riopelle (from his ridged pallet period) and a Lismer. He has a permanent staff of only ten people, including his two brothers. His working files consist of small piles of documents on his office floor through which visitors pick their way toward his desk. Each pile, which suggests the droppings of some mammoth paper-fed pigeon, represents a deal under active consideration. His secretary types up summaries of the fifty or so deals he is offered every working day. Nothing is too unlikely for him to touch. He did turn down the

transatlantic balloonist who wanted up-front financing for his journey and the group of adventurers who wanted to raise the *Titanic*
by pumping the hull full of ping-pong balls. But he bought into
Canadian Underwater Vehicles, a Vancouver-based firm that claims
to have a $20 million contract to build a deep-water, titanium-hulled
submarine for the Russians ("I want to use it myself, maybe just to
see if *I* can find the *Titanic*"); he has formed an air cargo company
to run a fresh vegetable shuttle from Mexico to West Germany; and
he bought an open-pit silver-gold mine at Eureka City in Nevada
(and flipped it to Bethlehem Copper). He owns a piece of the
Canadian Gold Brewery in Prince George and half a dozen hotels,
as well as apartment units, shopping centres and office buildings
in Vancouver, Calgary, Edmonton, Toronto, Seattle, San Francisco
and Denver. His only long-standing investment is the 48 percent he
has of the engineering firm where he started.

In 1979 he fielded a new company called Stewart Forest
Products to make a $400 million bid on a 3.5-million-acre timber
tract in the Berland and Fox Creek areas of Alberta but didn't
have the management depth to carry it off. His only current
public company is Skalbania Enterprises, which took over the
Internetwork Realty listing on the Vancouver Stock Exchange in
the spring of 1981. The stock had a phenomenal gain of 785
percent during 1980. With an original capital of $2 million
(and Peter Thomas, the Victoria real estate entrepreneur, as a
partner), he is planning to move into the oil and gas fields. His
favourite word in business is "next," as in, "Well, the deal fell
apart and cost me a bundle. *Next.*"

A KEY ELEMENT in Skalbania's ability to flip properties at a profit is that he never falls in love with them. And no wonder. He so seldom sees what he buys or sells. He studies balance sheets, cash flows and locations but only infrequently takes the time for a personal tour of the actual site. "I once bought an apartment building in Vancouver," he explains. "It had seventy-four suites, cost me nearly $2.6 million. I didn't go into the building, didn't really *look* at it—just drove by, that's all. I didn't have to look inside to know the replacement value. I didn't give a damn whether the suites were dirty or not, because the land was worth $50,000 a unit, and I was paying $35,000 per suite. I needed $1 million for a baseball team by the end of the month, so I spun it off for $3.6 million to a developer in West Vancouver. Buying right doesn't only mean buying the right property in the right place at the right time but also financing it right, so that it's easily resaleable. I usually avoid being hurt by knowing the people I'm dealing with, taking their word for things. It saves a lot of energy."

He operates out of a dog-eared address book and telephone booths, with most deals concluded in hotel rooms, exercise gyms or aboard private jets. (When he doesn't use his own jet, he goes commercial and buys three seats on the Redeye, removes the armrests and sleeps across them.) He's a master bargainer, keeping his emotions in check like a streetwise poker player. The moment the deal is done, the sense of excitement that grips him is almost sexual in its intensity. His cheeks glow with the flush of conquest as he performs his bargaining ploys.

"I'm totally disorganized," he admits. "I don't do proper accounting and that kind of stuff, sell too many things too idiotically quickly." His Meadowlark Mall in the west end of Edmonton went into receivership, and he lost $350,000 on the purchase of eighteen houses in Regina. But it's highly unlikely that Skalbania will ever spin himself into bankruptcy. "It's difficult to go bankrupt without bank loans," he chortles. "I usually buy everything on my own account or with individual partners. Without having extended a major line of credit, the banks can't foreclose on me."

Skalbania hardly qualifies as the meticulous banker's dream loan prospect. He can't be bothered to fill out the required forms, and whatever assets he pledges as collateral are usually flipped before the bank has time to process his application. In the late fall of 1976, he was in Toronto negotiating with the National Hockey League, doing his final deal with Fred Eaton for the Eaton Place project in Winnipeg and in the process of buying up 2,500 apartment units from Peel-Elder Developments, which he promptly flipped to Peter Pocklington. He was in his hotel room on a Friday afternoon with Fred Stimpson, a Vancouver developer who is his occasional partner and was then part-owner of Nelson's jet. "I was on my second martini," he recalls, "and Fred leaned over to me and said, 'This morning your comptroller and mine crossed cheques for $130,000. Mine was to pay for the jet's operations for the past couple of months, yours for some money you still owe me on the Bel Air Apartments deal. My cheque went through. But yours sort of came back.'

"'You mean it bounced?'

"'Yeah . . .'

"Son of a bitch . . . It was three o'clock Vancouver time. I telephoned the Royal Bank guy in B.C., who said, 'Well, Nelson, your loan is up to a million-fifty, and you don't talk to us. We couldn't find you, so we figured this way you'd listen.' I blew up and said I'd have them paid off by Monday and hung up. Son of a bitch. Where in hell do I get a million-fifty by Monday morning? I raped every goddamn apartment block, every goddamn thing I had. Paid them off on Monday and wrote a long note to Earle McLaughlin [then the Royal's chairman]. I got back a five-page letter from their B.C. guy four weeks later in which the last paragraph went something like this: 'Skalbania, we've been in business longer than you have, and we don't quite understand how you earn a living. Maybe you should take your business elsewhere.'"

He did.

His real estate technique is neither new nor particularly inventive. What's different about Skalbania's operation is the skill and scale of his flips. In 1978, for example, he bought the Dufferin Mall in Toronto for $23.4 million ($100,000 down) and resold it on closing day to CPR's Marathon Realty for $25 million, using the $1.6 million difference as down payment for a package of buildings owned by Marathon in Vancouver. He purchased Vancouver's Avord Building for $10.2 million in 1974, sold it for $11 million to Dr. Charles Allard of Edmonton six months later, bought it back for $13 million and before closing resold it to Sam Belzberg for $13.25 million. Similarly, he spun the 775-suite Bel Air Apartments in Edmonton from an original purchase price of $5.8 million to $24 million in 1980, being in and out of the project himself three times. When Eaton's closed its catalogue department, he bought, sight unseen, the company's twenty-four outlets across the country. These included the Edmonton warehouse (at $2.3 million for $100,000 down), which he flipped for $3.9 million a year later to Charlie Shon, an Edmonton developer. "That's not bad leverage," he says, "but Shon has since turned down $22 million for it. So who's smart in this business? Not Skalbania."

Shon also figured in what may have been Nelson's greatest coup: being paid $2.4 million *not* to buy something. "That was cute," he recalls. "I had put down $200,000 on 2,800 apartment suites owned by Abbey Glen. The price was $59 million, with $9 million cash in thirty days, another nine a year later and the rest in mortgages. When I told Shon about it, he gave me the $200,000 back, so I only had it out overnight. We had this arrangement that he would put up all the money, and if I sold out before closing, we'd share in the profits, with me getting 60 percent and him 40; after closing, the percentages would reverse. A week goes by, and he says, 'Nelson, I think it's a heck of a deal; I'd like to own it all for my retirement. Let me close and give you a cheque for $2.4 million.' So I sold out my fictitious interest in something I hadn't bought yet—for $2.4 million. Of course, Shon did very well. He sold one of the buildings for $2.5 million more than he paid for it, and they're now probably worth $45 million."

Skalbania's biggest deal was the $100 million worth of properties he bought from Genstar in December 1978. He put $500,000 down and had sixty days to raise the $60 million needed to close. He pre-sold enough of the units to cut his cash requirements to $21 million, which was supposed to come in from a Montreal mortgage firm. The funds didn't arrive in time. "It was a Saturday morning and the deal was supposed to close on Monday," he remembers, "so I called four friends of mine: Bob Lee, Ronnie Shon, Geoffrey Lau and Michael Cytrynbaum at Sam Belzberg's First City outfit. It took them only a couple of hours to commit the $21 million, though I had to give up a large piece of the action. Then the guy from Montreal phoned that he'd put the money into my account after all. I went back to my guys, and they all wanted to stay in, which left me out. So I telephoned Cytrynbaum, who was in for $6 million, and asked him what he wanted for taking his money back, but in such a way that next Saturday he'd show up again if I got into trouble. Mike took all of five seconds to think it over and said, 'I'll take $500,000.' I said, 'Okay,' which meant that he got half a million without having to pay even one day's interest. The deal closed on February 12, which happens to be my birthday. I still owned the Devonshire Hotel, so I went there and got really blasted. Drunk as hell."

NELSON SKALBANIA'S SWEEP of six franchises in six months during the latter half of 1980 and first months of 1981 made him an instant power in Canada's sports establishment. In a series of daring moves, he bought the Atlanta Flames of the NHL for $16 million and moved them to Calgary; bought two junior hockey teams (the Calgary Wranglers and the New Westminster Bruins); bought the Memphis Rogues of the North American Soccer League, renamed them Boomers and moved them also to Calgary; along with Jimmy Pattison acquired the Vancouver Canadians of baseball's Triple-A Pacific Coast League; tried to buy the Seattle Mariners of the American Basketball League; and purchased the Montreal Alouette football team.

His association with commercial sport dated back to 1976, when he found himself owner of the money-losing Edmonton Oilers, then fighting for a cellar spot in the World Hockey Association. He didn't particularly like the sport ("I'd seen the odd game on TV but never played hockey as a kid and had never seen a live game"). But when he was approached by Cam Allard, whose father owned the team, it was on the basis that the Oilers were an irresistible bargain. The Allards wanted to get rid of their sports involvement because it had brought them unwanted publicity. They had done a series of profitable deals with Skalbania through their family-owned North West Trust Company and offered him the team for only $300,000, which would become its working capital. Nelson agreed but soon discovered that the Oilers were in worse financial shape than he had thought. He went to see his friend Peter Pocklington, the

Edmonton financier with whom he had done real estate flips worth about $200 million, and said, "Peter, I've drilled this oil well and it's dry. I want you to come in for half."

"I don't know whether we enjoy a real friendship," says Pocklington, "but we certainly have respect for each other. Denny stands up during any deal and says, 'That's what I'll pay you,' and it's likely too much. Then, just before the ink is dry, he's off trying to sell it to me or somebody else. It's sheer balls. At the time, the Oilers deal was just a ridiculous thing, strictly an ego trip. But I've got a bit of that too." The two men went out to lunch and began their bargaining. Pocklington didn't have any spare cash at the time, so the issue quickly became what possessions he could offer that Skalbania would consider worth half his bankrupt team.

"Look, I'll throw in this seven-carat diamond ring. It's off my wife's finger, worth a hundred and fifty thou, easy."

"Well, ahh, Peter . . ."

"Jesus, do you want her finger too? Okay. I'll throw in the Rolls and a Krieghoff. But that's final."

"You've got a deal."

The Rolls in question was the 1928 phaeton that became the flagship of Nelson's car fleet, and the deal also included two A.Y. Jacksons and a Maurice Utrillo. At the time, the package was easily worth $700,000; a year later Skalbania sold Pocklington the other half of the Oilers for half a million dollars' worth of real estate.

Having been bitten by the hockey bug, Skalbania went on to buy another WHA team, the hapless Indianapolis Racers. The club was in receivership at the time, and even though Skalbania paid only a dollar for it, he overpaid. With his purchase price, he had to guarantee the Racers' debts, which quickly mounted to $2 million. "For each game I saw, it cost me twice as much as the full stadium," he recalls a trifle acidly, but adds, "watching the games when you know you're losing your ass dollar-wise is relatively exhilarating." His chief accomplishment was to bring into big-time hockey a youngster from Brantford, Ontario, then playing with the Sault Ste. Marie Greyhounds, named Wayne Gretzky. Skalbania flew Wayne, his parents and his agent to Vancouver for the final bargaining session. "I had never seen Gretzky play, but I heard all the reports and went from there. We went on a six-mile run, and when he beat me, that was it." The seventeen-year-old prodigy was signed to a seven-year contract worth $1.75 million. The letter of intent was drawn up and signed on a piece of blank paper while they were sitting on the grass, still sweating after the run. It was later formalized.

Even Gretzky couldn't rescue the skidding Racers. "We put on a big campaign to attract more ticket buyers. At the time, we had 2,500 season-ticket holders; after our great promotion drive, we went up to 2,700. That's when I knew Indy wasn't a hockey town. Hell, they used to run basketball headlines in the paper: 'ROOSEVELT HIGH EKES OUT 108–107 WIN OVER TRUMAN HIGH' or something like that. Never a word about hockey." The Vancouver entrepreneur made the headlines himself when he folded the team, on December 12, 1978, and left season-ticket holders in the lurch. "NELSON, GO BACK TO SKALBANIA," suggested the *Indianapolis Star.* Gretzky's contract was sold for $400,000 to Pocklington, who immediately extended it to twenty-one years, the longest in the history of professional sports.

Skalbania's first choice for Gretzky was the Winnipeg Jets. He flew him in on his private jet and went to see his pal Michael Gobuty (who has been a frequent real estate partner of his and owned a controlling piece of the Jets). The two men couldn't agree on a price. In one final bargaining session, Skalbania offered to play Gobuty a game of backgammon: "If you win, you can have Gretzky at your figure. If I win, I get a piece of the Jets." Gobuty declined on the grounds that backgammon wasn't his big game, and Nelson flew off to make his deal with Pocklington.

———

SKALBANIA'S NEXT VENTURE into hockey was to buy the Major Junior A New Westminster Bruins of the Western Hockey League as a birthday present for his twenty-year-old daughter, Rozanda. (His second daughter, Taryn, is studying Greek archaeology.) "I was close to getting remarried in Athens when I read in the papers that the Atlanta NHL franchise could be moved without anybody's approval," he recalls. "I thought to myself, 'Holy shit, I could move them to Calgary, but I've got no time to do anything about it.' So I typed up a letter offering to buy the team for $20 million and sent Rozanda to Atlanta with it. Tom Cousins, who owned the team, later told me, 'I'm in Atlanta, and I'm dealing with people who don't want to pay $11 million for my team when this goddamn girl walks in with a $20 million offer. So I thought I've got to at least talk to this guy.'"

The two men eventually agreed to a $16 million price tag, with a $100,000 deposit. Skalbania promptly pre-sold TV rights to Molson's for $6 million, negotiated another $6 million in loans, got his deposit back and sold 49 percent of the team to a group of Calgary businessmen (including Ralph Scurfield of Nu-West Group and the Seaman brothers of Bow Valley Industries, who had originally bid $14 million). The net effect of these lightning transactions was to make him effective owner of the Calgary Flames for an investment of minus $100,000. (Skalbania later reduced his ownership to 30 percent.) Until a new coliseum is erected, the games have to be played in the dilapidated 6,492-seat Corral, but the first season tickets (in lots of twenty games for $420) sold out in one day. "There's tons of money in Calgary, and they don't know what to do with it," growled a jealous Harold Ballard. "Now that they have a hockey team, it's like a hooker walking into a lumber camp."

Skalbania went on to buy the Memphis Rogues, Calgary Wranglers and Vancouver Canadians in similar deals. But his most remarkable achievement was extending his franchises to the Montreal Alouettes of the Canadian Football League. Although the club had lost $6.5 million during the decade that it was owned by Sam Berger, its home base at Olympic Stadium gives it unlimited cash-flow potential. Montreal's sports fraternity wasn't overjoyed by the purchase, particularly since Skalbania outbid one of the Molsons. "The prospect of Nelson Skalbania moving to Montreal from Vancouver is about as remote as shifting the tar sands to Ste. Scholastique," commented Tim Burke in the *Gazette*. Skalbania made headlines by signing Vince Ferragamo, the matinee-idol Los Angeles Rams quarterback, to a $1.6 million four-year contract and backing him up with James Scott, formerly of the Chicago Bears, and Billy "White Shoes" Johnson of the Houston Oilers as receivers. He is in the process of attempting to turn the Canadian Football League into an amalgamation with the National Football League of the United States to form a continental roster.

One reason Skalbania can afford to be generous with his teams is that he takes full advantage of a tax ruling that allows players' contracts to be depreciated off other income in much the same way farmers can write off breeding cattle. In the $16 million Calgary Flames deal, for example, he was allowed $12 million in depreciation. With Vancouver due to get a domed stadium seating at least fifty thousand, Skalbania is looking forward to converting the Triple-A baseball club to major league status. "I've always wanted to have a team in the city where I live," he says. "No more of this flying to Indianapolis bullshit."

Nelson Skalbania is impossible to capture in any moment of time. The furies of his ego will never be stilled because he is riding a streak of existential risk that can only end in triumph or catastrophe. "I've changed professions from engineering, to real estate, to sports, and God, it's fun," he says. "I'd probably like to slow down a little, do more quality deals, get into oil and gas, have a steady cash flow, play tennis in the sunshine—that kind of stuff."

Meanwhile, he's out there, vital signs pumping, flipping his properties, flinging change into the pay phones that serve as his office outposts. He exists as a kind of mirror image of himself, leaving those whose lives he touches with the eerie sensation that if no one were on the other side of the deals to reflect his presence, Nelson Skalbania would vanish, a figment of his own imagination.

———

CANADIAN CAPITALISM, which alternates between piracy and alchemy, has produced few more fascinating specimens than Nelson Skalbania. His strength was his negotiating skill. Like the master poker player he was, he knew how to keep his emotions in check; he so seldom fell in love with his properties because he so seldom saw them. His problem was that he wrote most deals on napkins and the insides of matchbook covers. What brought him down was that his business depended on continuing inflation to keep increasing the value of most of the assets he bought, even when they had negative cash flows.

On December 7, 1982, he ran out of money, credit and love. His second wife, Eleni, became fed up with his antics and temporarily left him. He offered the Vancouver Opera Company $20,000 for permission to publicly beg his wife's forgiveness during the intermission of one of their performances but settled for making his apology at a private party for more than 250 of his best friends. ("I'll be the most honest, loving, considerate husband possible. I just have to get rid of all the shackles that are draped over my skinny shoulders.") She agreed to a trial reunion, which is still in effect, and on the same evening, he declared that he was $39 million in the hole.

Skalbania's creditors agreed to let him work out his debts instead of declaring bankrupycy—and, amazingly, he still managed to attract backers. The pattern was set with his next investment: Radio Caroline, a pirate broadcaster anchored eighteen miles off the English coast. It was meant to mint money by bypassing British commercial radio regulations, which were promptly changed to sink the venture.

There followed the purchase of a match factory, a mothballed cruise ship, a company that operated fifty miniature theme parks across the United States, a Beatles museum, something called Club West (modelled on Club Med, with horses instead of beaches), a bar in Denver and an Australian aerospace firm promising to launch satellites.

Then he ran out of options. Not only were there sixty-one civil suits outstanding against him, but Skalbania had used a partner's $100,000 deposit in a real estate deal for his own private purposes, such as paying an overdue dry-cleaning bill. He did return the money with interest after three months, but the damage was done. Skalbania was first acquitted by a lower court, but he lost on appeal. Nelson Skalbania was certainly down, but only the brave would count him out.

—1981, 1997

K.C. Irving: How Could He Top the List?

I'VE BEEN HANGING around *Maclean's* for something like forty years but never realized how helpful the magazine can be.

In the July 1, 1998, edition, with its usual dedication to what's best for Canada and its customary dash of diligent research, *Maclean's* picked the country's leaders in every category over the past hundred years. The best of the best.

"Canada," trumpeted its headline in the business section, "is famous for entrepreneurs. The greatest of them all, *Maclean's* believes, was K.C. Irving, the man who built an empire in New Brunswick and, in the process, made himself one of the world's richest men."

I was delighted to find out about K.C., whose corporate enlightenment and creative accomplishments had somehow slipped my attention. Since the 1990s are the age of the entrepreneur, I am happy to pass on some of K.C.'s entrepreneurial qualifications that were somehow missed by Jack Granatstein, the history professor who wrote the accompanying cloying commentary.

Nothing is more important than to provide role models for today's bright and bushy-tailed young entrepreneurs. How else can they have a shot at the top slot when *Maclean's* repeats its contest in the year 2998?

It's not that hard.

The first rule, according to K.C., is to eliminate your competition. Not some of it; all of it. Irving, for example, was a great champion of the free press, as long as he owned every English-speaking newspaper, as well as most TV and radio stations in the province. When he left the country for Bermuda, the Saint John *Telegraph-Journal* editorialized: "Is New Brunswick richer or poorer because he has taken his leave? Does the sun shine? Is there water in the ocean? Is it dark at night? There are some questions which do not need answers . . . ." (Actually there were, but the Saint John *Telegraph-Journal* wasn't about to answer them.)

David Walsh of Bre-X was not on the list, but he and Irving shared at least one attitude important to aspiring entrepreneurs: take the money and run. Taxes are for losers. K.C. abandoned his Canadian residency on January 10, 1972, though he ran his empire with an iron fist for the next twenty years. Except for the $899,156 he willed to Winnifred (his secretary and second wife), his estate of $7 billion was left to a Bermuda Trust with very precise instructions: his sons could not claim the money unless they, too, became non-residents of Canada, to ensure that Ottawa never got a penny in taxes.

Another important lesson: it's much more fun to make your money from governments, and then not pay taxes. Most of Irving's biggest profits were from his $9.3 billion federal contract to build a dozen patrol frigates for Canada's navy. His other great money-making source was cutting trees on Crown lands, leased at the most favourable stumpage rates anywhere on earth.

Here again, an important lesson: great entrepreneurs waste nothing. The shore dwellers along the rivers that carried Irving timber to his mills dared not pick up the odd log that had separated from his rafts for use as firewood, out of fear of being prosecuted for possessing stolen property.

Somehow, K.C. also had a law put on the books that if one of his logs sank a pleasure craft or fishing boat, he wouldn't be held responsible.

Another clue: never give any money away. K.C. wouldn't allow his workers to donate to local charities. When Philip Oland was running Moosehead Breweries in Saint John and also headed the local United Way, he gave K.C. a lift to the airport and mildly suggested that he allow voluntary payroll deductions for his employees so they could give ten dollars a month to their community. "K.C. went berserk," Oland told me, recalling the incident. "He started banging the car's instrument panel and said he would never allow such a thing."

Ignore the environment. When his barge, the *Irving Whale*, sank in the St. Lawrence and began leaking the dangerous heating fluid it had been carrying, K.C. refused to pay the $42 million it cost the Canadian Coast Guard to raise it.

Make certain your corporate structure is too complicated to follow. When the crew of one of K.C.'s tankers, the *Irving Ours Polaire*, sought union certification, they were literally unable to obtain the name of the Irving subsidiary that owned the vessel and couldn't proceed with their application.

Control politicians. K.C. supported most New Brunswick Liberals, including Premier John McNair, until he noticed that one of his small bus lines, from St. Anthony in Kent County to Moncton, wasn't making enough profit. He was overcharging so much that local commuters started to organize car pools. K.C. went to Fredericton and ordered McNair to outlaw car pools. When the premier calmly pointed out that this couldn't be done, Irving helped throw him out of office by backing his Conservative opponent.

Finally, don't hire Charlie McElman as your PR guy. "That Irving Empire," McElman, a New Brunswick senator once told me, hiding behind his parliamentary privilege, "operates with the power of a lion, the appetite of a vulture, the grace of an elephant, the instinct of a barracuda and the principles of an alley cat." But then, if you were K.C. Irving, you wouldn't need PR guys. There is always historian Jack Granatstein.

—1998

The Eatons: Spoiled Kids Who Destroyed an Empire

THERE ARE FAMILY DYNASTIES, and then there were the Eatons. Their fall from grace was even more momentous than it appeared. They were an integral part of the Canadian mosaic, and we felt a special kinship to the family's four generations. Their catalogues had circulations of 18 million; their sixty-two stores sold goods worth $25 million a week. The family was as close as we had come to having an aristocracy of our own. We were proud to rub founder Timothy's brass toe in their flagship stores and grew up cheering the Eaton's Santa. ("Eaton's Santa was the real one," recalled Rick Rabin, of Gander, Newfoundland, who habitually lined the parade route. "You can't fool kids about anything as important as that.")

The private company was founded in 1869 by Timothy, brought to its initial flowering by Sir John Craig, extended to cross-country dimensions by Robert Young Eaton and modernized by John David. Probably the best-known Eaton of them all was Florence McCrea (better known as Flora), youngest daughter of a carpenter from Omemee, Ontario, who married Sir John in 1901. As a token of her special status, Lady Eaton retained the fifty-cent cheque issued to her when she had served an hour behind the ribbon counter during the opening ceremonies of the family's Winnipeg store. She built a Norman castle with seventy rooms at King, just north of Toronto, leased a villa in Florence (originally built for Queen Elizabeth of Romania) and travelled about the country in her private railway car. In a 1927 interview with the *Toronto Daily Star*, after her return from a summer in Italy, Lady Eaton praised Mussolini's reforms ("No more do the beggars around the cathedrals annoy anyone") and lamented that the dictator "is not really in good health, and the only relief is in distracting his thoughts by playing the violin."

"The Eaton name, as a general rule of thumb, appeared in the press only when an Eaton wanted it to," wrote Ron Haggart in the *Toronto Star*. "When a hold-up man murdered a finance company manager on Yonge St., fleeing through Eaton's store and then Simpson's in an attempt to get lost in the crowds, the dramatic chase was delicately described in the press as being 'through a downtown department store and south across Queen St. into another downtown department store.'"

John David Eaton was raised in a Toronto mansion called Ardwold, a house with fifty rooms, fourteen bathrooms and its own hospital that stood a little to the northeast of Casa Loma. In 1933 he married Signy Hildur Stephenson, whom he courted

while he ran the family's Winnipeg store. He served as the president of Eaton's from 1942 until 1969 and maintained a large
house in Toronto's Forest Hill Village, a country seat in the
Caledon Hills, a villa in Antigua and an island in Georgian Bay,
commuting to work in a helicopter he'd learned to fly. (John
David was chosen to head the firm over Sir John's eldest son,
Timothy Craig, who lived in England and spent his life pursuing
his hobby of operating model trains.)

Three of John David's sons, Fred, John and George, took an
active interest in the store. "They are rich men's sons of the most
attractive sort," wrote Alexander Ross in *Maclean's*. "Handsome,
soft-spoken, unobtrusively well-mannered, utterly assured, and
quietly confident of the fact that being born an Eaton is nothing
to be ashamed of. They would not be out of place as constitutional monarchs of some clean little country like Denmark or
Holland." (The family also founded its own Toronto church,
Timothy Eaton Memorial on St. Clair Avenue, now worth about
$7.2 million in real estate alone.)

Fred, who is president of Eaton's of Canada, lives in Forest
Hill and has a summer Rolls (a 1950 model with a space specially
provided by the maker for a picnic hamper) and a 1962 Rolls for
winter driving. Young John, who is the firm's chairman, lives in
a Rathnelly townhouse, drives a maroon Rolls and spends useful
time on reserve military matters.

One of the great mysteries about the Eaton empire was how
the family managed to pass it on from generation to generation
without paying the succession duties that cripple enterprises

many times smaller. The secret was a process called "estate freezing," which involved hiving off assets to a holding company (Eaton's of Canada) that controlled all the common stock, placed in the hands of each succeeding generation after payment of a relatively modest gift tax.

Despite its size and clout, Eaton's did not keep pace with the expansion of Canada's retail trade. Only a quarter century ago, the family's department store chain still ruled Canadian retailing. Eaton's was the country's fourth-largest private employer, ranking right behind the two railways and Bell.

One of the family's many legends was that John David's mistress, whom he had set up in an apartment in Côte-des-Neiges, Montreal, when asked what would make her happy, brazenly declared that she wanted "one of everything" from the family's Montreal store. The merchandise kept pouring into her apartment (that featured a bedroom lined entirely in mink) until a load of bicycle tires was delivered and there was no place to stack them.

John David, father of the four brothers whose flawed stewardship reduced the once-proud firm to near-pauper status, headed the firm from 1942 to 1969 and, like his predecessors, prided himself on never going to the market for new investment capital. That maintained the family's obsession with keeping balance sheets secret, but it also kept the stores from being modernized.

The last time I saw Fred Eaton was in Toronto on December 20, 1996. It was the Christmas rush and he was following family tradition by cruising the stores and wishing his underpaid, non-

unionized staff carefree holidays. He told me there was no truth
to the rumours that Eatons was seeking bankruptcy protection,
even though I found out later that he was lying. Earlier that same
week, the retail chain was declared insolvent. And that's how
dynasties die.

—1997, 1998

Lord Strathcona: Lord of All He Surveyed—and Then Some

MOST CANADIANS REMEMBER Lord Strathcona—if at all— only as a bearded history-book gentleman in a swallow-tailed coat, uncomfortably bashing in the last spike of the Canadian Pacific Railway. Behind this fuzzy public memory was the most remarkable business career in Canadian history. His empire-scale manipulations touched the lives of many men, leaving them with a brooding sense of awe and disquiet, like the first of a month of rainy days.

Although he spent more than half his manhood in tattered exile as an obscure Labrador fur trader, Strathcona more than any other businessman became a major determining force in the early evolution of Canadian economics and politics. His remarkable skill as an international financier made possible the construction of the CPR—a feat that united the country economically as Confederation had politically. During his four decades as governor of the Hudson's Bay Company, he transformed a dominion of wilderness into a highly profitable commercial enterprise. As its president for twenty-seven years, he made the Bank of Montreal Canada's largest financial institution of his time.

Strathcona is rarely remembered now as a statesman, but it was his diplomacy that settled the first Riel Rebellion and his dramatic political switch away from the reigning Tories that toppled Sir John A. Macdonald's first Canadian government. Even less well remembered is the fact that Strathcona was responsible for the establishment of the predecessor forces to the Royal Canadian Mounted Police and Canada's reserve army.

When Lord Strathcona died at ninety-four, in 1914, he had outlived most of the violent animosities that he created as plain Donald Alexander Smith. During the last three decades of his life—alone left of his generation—he listened to his legend and began to believe it. He wished desperately to be remembered not only as a man who had never sinned, but as a man intrinsically incapable of sinning. He regarded his House of Commons seat as a patriotic trust and would not accept his MP's salary. Yet he was tossed out of Parliament for bribing voters to re-elect him, and the success of his companies depended on the loans and stock options his agents distributed to cabinet ministers of both parties.

His contemporaries were sharply divided in their verdicts of the man and his achievements. Sir John A. Macdonald bluntly declared: "That fellow Smith is the biggest liar I ever met." W.T.R. Preston, the chief Ontario Liberal organizer, wrote: "The Smith syndicate was entirely responsible for using Canadian Parliament for the most improper purposes that ever became operative among a free people."

Those who defended Smith were equally vocal. After presenting him with the tenth of his twelve honorary degrees, the Very Reverend Daniel M. Gordon, vice-chancellor of Queen's University, proclaimed: "As a Canadian, I am grateful to God for the large service He has enabled Lord Strathcona to render for Canada." Because Smith spent the first thirty years of his business life forgotten in Labrador, the record of his appearance is almost entirely that of his old age.

He liked to picture himself as a Viking prince, moving the limbs of his six-foot frame with military precision. The formidable penthouse of his gnarled brows gave his snow-squinted eyes a telescopic effect. When he spoke, there was not a quiver in his meticulously trimmed beard. His sentences were ridiculously cumbersome, lacking any flash of wit. Rather than use a word of abuse, even in the most aggravating circumstances, Smith preferred merely to signify his agreement with the a blizzard of words. On the night of his humiliating defeat by Manitoba voters in 1880, for instance, he remarked to James Cole, a Hudson's Bay factor: "I am sorry to say that a majority of the intelligent electorate of my late Selkirk constituency have, in the exercise of their undoubted privilege and right to choose the most fit and proper person available for the purpose of representing them in the Dominion Parliament, seen fit to reject my own humble, not hitherto unacceptable person." Cole described the upset more succinctly: "The damn voters took your money and voted against you!"

"You have properly expressed the situation," Smith replied.

DURING THE DECADES before and after the turn of the century, Smith was one of Canada's best-known public figures. Invitations to the many receptions at the largest of his four homes—a baronial red-stone castle at 1157 Dorchester Street in Montreal's fabled Square Mile—were sought by every social climber. Smith was a snob to the point of keeping a secret guest tally, classifying his visitors according to rank. The impressive roll call included a future king and queen (George V and Queen Mary, who came to Canada in 1901 as the Duke and Duchess of Cornwall and York), a prince and princess, eight dukes, seven marquises, twenty-one earls, six viscounts, six governors general, twenty-six lieutenants-governor, seven prime ministers, twenty-seven provincial premiers, four archbishops, seventeen bishops, twenty-nine Supreme Court judges, fourteen chief justices, thirty-one mayors and fifty-eight generals. (Smith's list even separated this last group into forty-seven generals of the Imperial Army and eleven colonial troop commanders.)

The dining room of the house opened into a garden for summer tea parties often attended by more than two thousand guests. When the future king and queen of England stayed with Smith, he built a special balcony off the second floor so that the royal couple might have a better view of the fireworks display exploded from the top of Mount Royal in their honour. The home's custom-made furniture was carved out of bird's-eye maple; bisecting the house was a dramatic, three-storey staircase, all its mahogany components faultlessly dove-tailed with wooden pegs. Below stairs and out of hearing, a row of eight rooms was partitioned off for the more than a dozen maids and flunkeys.

Fitted more by temperament than by birth for the aristocratic life, Smith ruled his household with humourless mastery. Once, while he was eating breakfast with the missionary-explorer Dr. Wilfred Grenfell, he watched the lamp under the hot-water kettle falter and die. When the missionary wanted to re-light it, Smith stopped him and angrily summoned his butler. "Remember, James," he said, "you have only certain duties to perform. This is one. Never, under any circumstances, let such an omission occur again."

———

SUCH HAUTEUR WAS particularly maddening to those who remembered Smith's inconspicuous background. He was born on August 6, 1820, at Forres, a Scottish milling town in the middle of that brooding countryside where Shakespeare pictured Macbeth and Banquo meeting the doom-happy witches. His adolescence was much less influenced by his father—a tradesman clinging to solvency with alcoholic indecision—than by his uncle, John Stuart, who had been second-in-command during Simon Fraser's exploration of the Fraser River's headwaters in 1808 and later became factor of the Hudson's Bay Company trading post on Lesser Slave Lake. Following his unspectacular graduation from the local grammar school, young Donald began to toil as a clerk in the office of the town lawyer.

When Donald was eighteen, John Stuart came home on furlough and offered to recommend him for a junior clerkship in the HBC. The youngster accepted eagerly. In May 1838, a year after Queen Victoria had succeeded her uncle on the British throne, he sailed for Canada aboard the *Royal William*, a five-hundred-ton timber-trade windjammer. Much of Smith's time was spent reading about the country of his destination. The main reference in the ship's library was Evans's *Guide to Canada*, which contained advice that was more well-meaning than informative. "Canada is a country," he wrote, "where immigrants should not expect to eat the bread of idleness, but where they may expect what is more worthy to be denominated as happiness—the comfortable fruits of industry."

Smith landed in Canada at a time when nationalist stirrings were reaching their culmination in the Mackenzie and Papineau rebellions. British North America then had a population of 1.2 million. The country west of Ontario belonged to "The Governor and Gentlemen Adventurers of England Trading into Hudson Bay" under a charter granted by Charles II in 1670, as an inducement to find a northwest passage—a task the company never took seriously. Inside the quarter continent they ruled, Hudson's Bay officials made all the laws and enforced them. They could marry a man or hang him; they coined money, raised armies and fought wars. At its peak the company's power extended into Russia, Alaska, California and Hawaii.

Montreal, at the time of Smith's arrival, was a puppy bush settlement with a population of barely thirty thousand; its only patch of sidewalk was the approach to Notre Dame Cathedral. McGill University consisted of a medical faculty with two part-time professors. Smith's first job was counting muskrat skins in the stuffy Hudson's Bay warehouse at Lachine for "twenty pounds a year and all found." For three years he lugged around the stacks of pungent pelts. Then he was promoted to junior trader at Tadoussac, an isolated St. Lawrence River trading post near the mouth of the Saguenay. There he spent the most unhappy and unproductive years of his life.

Being forced to mature away from a world he had just begun to know and where he felt the things in which he wanted to participate were happening, he began to feel the gnawing need for self-assertion which never left him. The pressures which made him one of the most frigid aristocrats of his era had their roots here, on his lonely treks through the Saguenay forests, apparently forgotten by his world.

When his cabin caught fire during the summer of 1847, Smith fed the flames with his clothes and private papers, cackling incoherently in hope-exhausted frustration. That fall he began to feel the symptoms of increasing snow blindness. His requests for compassionate leave were repeatedly denied. When the schooner *Marten* called in at Tadoussac on her way to Montreal, he deserted. After Montreal doctors had examined him and declared there was nothing wrong with his eyes, Sir George Simpson, the autocratic Hudson's Bay governor, punished Smith for breaking the rules by assigning him to the company's version of hell: North West River (now Fort Chimo), a derelict trading post in the northeast corner of Labrador.

————

THE NORTH WEST RIVER station was tucked into a clearing on the shore of Hamilton Inlet, a hundred-mile-deep saltwater gash in the frowning eminence of the unexplored Labrador coast. With mountain ranges rolling out of both horizons in the mammoth undulations of a tornado-whipped ocean, the little outpost appeared to be an unwanted chunk of flotsam at the edge of the world. During Smith's thirty years in Labrador, the local Indians and Eskimos regarded him as such a benevolent monarch that after he became rich, a delegation of Nascopies journeyed all the way to Montreal and demanded that he buy Labrador, kick out the Moravian missionaries who followed him and become its king. "It wasn't solitude for me," Smith reminisced about Labrador. "I knew everybody there from the oldest white trader to the youngest Indian hunter and his dogs. I was always busy, and when I had no definite task, I was planning." Smith was the third white man to follow the Hamilton River

up from its mouth at Goose Bay to the awesome view of Grand
Fall—a wilderness-encased waterfall twice the height of Niagara,
where the river plunges over a 302-foot precipice into Bowdoin
Canyon with a roar audible fifty miles away.

Dressed in a flaming flannel shirt and homespun trousers,
Smith spent most of his time bartering blankets and tobacco for
furs. He also acted as judge and doctor. His treatment of wounds
with a pulp made from the boiled inner bark of juniper trees was
later studied by Lord Lister, who introduced the principles of
antiseptics to surgery in 1865. To provide himself with a city diet,
Smith sent to the Orkney Islands for poultry, to Quebec City for a
dozen cattle, six sheep, some goats and an ox. On seven painfully
cleared acres, he grew turnips, cucumbers, potatoes and peas. To
connect his farm with the trading post, he built a two-mile track
for his ox-drawn sulky—Labrador's first road.

With the remarkable foresight that characterized his later
decisions, Smith demanded that the Hudson's Bay Company
assign a trained geologist to North West River. "I believe," he
wrote Governor Simpson, "that there are minerals here which
will one day astonish the world." His superiors ridiculed the
requests and refused to act on them, even after he had sent them
samples of "magnetic iron." Diamond drills have since confirmed
that Smith's "area of astonishing minerals" contains commercial
quantities of iron ore, titanium, lead, zinc, nickel, asbestos and
columbium.

As the fur revenues of North West River declined, Smith
began to trade in seal oil and established a lively export business

with Britain in Labrador cranberries and salmon packed in ice. He even built a small but not very successful cannery. After Sir Leopold McClintock, the British Arctic explorer, surveyed the Labrador coast for the best landing place of the transatlantic telegraph cable, he reported on Smith's unusual activities to the Hudson's Bay Company board of directors in London. "Labrador won't hold that man much longer," he predicted. Smith had meanwhile married Isabella Hardisty, the daughter of a retired army officer. She had come north with her family and had married James Grant, one of Smith's fellow traders, but without church ritual. A few months later, she changed her mind and picked Smith as her husband. The marriage was legalized half a century later in a secret ceremony at the British Embassy in Paris.

Smith returned to England for a holiday and so impressed Hudson's Bay officials in London that five years later, he was transferred out of Labrador to Montreal as the company's chief factor. Canada was then barely two years old. Electricity was still considered a risky innovation; the telephone and typewriter had not yet appeared. Talk at the Saint James Club concerned the purple imagery in the latest rhymes of Alfred, Lord Tennyson, and William Gladstone's surprising eloquence in the British House of Commons.

The bearded Labrador trader had arrived at the company's Canadian headquarters at a strategic moment. The new federal government had just completed negotiations in London for the purchase of nineteen-twentieths of the Hudson's Bay territories for $1.5 million. The transfer might have been uneventful but for the Métis—six thousand French Half-Breeds who farmed around Fort Garry in southern Manitoba. They resented the company's disregard for their rights through settlement and feared the domination of a centralized, English-speaking Protestant government. The incendiary spark was provided by Louis Riel, a fanatic partially educated for the priesthood, called by Smith "a remarkable but ill-balanced man." Riel and his followers marshalled the discontent of the Fort Garry settlers, urging either annexation to the United States or formation of a separate republic.

It is doubtful whether many Canadians today realize by how delicate a margin the Prairies were saved for Canada. "The tendency of North American events is plainly towards the consolidation into one great nation," chirped the *New York Sun* in 1871. "From the Polar Sea to the Isthmus of Darien, there will in time be only one national government—that of the United States. Who among us can say that ours is not a glorious destiny or reflect without exultation that he is an American citizen?"

The Canadian government sent surveyors to the Prairies with instructions to parcel the land into mile-square sections, with no regard for the traditional strip-farming methods of the French and Half-Breed settlers. The move rallied Riel's supporters. They stopped William McDougall, the Ottawa-appointed governor of the region, from entering his territory at Pembina (now Emerson, Manitoba) and captured Fort Garry. In Ottawa Sir John A. Macdonald realized that the country did not have adequate transportation facilities for the dispatch in winter of troops to quell the rebellion by force. Because Hudson's Bay Company interests were so vitally concerned, he appointed Smith government commissioner to investigate the insurrection.

After a two-week journey by train, stagecoach and sleigh, Smith reached Fort Garry on December 27, 1869. Riel promptly arrested him. At a public meeting in the fort square three weeks later, he allowed Smith to proclaim Ottawa's intentions. Icicles hung from Smith's beard as, standing beside Riel in a numbing, twenty-below wind, he promised fair treatment to the mustered settlers. The meeting elected forty representatives to study the proposals. In an attempt to reassert his authority, Riel executed Thomas Scott, a particularly quarrelsome Portage-la-Prairie Orangeman.

When Smith returned to Ottawa, he recommended that an armed expedition be sent to Fort Garry in the summer to impose the rule of law. The troops entered the fort on August 21, 1870, without firing a shot. In his report to Macdonald, Smith also suggested that a permanent semi-military force should be established in the region. This resulted in the formation of the North West Mounted Police, predecessors of the Royal Canadian Mounted Police. Smith capitalized on his popularity with the Fort Garry settlers by winning the Winnipeg seat in the first Manitoba legislature. He became federal MP for Selkirk in 1871. But politics occupied little of his time. He was quietly becoming one of the new dominion's up-and-coming tycoons.

NAMED THE HUDSON'S BAY resident governor in 1871, Smith realized the potential of the assets retained by the company after the sale of the greater part of its lands to the Crown. He foresaw that where buffalo grazed, cattle would one day feed and that much of the prairie was favoured with two hours more sunshine per day during the wheat-maturing season than any other farming region in the world. While other shareholders panicked, he bought up great blocks of Hudson's Bay stock at depressed prices. He gradually acquired enough shares to exercise a working control of the company. On some of this stock, he later realized a 1,300 percent profit. He changed the emphasis of the company's operations from fur to land. So much of its remaining territory was sold by Smith that the Hudson's Bay Company eventually had to repurchase chunks of it for the construction of department stores at many times the original price.

Smith's business reputation prompted many of the Hudson's Bay factors to send him their savings for investment. With these funds and his own growing fortune, he captured stock control of the Bank of Montreal in 1887. For the next twenty-seven years, he was the bank's president, backing many of Canada's most profitable early commercial enterprises. He personally bought a textile mill at Cornwall and built a railroad rolling-stock plant in Montreal.

The flagrant business piracy which accompanies the embryonic stage of most developing economies dominated Canadian railroad construction in the last quarter of the nineteenth century. The twenty-six thousand miles of railway line operating at the beginning of World War I were built with government cash subventions and bond guarantees totalling $489 million. Ottawa also gave the railroad promoters more than fifty-six million acres of land and some of Canada's best timber and mineral tracts. Yet every mile of railway track in the country was privately owned. During the heyday of railway building, one CPR lobbyist boasted that whenever the speaker's bell rang for a division, there were almost always more MPs in his apartment, drinking free liquor and puffing free cigars, than anywhere else in Ottawa.

———

BUILDING THE CPR was the dominant issue in Canada's fledgling Parliament for thirty years, especially after British Columbia made a railway link with the East a condition of Confederation. Smith became a central figure in the first attempt to finance a transcontinental railway.

Sir Hugh Allan, head of Montreal Steamships and sixteen other important telegraph, coal, iron, cotton, tobacco and paper companies, was promised a government grant of fifty million acres and $30 million for the syndicate he organized to build the line. To enlist the support of Donald Smith—by then Macdonald's most influential backbencher—Allan included him on his provisional board of directors and proposed giving him $100,000 worth of stock.

The scheme exploded in Parliament on April 2, 1873, when the tabling of confidential correspondence revealed that Sir

John A. Macdonald had given the charter to Allan in return for $350,000 in election fund contributions. A royal commission confirmed the bribery attempt, forcing Macdonald's resignation. Had he been able to gain parliamentary support, however, he could have picked his successor, possibly even retained his party in power.

When the vote which would determine the fate of Canada's first Parliament was approaching, Smith was in the West. Macdonald ordered him back. "Upon you," he wrote, "and the influence you can bring to bear, may depend the fate of this administration." When he arrived in Ottawa, Macdonald tried to get a pledge of support from him, but Smith would say only that he would support his party if he might do so conscientiously.

The night of the crucial debate, November 5, 1873, was a cloudless, moon-washed autumn evening. The galleries were packed; visitors overflowed onto the floor of the House. At five minutes after one, Smith rose. "I would be most willing to vote confidence in the Government," he said, as the treasury benches yelled support, "if I could do so conscientiously." Then, speaking in the hushed tones of a judge pronouncing his verdict, he dealt the death blow: "For the honour of the country, no government should exist which has a shadow of suspicion resting on it; and for that reason, I cannot give it my support." (The more cynical commentators of the time were convinced that what *really* bothered Smith was that the government's contract with Allan did not give him personal control over the CPR charter.)

Smith's speech nearly caused a riot in the House. Macdonald, incoherent with rage, shouted at him, "Coward! Mean, treacherous coward!" Later he remarked to one of his cabinet ministers, "I could lick that man Smith quicker than hell could frizzle a feather." Those who sat in the galleries that evening claimed that only the presence of the sergeant-at-arms and the immediate dissolution of the House prevented fisticuffs between Macdonald and his former supporter.

In the election that followed, Smith returned to the House as one of the most influential members in the Liberal government under Alexander Mackenzie, a working stonemason who had led the Opposition during Macdonald's regime. Smith fought hard for his seat under his new colours. "His audiences," reported a writer of the times, "were abundantly supplied with eggs of an uncertain age." He won by 102 ballots, but his even narrower margin in the next general election was ruled illegal. To guarantee victory, he had temporarily transferred twenty-six Hudson's Bay families into his riding and bribed them to vote for him. A Manitoba judge, Mr. Justice Betourney, confirmed Smith in his seat, but when a reporter discovered that Smith held a $4,000 mortgage on the judge's home, a Supreme Court appeal reversed the decision.

Smith's parliamentary expulsion was humiliating, but he had long before switched most of the spare-time interests that his Hudson's Bay governorship allowed him to railroading—then the country's most profitable industry. With his cousin, George Stephen, he formed a syndicate to buy the defunct St. Paul & Pacific Railway from its Dutch bondholders. The road had been started in 1857 as a link between Minnesota and the West Coast, but the Civil War intervened after the completion of only 217 miles. Construction had originally been financed through the sale of $28 million worth of bonds to Dutch investors. By the time Smith became involved, interest on the securities had not been paid for seventeen years; the unhappy Dutchmen sold their holdings for less than a quarter of their par value. Smith renamed his property The St. Paul, Minneapolis & Manitoba Railroad (now part of the Great Northern), extended its tracks into Winnipeg and quickly made it one of the continent's most profitable railroads.

This venture convinced Smith that he should somehow obtain a major financial interest in the building and operation of the CPR. Although he was probably the only member of the Mackenzie government who fully appreciated the problems of railway building, he allowed the Liberals to flounder with the project as a federal enterprise. During the five years of the Mackenzie regime, only a hundred miles of track were laid. Partly because of the government's obvious incompetence in railway building, Macdonald was returned to power in 1878. Two years later, persuaded that the CPR would be built faster by private interests, Macdonald awarded the charter to George Stephen, then the Bank of Montreal president and a major shareholder with Donald Smith in the St. Paul, Minneapolis & Manitoba Railroad.

The terms were so generous that W.T.R. Preston, the Ontario Liberal organizer, called the deal "the most stupendous contract ever made under responsible government in the history of the world." The railway company's loans, cash subsidy and capital stock guarantees eventually amounted to $206 million. Completed government roadbeds were transferred to the CPR without charge. The land grant consisted of twenty-five million acres given in alternate sections of 640 acres in a belt twenty-four miles deep on each side of the tracks, with deficiencies in fertile lands made up in other regions. The CPR was also promised a twenty-year railway monopoly in its western areas, perpetual tax exemption over part of its lands and extraordinary authority over passenger and freight rates. In return, Stephen's syndicate guaranteed to complete the work by 1891.

———

ALTHOUGH SMITH AND SMITH'S MONEY provided a major support of the CPR syndicate, his name was left off all company papers and government submissions, in case Macdonald, remembering his treachery, would grant the charter to one of the other interested groups. Smith organized the Canada North West Land Company to get the maximum profit from the territorial land grants. Nearly five million of the free acres were eventually sold to settlers at an average price of six dollars per acre. Smith and other members of the CPR syndicate sold themselves treasury stock at twenty-five cents on the dollar, ensuring personal profits even before the first locomotive was purchased. Smith officially became a CPR director in 1883. For the next decade, he was the most influential member of the board's executive committee.

The ruggedness of the terrain which William Van Horne, the construction chief hired by Smith and Stephen, had to cross, rapidly drained the company's treasury. Stock sales went badly. Dutch bankers, disillusioned by their loss on the St. Paul & Pacific and other railroads, campaigned in European money centres to discredit the CPR securities. Many of the shares had to be sold for ridiculously low prices. Canadian banks floated loans up to their limit. Smith, Stephen and the other directors threw most of their personal fortunes into an ever more hopeless race with construction payrolls and supply bills. Finally, only a further appeal to the government for more cash could save the venture. Van Horne sent Smith a coded cable in the spring of 1884, which climaxed the hunt for funds: "Have no means paying wages, pay car can't be sent out. Unless you send immediate relief, we must stop."

In one of his rare short sentences, Smith summed up the CPR's plight. "It's to the government, or to the penitentiary," he told Stephen. When Macdonald was first approached about giving the CPR more funds out of the federal treasury, he flatly refused. "You may as well ask," he declared, "for the planet Jupiter as for more money." But the CPR directors decided to remain in Ottawa. "The day the CPR busts," one of them remarked, "the Conservative Party busts the day after."

During a party caucus which followed the interview with Macdonald, Tory members agreed to vote an extra subsidy, provided some way could be found of humiliating Smith for his treachery of 1873. Smith was told that the CPR would get the money only if he agreed to contest a Montreal constituency in the next election, not just as a Tory, but as a personal admirer of Sir John A. Macdonald. Smith agreed. He re-entered the House as the Conservative member for Montreal West but rarely attended sittings.

———————

RIEL'S SECOND REBELLION provided the revenues that ultimately saved the CPR. The railroad was completed on November 7, 1885. The first transcontinental consisted of Smith's private car, *The Matapedia,* Van Horne's *Saskatchewan,* an engine and a baggage car. Smith climbed off the train at Craigellachie, a flag stop in Eagle Pass in the Monashee Mountains, to pound the last spike through its iron holding plate into the wooden tie. His first blow merely turned the head of the spike over. Roadmaster F.B. Brothers yanked it out and replaced it with a new one, which Smith carefully tapped in with slow, measured strokes. (The engine that pulled the historic train was scrapped, *The Matapedia* burned to her trucks at Princeton, B.C., in 1925, but Van Horne's private car has been preserved by the Canadian Railroad Historical Association. The maul used by Smith to pound in the last spike was last seen in the basement of his Montreal house, being used to break coal for the furnace. The spike itself was cut into pieces which were set with diamonds to make brooches for the wives of the financiers mainly responsible for the CPR's construction.)

A year after the railroad's completion, Smith was knighted. He remained member for Montreal West until 1896. Afraid that he might swing behind the new Liberal leader, Sir Wilfrid Laurier, the Tories appointed the seventy-six-year-old financier-politician Canadian High Commissioner to the United Kingdom.

London society immediately adopted the former Labrador fur trader as its favourite colonial character. Queen Victoria called him "His Labrador Lordship" or, in kinder moods, "Uncle Donald." "You talk with him," wrote A.G. Gardiner, editor of the *London Daily News*, "and it is as if Canada stands before you, telling her astonishing story."

The *Montreal Star* campaigned for the naming of Smith as governor general of Canada, but he put down the suggestion, preferring his life in London. When the queen elevated him to the peerage in 1897, he chose as his official crest a beaver gnawing a maple tree. As "Baron Strathcona and Mount Royal, of Glencoe, in the County of Argyll, and of Mount Royal, in the Province of Quebec and Dominion of Canada," he represented this country in London for eighteen years. His appointment, oddly enough, was extended by both Laurier and Sir Robert Borden, his Conservative successor.

———

HE WORKED TWELVE hours a day. The lights of his office on Victoria Street burned late so often that the building was nicknamed "the lighthouse." During one holiday in rural England, he began dictating letters to a newly hired secretary on Sunday morning. The assistant politely but firmly declared that he could not work on the Sabbath. Smith paced his room all day and promptly at midnight woke up his startled clerk with the command: "The Sabbath is now over. We must make haste with those letters!"

Under his direction, the first Canadian immigration offices were opened in London. The transatlantic flow of Englishmen increased from ten thousand in 1897 to one hundred and thirty-eight thousand in 1912. On one immigrant-hunting trip to Hamburg, he was so successful that the German government officially notified Canada it would arrest Lord Strathcona if he ever returned to entice away the country's productive citizens.

In the last two decades of his life, Smith's business interests were limited to the stock market and his governorship of the Hudson's Bay Company. The CPR shares he had acquired for $25 reached $280 within his lifetime. This investment, plus his profitable holdings in the Hudson's Bay Company, the Bank of Montreal and other enterprises, including the Dominion Steel Corporation, the Anglo-Persian Oil Company and the Laurentide Company, made him one of the richest Canadians of his day. Finally in a position to compensate for the hardships of his decades in Labrador, Smith became the country's most generous philanthropist.

He gave away $12 million during his lifetime, $20 million in his will. Easily his most dramatic gift—and probably the most deliberately spectacular action in his life—was his donation in 1900 of a fully equipped mounted regiment to help the British fight the South African War. Smith analyzed reports of the Boer successes against the sedulously drilled British infantry and quickly recognized the need for a mobile troop of mounted scouts. He offered a million dollars to raise the Lord Strathcona's Horse—an army of six hundred North West Mounted Police veterans. Volunteers included a hundred adventurous Arizona cowboys who offered to enlist their own horses, but Smith turned them down.

In the fall of 1900, the troops travelled by train across the country to their embarkation headquarters at Halifax. Well-wishers thronged them at every stop. The citizens of Sudbury presented Colonel S.B. Steele, the commanding officer, with a battle flag on which was stitched the earnest tribute: "We are proud of the Empire. We are proud of our Queen. We are proud of Lord Strathcona." The regiment fought in South Africa for a year with considerable success.

After its much-heralded return to England, Strathcona entertained his army at a banquet in London's Savoy Hotel. "The occasion of his own toast being drunk," the *Times* dutifully reported, "produced the wildest enthusiasm, the officers and men springing to their feet, making the roof echo with their ardent cheering." During World War I, the Strathconas were part of the Canadian Cavalry Brigade. In World War II, they fought with distinction in Italy and northwestern Europe as part of the 5th Armoured Division. A, B and C squadrons were sent into action again in 1950 as front-line replacements in Korea.

The gift of the Strathconas gave Smith a worldwide reputation for philanthropy. All the requests for financial aid in his mail were placed on a silver tray. Every Sunday he would fish out a dozen or so. Those which satisfied his strict tenets of being "properly deserving" received a donation. Sometimes he would write for more details. One exception to this ritual occurred during his time as Canadian High Commissioner in London. A youthfully arrogant tramp ordered Smith's secretary to inform him that he was the son of the man who had driven young Donald to Aberdeen when he had left home to sail for Canada. The tramp came out of Smith's office with a five-pound note. Next day he was back. He received more money. But when he was announced again, Smith quietly told his secretary: "Give the gentleman another five pounds and tell him he need not return. You may add that his father did not drive me to Aberdeen. I walked."

———

SMITH'S BIGGEST GIFTS were to English, Canadian and American universities and Montreal hospitals. He financed the university education of nine young Montreal girls in 1884. Nicknamed "the Donaldas," they were the first women admitted to McGill. He donated a million dollars to found Montreal's Royal Victoria Hospital and gave the Grenfell Mission two hospital ships.

In his will Smith divided $6 million among McGill, Yale, Cambridge and the University of Aberdeen. He also set up the half-million-dollar Strathcona Trust for Physical and Patriotic Education in Canada—the forerunner of Canada's reserve army. It still operates from Ottawa, allocating about $30,000 a year for school cadet equipment, scholarships for physical training instructors and other activities "designed to foster a spirit of patriotism in young boys, leading them to realize that the first duty of a free citizen is to be prepared to defend his country." The strangest section in his will provided for the cancellation of debts owed him by the estates of Sir Richard Cartwright and Sir George Foster—finance ministers in the Liberal and Tory governments during the CPR negotiations. While there was no evidence of bribery, the personal necessities of these men that made them borrow from Smith may well have influenced their governmental decisions.

Despite his liberal philanthropy, Smith never forgave Manitoba voters for his defeat at the polls in 1880. He donated no charitable dollars to Winnipeg schools or hospitals during his lifetime and mentioned none of its institutions in his will. He timed his return from an inspection of the railroad's Rockies section in 1909 so that he would pass through Winnipeg at midnight. A deputation of citizens waited to greet him. There was no invitation to enter his darkened private coach. His secretary insisted that he could not possibly allow His Lordship to be disturbed.

Although he understood little about painting, Smith, during his last years, brought together one of North America's finest private art collections. He had works by Raphael, Titian,

Gainsborough, Reynolds, Romney and Constable. Most of the canvases were donated to the Montreal Museum of Fine Arts by his descendants in 1927, when his house was sold to Lord Atholstan, the *Montreal Star* publisher. (The latter converted it into a home for elderly Presbyterian ladies of good but bankrupt Montreal families. The building was destroyed in 1941 to make way for an office skyscraper.)

———

SMITH MADE THE error of many successful men in holding on to his power after age had diminished his capacity for rational command. In the last years, he became unbearably stuffy. When he heard that W.H. Duff-Millar, the agent-general for New Brunswick, had ordered a ceremonial uniform for a royal reception, he tracked down the tailor. Work on the outfit was stopped when Smith personally visited the shop and furiously insisted that, as far as he was concerned, provincial agents-general had no official standing and were therefore not entitled to special dress.

Lord Strathcona died of a heart attack on January 21, 1914, and his snobbery extended beyond the grave. His will directed that money be set aside for the establishment of a leper colony. But it had a strict entrance requirement—only leprous English gentlemen of good standing could apply.

—1958

Bud McDougald: The Tycoon
Who Never Gave an Interview

BUD MCDOUGALD AND I were sitting in the sunroom of Green Meadows, his great Toronto house, with its Georgian stables, willow-lined strolling avenues and thirty-car garage, discussing his death.

I had inquired about the provisions for succession at Argus Corporation, which he had chaired after E.P. Taylor's departure, and he started to reply with the comment "*If*, as and when I croak . . . ."

The unfinished phrase hung between us. I ventured to ask, "How do you mean, '*If*'?"

He looked at me for a long, revealing moment as if staring into the camera of history. Then he shrugged, raised his eyebrows and waved his hand in a gesture of dismissal that seemed to indicate that both of us were well aware of the complexities of human existence and what the hell was the point of adding to them.

We went on to talk of other things. But I vividly recalled our exchange last week when word came through from his mansion at Palm Beach that John Angus McDougald had died. Even though we'd had one terrible fight, we had grown fond of each other. He would telephone me every month or so to see how my next Establishment volume was progressing, offer advice on making *Maclean's* grow faster, use me as a listening post to deride Pierre Trudeau's latest perfidies and invariably tell me at least one new story.

My favourite anecdote concerned a large ranch he had recently acquired in Florida, which had housed a private zoo on its grounds. Under the terms of his purchase, the animals were to be removed, and when he discovered that the crocodiles had been left behind, dozing in the sun, McDougald demanded to know why. The former owner informed him that it was because she had read in my book about his preference for alligator shoes.

McDougald thought this was all great fun but chided me for his now having to bear the expense of removing the animals himself, since he didn't wish to disappoint the previous landlord about the accuracy of my research. (He did have a penchant for alligator shoes, but only for the English bench-made variety that he would buy at a small shop near Claridge's in London.)

McDougald had rebuffed my repeated attempts to interview him, since at the time I wrote my first volume of *The Canadian Establishment,* he unarguably was its dean, having inherited Argus

Corp. from E.P. Taylor and enlarged the assets it controlled to about $2 billion. When he turned me down, I was fortunate enough to get a list of his friends, and started a round of lunches with them, when I would complain that he wasn't co-operating with me, so that I would have to write about his $10 billion empire on my own. As I knew they would, they immediately objected, pointing out that he'd be lucky if his assets added up to $2 billion—but I dug in and made it clear I was going to use the higher figure. The campaign was successful. I knew that as soon as our lunch was over, his friends would be phoning Bud, saying: "There's this crazy guy out here who is going to seriously exaggerate your holdings. You better do something and shut him up."

The call came in, as I expected, inviting me for lunch, and we got along well enough for his first interview, followed by many more.

———

WE ALL HATE to get older, but it was typical of McDougald that he would actually try to do something about it. During the final two years of his life, he engaged himself in a private battle of documents with the archives of the 48th Highlanders, attempting to prove that he really was two years younger than his recorded age, vaguely maintaining he had faked his birthdate in order to enlist as a youngster. (His strength of will did find at least one posthumous expression. When reviewing the arrangements for his burial, a thoughtful member of his family realized that Bud would have been appalled by the length of the hair on the young sextet of professional attendants supplied by Rosar-Morrison, the funeral directors. He telephoned the firm and requested they get haircuts. They did.)

The few friends who were aware of his age realized it was all part of a half-serious attempt to extend past the compulsory retirement age his term as a director of the Canadian Imperial Bank of Commerce—an institution on whose board he had served since 1950. But even though he died the day after reaching his seventieth birthday, it's highly doubtful if any official of the bank would have had either the nerve or the inclination to press the Argus chairman for his resignation. Hardly anyone treated him in accordance with the rules that apply to ordinary mortals. And with good reason.

Bud McDougald was the last of his kind. He was possessed by a Jamesian sensibility—a highly developed sense of the urbane, a limitless faith in manners, a deep respect for privacy and the proper order of things. He would no more question a man about his monetary worth than ask him about his favourite sex position.

In all his dealings—and he maintained an amazing variety of high-level contacts around the free world—he deliberately cultivated the absence of public visibility. He had such a strong sense of inner identity that he required nobody to remind him of exactly who he was.

He viewed the world with the undisrupted gaze of a sentinel scanning distant fields through the battlements of his own castle walls. He had opinions on everything but hesitated to disseminate them, never once making a speech outside of his companies' annual meetings, refusing to appear on radio or TV. Discretion was best, anonymity better. It took me a full year to negotiate our first interview, but I gradually gained his confidence so that he would call me in for lunchtime sessions in his Argus office, both of us sipping Richmello Instant Coffee and munching Dominion Store vanilla cookies, speculating on the state of the world, discussing how fast the country was going down the drain and tabulating who was moving up or down the Canadian corporate ladder.

Our only disagreement came when my book was done and McDougald asked to see a draft of my lead chapter, which was entirely about him. I pointed out that I never show anyone anything I write about them before publication and that he could be no exception. His blue-grey eyes flashed. He rose from his desk, expressed some not very complimentary thoughts about me, suggesting that his purchase of Maclean-Hunter was hardly worth the trouble of keeping me quiet, and finally calmed down when he recognized my position was not negotiable.

Our private lunch meetings continued into the fall of 1977, when he left Toronto for the last time. Once, he decided we should visit the Toronto Club together, "to show the flag a little." It was an amazing occasion. McDougald was ushered in with the punctilious flourish of a pope presuming worship, scattering small comments to favoured members like benedictions. Those he missed came over to his private table (reserved for him whether he was in town or not) to seek his glance or approbation.

He loved the insider's world he had created for himself but never really felt comfortable with the changing ethics of the society in which he prospered. The chairman of Argus lived by his own rules. He would probably have felt much more at home within the strictly defined hierarchies of the seventeenth-century England of Thomas Hobbes, who saw life "as a perpetual and restless desire of power after power that ceaseth onley in death."

Bud McDougald understood power very well and knew how to exercise it. He didn't need anyone to tell him precisely where he fitted into the Canadian Establishment's complicated structures. He knew. Right at the very top.

He took a fatherly interest in Conrad, gave him a membership to the Toronto Club for his twenty-first birthday, and while he didn't directly appoint him as his successor, he certainly made it known that he would have no objections to such an event. That was enough to push him over the top.

As he grew older, McDougald retreated into his various mansions and boardrooms, emerging to view the world ever more rarely, growling at the galloping imperfections of the liberal society he despised. That he paid personal income taxes of more than a million dollars a year accredited him in his own eyes as a roving commissioner free to criticize all government activities. He was never himself tempted to run for Parliament, dismissing the idea "because of the sort of people you have to meet—all that terrible going to strawberry festivals and the like."

He considered all politicians suspect by definition, and when I asked him to name an exception, he couldn't. Finally, after torturous effort and the running down of long lists of possible candidates, he allowed that perhaps Abraham Lincoln wasn't all that bad. Then a look of pure mischief came over his face. He winked at me and said, "But, of course, I like John Wilkes Booth even better!"

—1978

The Day Confederation Life Went Bust

THE CONTRACT BETWEEN Canadians and their insurance companies prior to 1994 was that, even if life on earth remained unpredictable, its three certainties were death, taxes and insurance payouts. Once they died, their surviving spouses, kids, relatives or favourite charities would be taken care of by their policies. That faith was terminally shattered with the bankruptcy of Confederation Life, once the country's fifth-largest insurer, whose roots stretched back to 1871. It turned out to be the largest insurance company failure in North American history. To run a company with a stellar reputation and assets of $20 billion into the ground could not have been easy—even for the crew of misguided incompetents who ran Confederation Life under CEO Patrick Burns.

A self-described "heavy drinker" with a W.C. Fields nose, Burns found his way around Ottawa's restrictive insurance firm regulations by establishing Confederation Trust. The subsidiary operated in a looser regulatory environment, pumping up the company's portfolio with commercial real estate investments in Ontario cities. When these values melted like Häagen-Dazs in the sun, the company went bust. That was a common enough occurrence in the 1990s; what made Confederation Life different was that it had taken horrendously risky gambles with policyholders' premiums, which it did not legally own and from which it was legally obliged to pay out death and other benefits. That was unforgivable in any business; in a mutually owned life insurance company, it was virtually criminal. That no one was held accountable for the irresponsible and devastating decisions of its executives and directors added potent fodder to the antibusiness mood of a growing number of Canadians. Some of Confederation Life's two hundred and thirty thousand policyholders were forced to take heavy losses on the funds they had invested for their retirements, their children's educations and all the other worthwhile reasons Confederation Life's sales agents had given them to buy the policies in the first place. Paul Cantor, the ex-Commerce executive who was appointed president in October of 1993, got there far too late to salvage the situation. His best efforts were frustrated by Great-West Life's prolonged hesitation about whether it should be a white knight and rescue Confed or wait and become a vulture. It chose the latter.

Until Confederation Life's downfall, there had been only two relatively small life insurance failures: Montreal's Coopérants, Mutual Life Insurance Society (with a resultant loss of $180 million) and Calgary's Sovereign Life ($75 million), both in 1992. Alan Graham, the reclusive British investor who ran Sovereign, had first come to Canada as an imported goalie for a Calgary soccer team and ran his company's public relations department with one simple rule: any staff member who allowed the Graham name to appear in print was automatically fired. Graham's favourite charity was helping to preserve a local ceremonial cavalry troop.

More to the point of revolutionary discontent was the highly questionable role played by Confederation Life's board of directors at the time its outrageous real estate acquisitions were being made. Adam Zimmerman, who joined the board after most of the harm had been done, publicly complained that "the company's control and reporting systems were inadequate to the task" and that the directors "didn't know what was happening and didn't understand, if they knew it." That seemed unlikely at best. In 1989, when most of the questionable investments were being made, Confed's board included some of the shrewdest and most respectable of the Canadian Establishment's luminaries, whose reputations seemed hardly worth endangering by negligence in one of their most important board appointments. They included former Confed chairman Jack Rhind (known for being the only corporate chairman, apart from the mutual fund guru, Fred Soyka, who rode his bicycle to work); former University of Toronto president Claude Bissell; Mitel Corp. turnaround artist Anthony Griffiths; Toronto great-causes icon George Mara; Montreal corporate legal genius André Monast; and some guy called Conrad Black. The responsibility of these and the other directors extended far beyond the duty of most board members. Theirs was an exacting task because Confederation Life was a mutual, not a stock, company. That meant it was literally owned by its policyholders, whose surrogates and protectors were supposed to be the directors. Until resurrected by the Confed incident, the time seemed long past when corporate directors could remain imbued with what a British judge had once characterized as "lovable dimness."

The dimness endured. The board had sanctioned Confederation's entry into real estate deals, many of which bordered on foolishness—to the point where Confederation Trust became known as "a lender of last resort." It was the place where desperate borrowers who had been turned down by careful credit officers elsewhere went for mercy money. By 1992 two-thirds of the company's assets had been invested in risky real estate. Confed had also become a major player in financial derivatives, the riskiest of investment vehicles that would be used in 1995 by Nick Leeson to bankrupt Barings Bank. Investing policyholders' premiums in the unpredictable swings of foreign currencies, interest rates, commodity prices and market indexes was the equivalent of getting Daffy Duck high on laughing gas to guard Granny's savings.

After a leading American mutual fund (Piper Jaffray) lost $950 million on derivatives, North Dakota senator Byron Dorgan compared derivatives to nitroglycerine and introduced legislation in the U.S. Congress to ban their use. Despite these risks, a desperate Confed moved massively into derivatives in 1991 through a subsidiary called Confederation Treasury Services Ltd. A year later, just as the company's financial situation was reaching its point of no return, an astounding $10.3 billion had been entered on its books as "*notional* principal amounts of outstanding contracts," which was the only way the value of derivatives could be measured. By the end of the following year, Confed's investment in derivatives had doubled, reaching an eye-popping $20.4 billion, including $4.3 billion in currency swaps, $9.2 billion in interest rates futures and $5.1 billion in foreign exchange contracts—the riskiest derivative category. None of these transactions had any intrinsic worth, and all were subject to random valuation—Confed might as well have invested in ostrich-egg futures, Dutch tulip bulbs or the South Sea bubble.

It might have been tempting for Confederation Life directors to deny any knowledge of these deals, but the amounts were so huge that such a defence was not credible. In fact, Chairman Burns was not only fully aware of these Monte Carlo–style investments, but he actively defended them despite at least one warning from a senior insider. When Frank DiPaolo, of Confederation Life's large U.S. operation, visited the Toronto headquarters in November of 1991, it was not a routine courtesy call. A distinguished insurance executive who had spent thirty-five years with Confed, di Paolo rose to be the American subsidiary's chief actuary and then its vice-president of finance. He had been invited to head office to celebrate his retirement. At a corporate dinner, he found himself seated next to the chairman. He took the chance to warn him against the proposed entry into derivatives. "I told him that this business could be very risky, because even though it might—theoretically—be possible for the company to hedge its risk, in a practical sense it could not be done," he later recalled. "I also mentioned that the new Canadian Insurance Companies Act, about to be enacted, did not permit life insurance companies to assume risks other than those 'related to the happening of an event or a contingency dependent upon human life.' Burns replied that no decision had yet been reached, but if the company did go into derivatives it would be through a subsidiary."

Di Paolo was shocked that Ottawa's financial regulators did nothing to cool down the directors' gambling instincts until it was too late. "It doesn't take the intellect of a Nathan Rothschild," he concluded after Confed's bankruptcy, "to figure out that if you pay the highest interest rate, you can attract enough deposits and see the trust company's assets grow geometrically. Of course, all that money had to be invested quickly. Hence the shift to derivatives, and to becoming a lender of last resort, modes which inexorably led Confederation Trust—and later Confederation Life—to ruin."

There was a postscript to the Confederation Life affair. Its directors had typically not allocated any funds to pay out the earned benefits of its retired employees. Jack Rhind and Patrick Burns deserved no prize for knowing how to run an insurance company, but they surely earned a special citation for brashness. In early 1995, they demanded a special hearing where they seriously requested the court-appointed liquidator pay them overdue bonuses of more than $1 million. Now, that's chutzpah.

Confederation Life's fate was entirely typical of the times. The uncontrolled greed of the 1980s and early 1990s, which eventually brought down most of its practitioners—Cohen, Campeau, Reichmann and many others—fed the Canadian Revolution of 1985 to 1995. It would never have materialized if the banks had not financed corporate treasuries way beyond their ability to repay. The banks, just like the insurance companies that played loose with their depositors' money, were responsible not only for the damage to confidence in their own institutions, but for the withdrawal of confidence in the free enterprise system as a whole.

Canada's bankers really had been the people's fiscal father-confessors; there was something reassuring about their very presence. Every small town or railway whistle stop with a bank branch felt it had a future. Then, like the other touchstones that failed during that decisive decade, the bankers forgot about the people they had been set up to serve and became instead demigods, serving their distorted ambitions and their star customers. Christopher Fildes, writing in the London *Spectator*, neatly summed up what had happened. "It is worrying in more ways than one," he wrote, "to hear international bankers proclaim, as they do, that they sleep like babies. 'Yes,' a City magnate is heard to say, 'these days I sleep just like a baby. Every two hours I wake up screaming.'"

—1995

PART 2: POLITICS

Tom d'Aquino: The Man Who Sold the Farm

TRYING TO MEDIATE between public and private initiatives used to be like going to the dentist. Just as he approached your molars with that nasty drill of his, you'd grab him by the gonads, and with the sweetest of smiles, suggest, "Now, we're not going to hurt each other, are we?"

That was how, in simpler times, business and government managed to maintain an uneasy peace. But ever since the Great Recession That Bugs Us Still, the two spheres of influence spilled into one another. That melding together of private and public purposes seems like an appropriate moment to celebrate the departure from Ottawa of Thomas d'Aquino, the most influential lobbyist in Canadian history.

To some, he was a capitalist hero; to Canadian nationalists like myself, he was a villain, not because he was evil but because his lobbying on behalf of American buyouts was so damn effective.

He once explained to me that he really didn't really mind being called a lobbyist, "since the pope is a lobbyist too." I never considered His Holiness in quite those terms, but on second thought, it seemed like a valid comparison: both men treated their positions not as jobs, but as missions—and each of their policy pronouncements was couched in the patois of unimpeachable papal bulls. D'Aquino's operational code was not so much to impose his private agenda on government priorities as to provide pro-business policy options, doing his damnedest to make their acceptance all but inevitable at crucial moments in Ottawa's policy imperatives.

He was an unassuming gent in terms of his public image, yet in terms of his self-imposed mandate of turning free enterprise into Canada's state religion, he walked on water. He was the first special interest pleader who broke the mould and instead of merely suggesting improvements to the laws of the land, actually authored some of them himself, or at least ghostwrote their intent. For most of three decades, he ran what amounted to a parallel government, first under the banner of the Business Council on National Issues (BCNI) and, since 2001, under the renamed Canadian Council of Chief Executives (CCCE).

As the major-domo of these über-organizations, which brought together the heads of 150 of Canada's most powerful business empires, representing $3.5 trillion in assets and $800 billion in annual revenues (four times the national budget), d'Aquino drastically escalated the corporate clout of his members. He inaugurated more right-wing causes and crusades than any active politician while remaining well nigh invisible, and pre-

ferred it that way. I once referred to him in print as Canada's
"prime-minister-in-waiting." But looking back at his spectacular
career, I realize that this was an inadequate description. When it
came to how government policies impact the business climate,
Tom considered himself to be Mr. Action Central, and he was
not fond of waiting. "If you ask yourself in which period since
1900 Canada's business community has had the most influence
on public policy, I would say it was in the last twenty years," he
told me in a rare late-1990s interview. "Look at what we at BCNI
stand for and look at what all the governments, all the major parties have done, and what they want to do. They have adopted the
agendas we've been fighting for in the past two decades."

That was an accurate assessment, and the fact that, during his
tenure, no federal budget was tabled without his comments on
draft copies made d'Aquino impossible to ignore. (As minister
of finance during the late 1970s, as d'Aquino remembers, Jean
Chrétien once publicly confessed, "I don't do my budgets without consulting with de Business Council on National Issues.").
D'Aquino was single-minded, possessed by an almost evangelical
fervour in the pursuit of his causes. But he was also a small-town
boy playing in the big leagues and remained awed by his own
accomplishments.

———

BORN AND RAISED in Nelson, B.C., he graduated with honours from the London School of Economics. "I took the very

first course that was offered on the law of European institutions, which really focused on European union," he recalled. "That got me very interested in the role of trans-nationals operating within the European Union, and when I went on to do management consulting in Paris, I worked for transnational companies, primarily in Europe. That and my studies at LSE hooked me into this idea that the winds of change were already sweeping over Europe and ultimately would sweep over North America."

When he returned to Canada, he spent three years in Prime Minister Pierre Trudeau's Privy Council Office, until 1981, when he made the shift into the private sector. The BCNI had been established four years before d'Aquino was recruited as its president and CEO by such Establishment pillars as Earle McLaughlin of the Royal Bank, Ian Sinclair of Canadian Pacific and Paul Desmarais of Power Corporation. The dedication of his organizations' members to their cause was hard to exaggerate. When Arthur Child, the CEO of Calgary's Burns Foods Ltd., died in the spring of 1996, for example, he bypassed some family obligations to leave a cool $1 million of his personal wealth dedicated to propelling d'Aquino's efforts.

As the animating agent of the organizations that brought together the nation's wealthiest and most influential corporate honchos, he met their epic expectations. They accorded him a virtually unlimited mandate to alter Canadian public policy so it would be more in line with their aspirations and balance sheets. It was a concentration of power that even the mighty C.D. Howe, at the height of his powers during the Second World War, might

have envied. Much reviled by his critics, d'Aquino was very good
at what he did. For one thing, whenever he made a policy pro-
nouncement, he was guaranteed an audience. In the fall of 1997,
for instance, when he was preaching a reduction in Canada's environmental goals at the Kyoto Conference on global warming, no
fewer than seventeen Ottawa deputy ministers gathered to watch
his slide show, a record seldom equalled and never surpassed. A
tall, humourless gent, he outmanoeuvred the few bureaucrats
who dared take him on by the simple gambit of being smarter—
and faster—than they ever dared to be.

D'Aquino's boldest venture was his success in dictating the
1981 revision of Ottawa's competition bill, the federal legislation
that is supposed to keep piratical corporate instincts in check. "We
had previously decided that Canada needed a new competition
law," he recalled. "But attempts to bring the business community to heel on the issue got nowhere. When André Ouellette
was named minister of consumer and corporate affairs, we had
lunch in his Centre Block office and he said, 'Look, one minister
of consumer affairs after another has tried to bring amendments
to the competition law, and they've all failed. What are we doing
wrong here?'

"'André,' I said, 'the time has come for Canada to have a new
act that is not antiquated, but I can tell you that if you pursue
what has been the historical approach—that business is bad, and
we've got to bring in a law to tame them—it will never work. If
you bring in a different approach, I'll turn the business community around and we'll work with you.'"

According to d'Aquino, the minister replied, "That's fine. You've got a deal." During the next three years, the BCNI spent $1 million on the project, hired its own team of twenty-five lawyers headed by Toronto's Bill Rowley, and by 1985 had produced a 236-page master plan. Incredibly, it became Canada's new Competition Act, virtually word for word. As might be expected, there were no provisions for class-action suits; corporate monopolistic conspiracies were so vaguely defined that they were just about impossible to prosecute; and the prosecutions themselves were moved from criminal to civil courts. It was the only time in the history of capitalism that any country allowed its antimonopoly legislation to be written by the very people it was meant to restrain.

———

D'AQUINO'S MOST DRAMATIC intervention was his pivotal advocacy of the pro-American side of the Great Free Trade Debate of 1985–88. His organization spent $20 million in Canada's most intense lobbying effort, ever. D'Aquino had launched the idea as early as 1981, when both the Liberals and the Conservatives were against even exploring its prospects. He became obsessed by the advantages of free trade without a moment's concern for its adverse effects on Canadian culture. His greatest roadblock was Brian Mulroney, the incoming prime minister at the time, who was dead set against such a deal with the Yanks—until a streetcorner conversion, when he ran into d'Aquino.

"After he was elected but just before Brian moved into 24 Sussex, and while he was still living in the Opposition leader's house at Stornoway," d'Aquino told me at the time, "I was walking along Acacia Avenue and ran into him. 'Lookit,' he said, 'I know you people have been promoting this idea of free trade now for a couple of years and I've read your most recent paper. It's got a lot of appeal and I'm really looking at it with great interest.'

"That was within ten days of the election and was the first favourable sign that I had seen from any of the Conservative leaders," d'Aquino exulted. "Brian had sufficiently high regard for the BCNI that if we thought it was a really important issue, he should at least take a good hard look at it. And he did. By the end of that autumn, he had bought the argument. The Shamrock Summit in Quebec City followed in April, and the rest is history."

Not all of d'Aquino's Ottawa assignments went smoothly. When Chrétien returned to Ottawa in the early 1990s as leader of the Liberal Opposition, one memorable winter evening, at a European ambassador's residence, there was a shouting match between d'Aquino and the veteran Quebec politician that shook up those who witnessed it. "There were four tables set out for dinner," d'Aquino recalled. "Jean and I were at the same one, but he was at one end and I at the other, talking with the ambassador. I could overhear him saying, in his brand of English, 'You know de business community of Canada, it's done me in. I been trying to raise money for de party and I can't get no pennies out of dose guys, after all I did for dem. See dat big shot d'Aquino over dere? He's my problem cause he's leading dose big business guys!'

"It was becoming somewhat embarrassing," d'Aquino confessed, "so I said, 'You know, Jean, I really don't know why you're so up in arms. You've accused us of being great supporters of Brian Mulroney. Let me remind you that corporate Canada was largely supportive of John Turner.' The discussion got so heated that at one point I said, 'You know, Jean, the party you lead bears no resemblance to the party I once served, none whatsoever. In fact, you people are not qualified to run Tanzania!'"

The feud didn't last very long. One summer day not long after the catfight, when the Liberals had been elected to office with a majority, Chrétien called d'Aquino and asked if he and Aline could come over and see Tom's house, cantilevered over McKay Lake, in the heart of Rockcliffe. The two couples spent three hours in pleasant chit-chat. After that, the prime minister had little problem implementing his lakeside host's BCNI agenda. The circle had been closed.

———

THE MOST FAR-REACHING of d'Aquino's many crusades was his unsuccessful bid to turn into law the Multilateral Agreement on Investment (MAI), which, until public protests flared and eventually forced an indefinite postponement, the Chrétien government was prepared to sign. The specific proceedings were kept so secret that there was no parliamentary debate on the issue, even though MAI represented the greatest potential threat to Canadian sovereignty since we traded Pamela Anderson for Howard Stern.

Former Liberal deputy prime minister John Manley took over as CEO of the CCCE on October 14. He boasts an appropriate pedigree, but it is doubtful if ever again Ottawa will buy the notion, so successfully propagated by Tom d'Aquino—that what's good for big business is necessarily good for Canada.

—2009

Brian Mulroney: Wooing New York's Millions

DRIFTING AROUND THE private receptions before the meeting of the Economic Club of New York in 1984, a reporter would have found it hard to name any Canadian power brokers who had stayed home. They turned out to pay visible homage to the new prime minister's official American debut. Dressed in their best regalia, the Canadians who owned and/or controlled the country's economy were sending Brian Mulroney a clear signal that they approved of his message.

More remarkable was the heft of the representatives from the U.S. investment community who had turned out for this, the 306th dinner in the seventy-seven years the Economic Club had been holding such shindigs. It was the most influential audience outside a joint session of Congress, representing a distillation of the decision makers who redistribute U.S. investments among the world's time zones.

These are the Wall Street big hitters, men with large corner offices who never dial their own telephones and would happily finance another assault on the Alps by Hannibal if he could only keep his books straight. Many of their wives were there, attracted by the reputation of Mila and Brian as North America's newest and most glamorous power couple. They looked like the kind of women who raise Lhasa Apsos, wear aviator glasses for walks in the country, air-kiss celebrities and never eat the top lid of their sandwiches. "Listen, Malaura," I overheard one of these creatures breathlessly briefing another, "this is really a big deal. That guy with the hair is the president of Canada!"

What Mulroney understood about the guests who thronged the huge hotel ballroom was that, even more than craving fat bottom lines (and thin female ones), his listeners wanted to be loved. At a time when any politician in the Third World and most of Europe can get elected by depicting Ronald Reagan as a senile Dr. Strangelove, these men and women chomping their filet mignons resented their isolation and ached for strangers to underwrite their righteousness.

Mulroney's message, delivered in his best Kirk Douglas whisper, was direct: send us your megabucks and we will be your pals. "To all who seek a definition of peaceful association between nations," he declared, "I say look no farther. It is unlikely you shall find a better illustration than the simple story of friendship and prosperity that has marked the evolution of our two countries over the years."

Mulroney understands these power paladins in a way that

Pierre Trudeau and René Lévesque, who addressed this same group, never did. These merchant adventurers are not frightened off by investment risks and were never bothered by Trudeau's anti-Americanism or Lévesque's noises about separation. What they couldn't tolerate was any politician who changed "the rules of the game" under which funds were originally committed. That was why the loudest ovation of the evening greeted Mulroney's declaration: "There shall be one game—building Canada—and one set of rules. These shall not be changed after the game has started to the detriment of any of the players."

Mulroney said little that was new, but his words carried a disproportionate impact because the chief executive officers of the Fortune 500 in the audience never bother with statements of policy issued by foreign governments or even the "situationers" prepared by their own PR flacks. They like to get the news directly from the source, the big guy who's running the country. That was why Mulroney made such a production of his retreat from his predecessor's Canadianization measures. He stuck yet another sword into the Foreign Investment Review Agency, surely history's most toothless dragon, declaring that it was really dead this time, done for, kaput.

Mulroney once again demonstrated his ability to place himself squarely in the centre of an audience's emotions, so that he seemed to be speaking on a one-to-one basis with each of the fifteen hundred diners. When he interrupted himself to ruminate on the undefended border between the United States and Canada, he ad libbed: "There hasn't been a shot fired in anger between our two countries since 1812. That wasn't much of a war. We captured Detroit, took one look around and gave it back." Even the bookend-Mounties guarding the dais managed to stay awake throughout his address.

At the time, most Canadians didn't realize that Mulroney was genuinely at home with the Wall Street barons who turned out for him. From 1980 to 1983 he had been a director of the Hanna Mining Company of Cleveland, the Iron Ore Company's corporate parent, which later slipped under the control of Conrad Black. But before that, Hanna was the centre of a giant spoked wheel, uniting investments from five great family fortunes: the Mellons of Pittsburgh, the Hannas and the Humphreys of Cleveland, the Bechtels of San Francisco and the Graces of New York. While he never became one of them, Mulroney established the connections and the credibility he was now exploiting to attract new investment funds into Canada.

As the evening ended and the crowd dispersed, the faces of the Economic Club members were relaxed in a post-coital glow of satisfaction: Canada is A-OK. The guy with the hair who's running America's attic was user-friendly. It had been a tough crowd to charm, and as they climbed back into their limos, the Wall Streeters were already reverting to type.

"Hey, Virgil," somebody yelled across the street. "What's the world's fastest animal?"

"Beats me."

"A chicken in Ethiopia!"

—1984

René Lévesque: Meeting the Wall Street Cowboys

THEY WERE THE really big fish in the Wall Street aquarium, but when Separatist Quebec premier René Lévesque came to address them within the solemn enclave of the Economic Club of New York, something went terribly wrong. A mutual fund guru sitting across the table from me kept leaning over to his partner and muttering, "Hell, this is a declaration of civil war, Harry. These guys want to do Gettysburg and George III all in one go."

"Oh, I don't know, Barney," his partner, a bright-eyed man with a broken nose and America's last crewcut, replied. "I've crunched these Quebec numbers backwards and forwards through our computer, and it still looks better than Gabon."

Maybe it was that damned tuxedo Lévesque had rented for the occasion. Imprisoned within its unfamiliar confines, he spoke with none of the speed and sky he usually radiated. I had watched Lévesque in action on the Quebec hustings, when his body seemed to be held together by elastics and the world was his ashtray, able to charm and enthrall even the most hostile of audiences. On such occasions, he made his listeners feel that Quebec independence was the most profound moral option of our time.

But not tonight. He went on, in that GI-Joe English he learned while serving with the U.S. infantry as a correspondent during the Second World War, describing the inevitability of Quebec separation, trying to wring some kind of reaction out of his phony comparisons with the American Revolution, returning constantly to his theme that Canada was conceived in sin and that those Canadians who refused to accept his thesis—because of not having been born in Quebec or their WASP cussedness—were dead wrong.

The performance didn't jell. The mask slipped. Instead of appearing to be one of the great political prophets of his time, René Lévesque stood revealed as a fanatic in a borrowed tux. In planning his appeal, the Parti Québécois leader forgot the cardinal rule of dealing with American money men: they insist on knowing the rules of the game. Now, Lévesque was telling them not only that he intended to alter the rules but that he was changing the game.

There is little ideology involved in measuring credit ratings. Even the worst risks of all, such as czarist promissory notes, seem to find buyers. Quebec will probably be able to raise all of the funds it needs, but the all-important interest rate—the cost of that money—will be higher than it was before Lévesque made his speech. The province already has long-term debt obligations of more than $3 billion outstanding, and the James Bay power development will eventually require another $16 billion.

So far, the difference between Ontario and Quebec issues has been about seventy-five basis points (one basis point is equivalent to 1/100th of 1 per cent), but no Quebec bonds have been sold. (The last Montreal issue of $214 million went for a considerably higher rate than some Venezuelan debentures floated the same week.)

The Economic Club speech was more of a turning point in the hardening of Lévesque's position than it need have been because it provoked the very first outright hostility he had encountered. But for the Quebec premier to accuse "English-Canadian businessmen out to spread their antediluvian ideas about Quebec south of the border" of having somehow sabotaged his performance was silly. He managed that trick all by himself.

Even though the overall reaction was clearly unfavourable, in retrospect it was not easy to tell exactly how uncomprehending Lévesque's audience really was. As I left the ballroom of the New York Hilton, I overheard two American bankers exchanging views on the evening's proceedings.

"I damned near fell asleep in there, Virgil. What did he say?"

"Not sure, Oswald. Something about a quiet revolution that didn't go far enough."

"Well, we're not going to put money out to finance any revolutions, that's for damn sure . . . Say, did you ever read my 'Let's Repeal the Twentieth Century' speech? Must send you a copy."

"You just do that."

—1977

Kim Campbell: Ah, We Hardly Knew Ye

AND WE'RE NOT going to know ye any better from this damp squib of a book. What a story: the self-confessed wood nymph conceived at a timber lookout near Port Alberni becomes the country's first woman (first British Columbian, first yuppie) justice minister, attorney general, national defence minister and, whammo, prime minister of Canada.

A CV to kill for.

Yet her book, *Time and Chance*, surfs instead of diving. We learn little about the real woman who had the chutzpah to grab all that, and survived to write about it. What we do learn is that politics at the top (she was PM for 132 days) is just as shoddy as we suspected it was. In some ways, Campbell's ingenue approach is useful because the book catches the nuances of promise and betrayal, describes the inner workings of the Mulroney cabinet and allows the reader to peek into the anat-

omy of her election campaign, even if it was among the worst
run in Canadian history.

Unfortunately, in its middle chapters, this book oozes like
overripe brie. Being a deferential Canadian despite her much-
touted irreverence, Campbell uses the awkward device of
criticizing her enemies—real and perceived—not by attacking
them, but by quoting from her stepdaughter's diary entries that
contain her adverse comments. That's a transparent and basically
silly device, but it serves to drive home her point that whatever
losses her party suffered (a wipeout, in fact) were not her fault.

If, indeed, the 1993 election was stolen from her by the pla-
toons of Mulroney strategists who ran her campaign, as she charges,
there is surprisingly little anger in the book. Too many crooks may
have spoiled her wrath. Yet as holder of the nation's highest political office, she must have been responsible for something. Allan
Gregg, the pollster she inherited from her predecessor, once told
me that the only way for an incumbent PM to lose a TV debate was
to eat a live rat on stage. Kim managed it without the snack.

She went into the campaign with the highest approval rating of any Canadian political leader in three decades; just six
weeks later, Campbell was running a poor fourth and facing
defeat in her own riding. The most interesting chapters deal
with her demise during that critical period. Instead of her usual
off-the-wall charm, she spent most of the campaign delivering
school-marmish economic lectures, while promising voters nothing they didn't already have. Probably the most telling moment
in her nightmarish election campaign was a stopover in Kelowna,

where a cornered and exhausted Campbell let the truth hang out. "I'm working hard to get re-elected," she told a small rally, "because if I get thrown out of office, I'm not sure I can find a job." Delivered in jest, it was the most honest moment of her campaign.

That lack of greater purpose was the ultimate condemnation of Campbell's brand of politics. Any woman or man who seeks to be prime minister in this bedevilled country of ours ought to approach that august office with the courage of her or his convictions, or at least intentions. There must come a moment in the lonely quest to be the *grand fromage*, when passion clambers up to endow policies and issues with something more illuminating than necessity.

For Campbell, that moment never came. She stumbled through the campaign like a Woody Allen in drag, comically inept, blaming others for her pratfalls—even for hotel-room temperatures not exactly to her liking. One of the fragments of hard evidence she produces to prove that she was being manipulated by Mulroney's former handlers is that they kept the temperature in whatever space she was occupying as cool as he had liked it, but not at the toasty temperature she preferred. Death by thermostat. If no executive decisions on radiator heat levels were forthcoming, neither was there any cogent policy analysis. *Nada.*

Campbell's decision to enter the Tory leadership race in the spring of 1993 seemed to swing on degrees of perceived loneliness. When she was speculating on whether or not to try for the brass ring, her prime concern was what sacrifices in privacy would be required. "I began to wonder if I wanted to subject myself to the loneliness that would come from being in the prime ministerial spotlight," she asked herself. "Weekend parties would be few and far between." So much for constitutional reform, balancing the trade deficit and boosting industrial productivity.

That paradox of reaching for power without really knowing why pervades the book. In an aside on page 281, Campbell recalls enjoying the attention of a friendly dog on her campaign travels. "You know, if I win this, I could have a dog," she remarks to one of her assistants. After that, whenever she hesitates in her resolve, members of her entourage whisper "bow-wow" in her ear—and the caravan lumbers on.

What portion of blame for reducing the Conservative party from 157 to 2 seats she doesn't apportion to the Mulroney team is placed squarely on an unco-operative media. Campbell confesses it wasn't until after the election that she discovered that the press was so hostile to her because they had been forced to endure spartan conditions aboard her campaign bus, while those dastardly Liberals plied reporters with free cappuccino. (I do not rise to defend my craft easily, but we can't be bought for cappuccino. Well, maybe rented.)

The American novelist Peter De Vries, describing a character similar to Campbell, wrote: "Deep down she's shallow." That was our Kim. Yet, occasionally, rays of wisdom shine through the book, such as her description of the Trudeau legacy. "Pierre Trudeau had been the unwitting architect of division in this country," she writes. "He had attempted to address the cultural concerns of

Quebeckers by giving them what they hadn't asked for—power in Ottawa—in a way that increasingly alienated the West; hence the arrival of Preston Manning and Lucien Bouchard as the leaders of the disaffected constituencies in 1993."

The author's sense of irreverence seems undiminished. Kim Campbell may not have been a miracle worker—or even a great line dancer—but at least she was relatively fresh, and still had an unexpired shelf life. She recalled, for example, being introduced to Nathan Divinsky, her first husband, during her third year at UBC. The good-natured mathematics prof was known to his friends as "Tuzie," because of his inability as a youngster to pronounce his Hebrew nickname, Tula. "My first reaction on hearing this," Campbell recalled, "was to ask: 'Does he have a brother called Threezie?'"

Campbell's fundamental weakness as a politician was that she never took time to serve an apprenticeship at anything except life. She became justice minister only seven years out of law school, counting the brief sixteen months she spent articling at a Vancouver legal factory. (The same leap from graduation to the justice ministry took Pierre Trudeau twenty-five years to complete.) She became a federal Tory only five years before being sworn in as prime minister and had little feel for her party or the perverse idiosyncrasies of Conservative politics.

No matter what her autobiography claims about how she achieved power, it was a fact that the country emerged from the Meech and Charlottetown disasters with only one consensus: no more guys in suits. Since Kim Campbell was clearly not a guy and, as the famous Barbara Woodley photograph proved, held her suits in front of her, Canadians quickly developed a crush on her. That brief affair went sour when the forest nymph turned out to be just another wooden politician, and not a very good one at that.

—1997

Louis Riel: The Mad Rebel Who
Was Our Founding Father

EVERY ONCE IN a while, almost in spite of itself, Canada's Parliament does something worthwhile. That was the case when the House of Commons granted speedy approval to Constitutional Affairs Minister Joe Clark's motion recognizing Louis Riel's "unique and historic role as a founder of Manitoba."

Clark went on to salute the Métis leader for "deep devotion to his people and his willingness to pay the ultimate price of his life," pointing out that recognition of Riel's crucial role in Canadian history is "an indication that we have matured as a nation."

True enough. When Riel was sentenced to be hanged in Regina in 1885, Sir John A. Macdonald, the Tory prime minister—who was not above playing up to the anti-Catholic voters of Protestant Ontario—told a friend who had requested clemency for the Métis leader: "He shall hang, though every dog in Quebec bark in his favour."

Hang he did, but Riel's strange saga—particularly his refusal to hide behind a justified plea of insanity that might have saved his life—remains Canada's most enduring myth. A messianic rebel in a nation of cloying conformists, Riel remains the perfect Canadian martyr: a well-meaning yet deluded mystic who died prematurely by pretending to be sane.

In his time Riel inspired hero worship and contempt in almost equal measure, being condemned by English Canadians as a traitor who well deserved to be hanged, while being worshipped in French Canada as a victim of Anglo-Saxon racial prejudice. The conflict that swirled around him, then and now, is as ancient and as contemporary as Canada itself—the clash between the semi-articulated collective demands of the Métis and the stubbornly held belief in individual rights of English Canadians.

Despite his humiliating defeat and death by hanging as a traitor at the age of forty-one, Riel's defiance salvaged the French-Canadian fact in Canada's North West, and in the process bestowed on the French-speaking Métis a degree of self-confidence and self-assertion they had never possessed. "His name marks a deep furrow in the soil of our young country," editorialized Montreal's *La Minerve* the day after Riel's hanging. "The hand that placed the gallows rope around his neck wounded a whole people."

At the time of Riel's exploits, the Métis around the Red River (the site of modern Winnipeg) had grown restless because their

main sources of livelihood—the fur trade and buffalo hunt—
were drying up. Possessed by the fierce pride of pioneers—they
had, after all, opened up western Canada—and now they felt
left out, recognizing that the newly evolving circumstances
would neither restore their past nor validate their future. That
was when, led by Riel, they decided to draw on their French and
Indian roots to fashion a peculiar world of their own—a new
nation, their nation.

Riel captured the local Hudson's Bay Company post and
declared himself president of the provisional government of
Rupert's Land and the North West, covering most of the Prairies
and the North. At the time, his republic was the world's second
largest, exceeded in size only by the United States. He chose
as his flag Samuel de Champlain's golden fleur-de-lys and a
green shamrock (to honour the new government's treasurer,
a professional Irishman named W.B. O'Donoghue) on a white
background. For eight months, he governed his people with
enlightened grace—and some considerable ambiguity.

He was caught between his French nationalism and loyalty to
the idea of a British Canada, never able to let go of either emo-
tion, eventually becoming trapped in a polarization of his own
making. While restlessly championing the rights of his people,
he was just as insistent on gaining "our rights as British sub-
jects." Riel calmly negotiated the terms for Manitoba's entry into
Confederation and told his tiny legislature how proud he was of
the people of the North West for "having trust enough in the
Crown of England to believe that ultimately they would obtain

their rights." Nonetheless, Macdonald soon dispatched an army brigade to bring the rebel to heel.

Riel's greatest error was executing a boisterous Irish Protestant drifter named Thomas Scott, a marginal frontier character who had amply demonstrated his anti-Métis prejudices. Although Scott's only recorded crime was yelling abuse at his Métis captors, he was sentenced to death, and the sole explanation Riel offered at the time was, "We must make Canada respect us." It was that senseless execution which empowered the violent anti-Riel reaction in Orange Ontario.

Even Riel's dress symbolized his split in loyalties. During the time he was president of his puppy republic, Riel received visitors while wearing a Victorian frock coat and hand-sewn moccasins. He drilled a Métis guard of honour to welcome the British troops and planned to preside at the ceremony turning the western territories over to Canada, but was instead chased out of the country.

Macdonald bribed him to stay away, but Riel returned and twice ran successfully for the House of Commons as an Independent from Provencher, though he never took his seat. After a nervous breakdown and a lengthy spell in a mental asylum at Beauport, Quebec, he moved to Montana, but returned in 1884 to lead the last rebellion fought on Canadian soil. This was not the dreamy statesman of his Manitoba period, but a hard-edged religious fanatic proclaiming himself as the "Prophet of the New World." Riel set up another provisional Métis government in Batoche, a fording place on the South Saskatchewan

River, forty-four kilometres southwest of Prince Albert. It was there that the Métis nation was defeated by a volunteer Canadian army; Riel was arrested and shipped to Regina for trial. (He was first taken to Winnipeg, but when the authorities discovered that under Manitoba law half the jury could be French-speaking, Riel was transferred to the territories court in Regina, which more readily guaranteed a guilty verdict.)

It's very Canadian that Parliament has now bestowed post-humous sainthood on Riel, the tame administrator of Red River, rather than Riel, the untamed rebel at Batoche. But at least we recognized him as one of our founding fathers—an eternal reminder of this country's divided soul.

—1992

Jack Pickersgill: "Sailor Jack"
and the Politics of Patronage

JOHN WHITNEY PICKERSGILL'S approach to government was so uniquely his own that his name found a place in
Canada's political dictionary. The expression "Pickersgillian"
came to signify any partisan ploy that was too clever by half. His
persuasive manner and encyclopedic knowledge of Ottawa and
its ways, his mastery of Commons rules and his intense loyalty
to Lester Pearson allowed him to exercise a decisive and not
always benign leverage on the course of federal events. But his
violent partisanship, dated view of Canadian society and erratic
political judgment made him a dubious asset to the hard-pressed
government. He interpreted each new suggestion not in terms
of its future potential, but merely by how it tallied with the past.
He judged policy initiatives on the basis of their administrative
acceptability and regarded any reform with suspicion.

"Jack is so firmly hooked on the past that I sometimes think he's wearing cement boots," commented one of his colleagues. Another minister swore that rare indeed were the meetings of the Pearson cabinet during which Pickersgill failed to mention the way Mackenzie King used to solve the crises of his day. Pickersgill readily billowed forth irrelevant historical data (such as the fact that John Bracken's Manitoba cabinet of 1922 was composed entirely of Presbyterians), but had little feeling for contemporary events.

Still, despite his dated view of Canadian politics, Pickersgill was a pivotal player among Ottawa insiders. First, as the only senior assistant Mackenzie King could tolerate and secondly as a senior adviser to two prime ministers: Louis St-Laurent and Lester Pearson. "Check it with Jack," became the validation for many a major policy shift.

Part of Pickersgill's problem was that he really had no contact with modern Canada. He had grown up on a Manitoba farm, attended a local university and then, except for summer holidays on the coast of northern Newfoundland, had spent the rest of his life entirely in Ottawa. "Metropolitan urban society is just outside my human experience. What the great majority of Canadians regard as a normal environment has not been my environment and this undoubtedly colours my outlook," he once admitted.

What allowed Pickersgill to prosper so long at such high levels of influence within the Ottawa hierarchy was his uncanny ability to manipulate the gears of bureaucratic control and his faith in Liberal patronage. His thirty years within the Ottawa power structure had taught him all the tricks both of how political control of the civil service could be exercised and of how bureaucratic methods could be used to drain the will of the politicians. He had the habit of power and knew the mechanics of the game.

———

PICKERSGILL'S UNUSUAL CAREER spanned four political eras and left a deep imprint on each. Between 1937 and 1948, he had functioned as Mackenzie King's chief adviser, and it was during this epoch that the phrase "clear it with Jack" first became a password to power in Ottawa. He was an even more important arbiter of influence during the administration of Louis St-Laurent, and in 1953 emerged, full-blown, as a cabinet minister and an MP for Bonavista-Twillingate on the Newfoundland coast.

His next guise was as one of the most effective Liberal Opposition frontbenchers during the Diefenbaker years. After the Liberals regained power in 1963, Pickersgill emerged once again as a prime ministerial confidant. Near the close of the Pearson period, when he could sense the draining away of his political power, Pickersgill smoothly slid into a self-created plum job as head of the Canadian Transport Commission. It may not have been exactly a noble career, but it was—well, cohesive.

Like Mackenzie King, Jack Pickersgill could not see much scope for public service away from power. Probably more than any other Liberal, he considered his party not so much an organ of the people as an organ of the state and in private would often refer to the Liberals as "the government party." His career and opinions made him the incarnation of the Ottawa Liberal Establishment. He acted as though he really believed that, by accepting the burdens of office, the Liberals were bestowing a benefaction on the nation at large and that any criticism of Liberalism was unpatriotic. Just before the 1957 election, Pickersgill declared with a straight face: "It is not merely for the well-being of Canadians but for the good of mankind in general that the present Liberal government should remain in office."

His party affiliation seemed so close to a religion that one wondered whether faith alone and not reason informed him. Questioned by a reporter about the characteristics of Liberal prime ministers, he replied: "They never, any one of them, ever told a conscious lie or allowed anything that was calculated to give a false impression. Mackenzie King, for instance, was meticulous to the point of being tiresome about it, putting in all sorts of qualifications so that nobody in any conceivable circumstances could ever show that there was anything about his statements that was untrue."

If the Liberals were lily white in the Pickersgillian lexicon, the Tories were jet black. "The real trouble with the Conservative Party," he once said, "is that basically it has been a party of Anglo-Saxon racists. They really don't believe in the equality of Canadians. They really don't believe the French have any rights in this country, unless they act like a conquered people." On another occasion, he remarked that Conservative governments are "like having the mumps—something you have to endure once in your lifetime, but when it's over you don't ever want it again."

Though Pickersgill's influence was exercised in the hush of his office and the privacy of the cabinet chamber, he was best known for the displays he put on in the House of Commons. His penguin shape was constantly bobbing up and down during the excitement of debates. Physically clumsy, he was utterly incapable of sitting still. When he was a youngster, his grandmother had made him a standing offer of five cents for every five minutes he could keep quiet. "I needed the money badly, but I never earned a penny of it," he recalled.

The thrift he learned growing up on a Prairie homestead dominated his life in the expenditure of both time and money. He never parted easily with the coins he carried in a woman's black, clasp-type change purse stuffed into his right hip pocket. He used pencils until they were inch-long stubs that could barely be gripped. He once complained at length in the House of Commons about the fifteen cents he had lost in an airport stamp-vending machine. On a twelve-day trip to British Columbia in 1952, as clerk of the Privy Council, he submitted an expense account of $30.35. He wore only two ties—his Oxford New College brown-and-silver stripe and a blue-and-white polka dot—depending on friends to notice when the ties became frayed and send him new ones.

———

PICKERSGILL'S FATHER HAD died in 1920 of wounds suffered at Passchendaele. He had to help run a small lumber business managed by the family to supplement the income from their quarter-section homestead at Ashern, near Lake Manitoba. Both before and after the death of the senior Pickersgill, politics was the family's main dinner-table topic. The father had been a hard-bitten Tory who gave his eldest son the middle name of Whitney after Sir James Pliny Whitney, a Conservative who became premier of Ontario in 1905. Young Jack grew up such an ardent Tory that at ten he converted to his faith two school chums who happened to be the sons of Ashern's leading Liberals. When the boys, in turn, tried clumsily to convert their families, the angry fathers called the elder Pickersgill and demanded that he order his son to give up the schoolyard politicking. "That didn't stop me," Pickersgill recalled. "I swore the little buggers to secrecy, took them into the woods at lunchtime and instructed them on the evils of giving the franchise to women and the glories of the Conservative Party."

Pickersgill's own conversion to Liberalism occurred in the fall of 1925 when, as a University of Manitoba history student, he went to hear Arthur Meighen, then Conservative party leader, speak at the Winnipeg Rink. "I was a Tory when I went in and a Liberal when I came out," he remembered. "I felt that Meighen was on the wrong side of three issues—racial tolerance, tariffs and colonialism. The Tories had not really accepted the implications of self-government; they were reluctant to see Canada become an adult nation." The young student's ideological transformation was further strengthened during his two years of studying nineteenth-century history at Oxford on an IODE scholarship. He qualified for two degrees at the end of his studies there but didn't have enough money to pay his diploma fees.

Pickersgill spent the eight years after his return from Oxford as an obscure lecturer in European history at Wesley College in Winnipeg. When he still hadn't received a salary increase or promotion by 1936, he wrote exams for the External Affairs Department, topping his group, and joined the civil service on October 14, 1937, at $2,280 a year. Mackenzie King was then in the habit of seconding to his office bright young men from the department, and O.D. Skelton, the undersecretary of state, nominated Pickersgill for the job. "You won't last more than six months," a colleague predicted. "Nobody ever does."

But the posting lasted eleven years and grew into a relationship unique in the history of Canadian politics. As King's main speech writer, private secretary and general confidant, Pickersgill grew closer to the prime minister than any other man in Ottawa. King, as he got older, found contact with new faces increasingly distasteful and learned to depend more and more on his trusted assistant to maintain touch with the political world. One reason Pickersgill's help was so acceptable to King was the younger man's instant realization of how useless it would be to attempt any alteration of the prime minister's style and vocabulary. "His language," Pickersgill said later, "appeared to have been frozen in the latter part of the nineteenth century. Mr King didn't like flamboyant phrases. He detested the word 'challenge' and would never use the adjectives 'sober' or 'decent.'" Pickersgill became such an expert in gauging King's reactions that he could point out to the other assistants who helped draft paragraphs for the prime minister's speeches exactly which words would be stroked out.

———————

THE RELATIONSHIP WASN'T always smooth. The two men quarrelled openly during the 1945 meeting in San Francisco that established the United Nations. Pickersgill had suggested to King that a good way of solving Canada's dilemma over a national flag would be to replace the Union Jack flying on Parliament Hill with the Red Ensign on VE Day and then pass a law adopting it as the official flag. King agreed to hoist the distinctive emblem for VE Day but insisted that Pickersgill tell Ottawa it would be removed the next morning. "If you once put it up, you'll never be able to take it down," Pickersgill snapped irritably at the prime minister. King angrily ordered him to do as he was told, and when after King's death Pickersgill read the diary entry for that day, he found himself referred to as "an impudent upstart."

To protect himself, Pickersgill maintained his job classification as a foreign service officer, temporarily assigned to the Prime Minister's Office. He admired King but doubted that the admiration was mutual. "To an extraordinary degree," he once remarked, "Mr. King regarded me as part of the furniture."

His relationship to Louis St-Laurent was vastly different. The obscure fixer of the King era became the true grey eminence of Canadian politics under King's successor. When he was sworn into office on November 15, 1948, St-Laurent had spent most of the preceding two years in the politically insulated External Affairs portfolio. He depended on the "special assistant" he had inherited from King for direction on how to operate the Prime Minister's Office. Political observers in Ottawa insisted that for the first three months of St-Laurent's term at least, the country was to an astonishing degree run by Jack Pickersgill. "I had a very great influence on Mr. St-Laurent," Pickersgill admitted. "He had more confidence in me than in any cabinet minister or anyone else." During the 1949 election, St-Laurent made a pact that he would commit himself to no appointments or public appearances that weren't "cleared with Jack."

MOST CANADIANS FIRST heard of Pickersgill in June 1952, when St-Laurent appointed him to succeed Norman Robertson as secretary to the cabinet and clerk of the Privy Council. This was a non-political job, but Pickersgill had become a political creature, and St-Laurent soon saw that it might be more useful to have Pickersgill in the cabinet. That meant not only promoting him over the heads of 160 Liberal backbenchers, but also finding a constituency he could win.

This problem was solved by Joey Smallwood, the premier of Newfoundland, who had become friendly with Pickersgill during the negotiations leading up to Confederation. At one critical moment, it was Pickersgill's quick thinking that had saved the whole project. Mackenzie King had felt that Newfoundland should join Canada only if a substantial majority of her people voted for Confederation. The first plebiscite ended in a stalemate. When Pickersgill heard on the morning news that a bare 52 percent had supported union in the second vote, he dug up the percentages of the popular vote received by the Liberals in every election under King. At ten o'clock that morning, King placed his first daily phone call to Pickersgill. "Well, did you hear the Newfoundland result?" he asked coolly, implying that the vote wasn't high enough to warrant Confederation. "Yes. Isn't it wonderful!" Pickersgill shot back gleefully. "Do you realize, sir, that the Newfoundlanders want union with Canada by a considerably higher percentage than Canadians voted for you in any election except 1940?" King, obviously surprised, replied with a snort, but the plebiscite figures suddenly became acceptable.

When Smallwood first suggested to Pickersgill that he should run in the Newfoundland seat about to be vacated by Gordon Bradley, the secretary of state, who was being retired to the Senate, Pickersgill didn't think it could be done, but Smallwood assured him: "Don't worry. When I'm through with you, you won't recognize yourself." Pickersgill agreed to run, providing he could limit his electioneering on the island to five days, so that he could spend the rest of the campaign at St-Laurent's side. He was appointed secretary of state on June 12, 1953, and a week later opened his brief campaign by sailing into Twillingate aboard the coastal steamer *Glencoe*. The local fishermen saluted him with a blast from thirty sealing guns, while on the flag-decked wharf a brass and drum band whacked out the hymn "Hold the Fort, For I Am Coming."

PICKERSGILL FOUND HIMSELF hailed more as a hero than as a vote seeker. Smallwood would get him up on a platform, point to him and thunder: "This is Pickersgill! Isn't that an incredible name?" Then the premier would lean down and confide to his audience: "You'd better like him despite his name. He's the second-most-important man in Canada . . . some day he'll be prime minister!"

Pickersgill won his seat with a 7,500-vote margin and earned the nickname "Sailor Jack" by buying a 115-foot schooner to make the rounds of his constituency. But Smallwood's assurances that Pickersgill would become prime minister were received less enthusiastically in Ottawa. C.D. Howe acidly remarked to a reporter: "I don't think the newest member of the cabinet should aspire to leadership right away." In the House of Commons, the Conservatives were delighted that they could finally taunt the man so long dedicated to advising prime ministers on how to keep them out of office. They treated Pickersgill as something of a performing animal. Tory hecklers called him, among other things, "Jumping Jack with springs in his trousers" and "Poor Old Pick" and asserted that he was "deaf in one ear and dumb in the other." Pickersgill didn't help matters by replying to every Opposition thrust with a smart-aleck retort. On July 1, 1954, St-Laurent astonished Pickersgill's critics by appointing him to the important and sensitive immigration portfolio.

The best-remembered legacy of his term in office is the report of a speech he made to a group of Liberals in Victoria in which he claimed that no immigrant was as good as a Canadian-born baby. He insisted that the Victoria *Colonist* had ripped his words out of context, leaving out his vital qualification that a child born and raised in this country is naturally better adapted to the Canadian way of life than any newcomer. But his denials never caught up with the original headlines.

Pickersgill's most controversial contribution to the St-Laurent government was to plan, along with Walter Harris, the disastrous Commons strategy of the 1956 pipeline debate. When C.D. Howe moved closure on each of the pipeline bill's three readings, he was acting on the instructions of Jack Pickersgill and seemed himself hardly aware of the significance or long-term legacy of what he was doing. After the Liberals moved into Opposition, Pickersgill's advice proved equally bad, but it was still taken. It was Pickersgill who drew up the ill-fated non-confidence motion which Lester Pearson moved on January 20, 1958, asking, in effect, that the Diefenbaker government resign and turn power back to the Liberals. This allowed John Diefenbaker to produce his so-called "hidden report" and to launch the 1958 election that won him a landslide.

———

DURING THE REST of the Liberals' Opposition period, Pickersgill's performance improved. Dedicated to the destruction of the Conservative government, he became one of the party's best infighters, taking the floor to hurl barbs across the House more often than any other Opposition member. He once broke into a sonorous speech by Donald Fleming sixty-two times with interjections that ranged in rudeness from the inelegant to the vulgar. He regularly called John Diefenbaker "utterly incompetent" and used every device to accuse him of lying without actually saying the word, which would have been against parliamentary rules. In one 1959 debate, he summed up the Diefenbaker record, and then, in a sweep of anger, declared that Diefenbaker and his promises were just like Humpty Dumpty—broken. The prime minister laughed, agreeably surprised by Pickersgill's mildness. Then Pickersgill bore in. Referring to Allister Grosart, the former vice-president of McKim Advertising in Toronto who had been Diefenbaker's campaign manager, Pickersgill chanted: "Yes. Just like Humpty Dumpty. And all McKim's horses and all McKim's men can never put him together again." Diefenbaker was furious.

During the 1960 debate on the Bill of Rights, Pickersgill hesitantly asked Immigration Minister Ellen Fairclough whether the government intended to deport a Chinese woman who had emigrated to Canada illegally two and a half years before and subsequently given birth to a child. As soon as Mrs. Fairclough had admitted that the deportation was proceeding, as Pickersgill knew she would, he reared up to ask Diefenbaker: "Can the Prime Minister tell us how the government squares its conduct, in attempting to exile a Canadian citizen, with the Bill of Rights?" The prime minister, obviously caught without an answer, could only mumble: "The Bill of Rights hasn't been passed yet."

Pickersgill's authority within the Pearson retinue continued to expand, and when the Liberals moved back into power, he was named to the key post of House leader. One of the few ministers Pearson's secretary, Mary Macdonald, would unhesitatingly put right through to the PM any time he called, he was a key influence throughout the Pearson period, particularly after Walter Gordon (following Pickersgill's whispered advice) proved so inept in defending his first budget.

His world was vanishing, but Pickersgill was shrewd enough to recognize it and proceeded to plan himself a new career. His long-time acquaintance with John C. Doyle, a fugitive from American justice, and Geoff Stirling, the Newfoundland broadcaster, had cast a shadow over his reputation.

In the summer of 1967, Transport Minister Pickersgill was busy piloting through the Commons the National Transportation Act, designed to rationalize Canada's obsolete railway system. Few MPs noticed that the presidency of the new Canadian Transport Commission set up by the legislation was made particularly attractive. The annual salary was set at $40,000 a year, and the retirement age (Pickersgill was then sixty-two) was not the usual sixty-five, but seventy. The position was never advertised by the Civil Service Commission. Having written himself a job description, Pickersgill resigned from cabinet and recommended himself for the opening. Pearson accepted and "Sailor Jack" launched himself on his fifth Ottawa incarnation, showing no qualms whatsoever about having left the public service, staying fourteen years in politics and now re-entering a bureaucracy which, in theory and practice, ought to be non-partisan.

The circumstances that allowed Jack Pickersgill to flourish were part of a cynical, old-style approach to politics in Canada. He was the last of his kind.

—1968

Bill Vander Zalm: The Kamikaze Premier

JUST FOUR FRANTIC days before British Columbians gave free rein to their gambling instincts by entrusting their future to Bill Vander Zalm, I went to one of the premier's final rallies of the campaign. Held at the Macaulay Elementary School gymnasium in Esquimalt, a sleepy suburb of Victoria, it turned out to be one of only three brief appearances that the Social Credit leader made in the provincial capital. But the political voodoo that made his remarkable victory possible was on open display.

The audience was made up mostly of decent, middle-aged, middle-class citizens confused and troubled by a world they never made. There were a few yuppie bungaloids looking for a cause to follow; the odd leftover sixties hippie, hair tied back Willie Nelson–style; a quartet of loud loggers with room-temperature IQs; a few stray dogs; and mutual fund salesmen—your typical Social Credit gathering.

Nothing much happened until Vander Zalm arrived, leaping off his tour bus, which had only one police car as its slim retinue. Because Esquimalt is so close to the capital, a few backroom Socred functionaries were cruising the hall, taking soundings of the crowd that numbered something less than 250. Big men with cruel mouths (scars in bloodless faces), they pranced around, obviously proud of their new boy.

Vander Zalm's smooth handling of what must have been the 419th stop on his four-week campaign, totally indistinguishable from all the others, was impressive. He has the rugged good looks of a safari guide in an old-fashioned jungle movie, with bronzed face, chestnut hair and restless limb movements. Much has been written about his smile, and it certainly is no ordinary grin. The choreography of arched eyebrows, flashing dimples, pulled-back lips, sparkling cuspids and crinkled eyes produces a Cheshire glow that envelops his audience.

Wife Lillian has a heart-shaped countenance (not much chin, lots of forehead for the obligatory headband), a perky, cheer-leading manner, almond-like nails trimmed short. Most noticeable is her smile, which seems wired to her husband's, so that they flash their ivories simultaneously, even if they're on opposite sides of a room and not looking at one another. They are not so much political cronies as lovers with an almost palpable flow of affection between them. Nice.

This campaign appearance, like all the others, has little to do with platform or policy. In fact, the party leader's mind hardly seems engaged with his vocal cords. But his nervous system is going full tilt. Suddenly, the source of Vander Zalm's political magic becomes clear: he is the first Canadian politician who transmits his essential message entirely through body language. And it works.

It works partly because the body language of his chief rival, Bob Skelly, emits precisely the opposite signals. Throughout most of his campaign, the NDP leader betrayed the stance of an irresolute rabbit caught in the headlights of a moving car, soiling the air with his hesitancy.

Before and after the election, Vander Zalm was being accused of being vague. Yet the message, at least that Saturday afternoon in Esquimalt, was as plain as the caps on his teeth: elect me and I'll worry for you. Sure, British Columbia may be on the verge of becoming the economic Manchuria of the Pacific Rim, but at least we'll all go down smiling. Somehow the notion is passed along that with Smilin' Billy and Smilin' Lillian safely ensconced in the Walt Disney pile of stones that passes for Victoria's Parliament buildings, neither Ottawa, Washington nor God will deal the province any more karate chops.

Vander Zalm's greatest asset—and the reason he won such a resounding mandate in his original foray to the polls—is that he has a fresh way of approaching the province's problems. Instead of attempting to preach specific options or pretending that he has all the answers, he limited himself throughout the campaign to the pledge of changing the climate in which solutions might be negotiated. "We're open about what we propose to do for the people of B.C.," he said in Esquimalt that afternoon. "We'll develop a trust, and with that trust will come a confidence, and as people develop confidence in their province, they'll want to invest in it, and when others see that investment, they too will invest." In British Columbia these days, that amounts to a major policy statement.

———

WHEN THE COMMONWEALTH Conference was being held in Vancouver in the summer of 1987, Nathan Nemetz, then British Columbia's chief justice, hosted a formal dinner party for Lee Kuan Yew, most senior of the attending prime ministers, who had ruled Singapore with an iron fist since 1959. Much of the Vancouver Establishment was on the guest list, and Bill Vander Zalm had been asked to propose a toast to the distinguished visitor. As we stood outside the dining room, I watched the premier in action.

Despite his Great White Hunter good looks, his face somehow lacks definition, as if it were painted on a balloon, and his eyes seem as unfocused as billiard balls. What's remarkable are the semaphore signals sent out by his piranha-perfect teeth, always visible, the enigmatic duck of the head and the arms parked akimbo, signalling that this man will not accept any assessment of himself except his own. Just before we were ushered in, the premier sidled up to me and whispered, as if to confirm a rumour he had once heard: "This Singapore—is it in the Commonwealth?" I allowed that it was. Aglow with this delicious secret (for which

I was rewarded with a dazzling flash of molars), Vander Zalm took his place at the table and, a few minutes later, delivered a remarkably spirited toast to the Far East dictator, with whom he got on discouragingly well.

I was reminded of that performance as the B.C. premier, faced with a decisive challenge to his authority, tried to smooth away the wrath of his disillusioned followers with oily semantics. "I know a strong government will be challenged," he declared. "But I would rather have a strong government that gets challenged than a weak government that doesn't get anywhere."

That constituted a curious defence because no one in the Pacific province was accusing Vander Zalm of being weak. Dumb, insensitive, certifiable—certainly. But never weak. The controversy over the resignations of Attorney General Brian Smith and former Deputy Premier Grace McCarthy had exposed to cold daylight the roots of Socred power. There are many misconceptions about the nature of the Social Credit movement, none more prevalent than the belief that it is composed largely of marginal misfits, former and future talk-show hosts, used-up used-car dealers and rednecks from bumper-sticker country who subscribe to the dotty dogmas of the party's official founder, Major C.H. Douglas.

That wasn't true when W.A.C. Bennett first used the Social Credit label to break the political deadlock that catapulted him into office in 1952, and it is even less true now. The party's followers include most of the province's mainstream voters. The common bond holding them together is a determination to keep the socialist hordes out of office so that the 1972–75 NDP interregnum is never repeated.

But that is only the public face of the Socred phenomenon. Behind the scenes, the province's business establishment has up to now squarely supported Social Credit, providing party funds, contacts with the country's national power sources and, above all, legitimacy. Vander Zalm was able to harness that support because, faced with the choice between the palavering left and the fanatic right, Vancouver's power brokers swallowed the premier's nutsy excesses.

———

THE REAL SIGNIFICANCE of the Smith and McCarthy resignations (and the firing of Highways Minister Stephen Rogers, the scion of a well-connected Vancouver family and a thirteen-year veteran of British Columbia's political wars) goes well beyond the fact that the cabinet has lost three of the premier's few ministers with any effective long-term experience in government. The move has irretrievably severed Vander Zalm's links with the province's business establishment. (And Vancouver itself. For the first time in its history, the city lacks representation in the provincial cabinet.)

Vander Zalm's predecessor, Bill Bennett, had established something called the Top Twenty Club, a closed circle of B.C. business elite, to hold private briefings with the premier. (There were actually sixty members; the club's designation represented the twenty swing ridings that the Socreds need to win.) The group, headed by Robert Hallbauer of Cominco and former MacMillan Bloedel chairman Jack Clyne, is now dormant. More significantly, Michael Burns, a former IBM executive who helped form the Top Twenty and was the party's chief fundraiser, has been replaced by Peter Toigo, Kentucky Fried Chicken King (he owns sixty-three franchises), who is as far removed from the B.C. Establishment as you can get. Vander Zalm's machinations on behalf of Toigo's bid to buy the former Expo 86 site for a gambling casino alienated Vancouver's business elite. Particularly put out was Canarim chairman Peter Brown, who headed the Crown-owned B.C. Enterprise Corporation, which held the disputed lands.

Whether Vander Zalm can (or wants to) heal the rift between his office and the business community remains an open question. Whether he will change his kamikaze style of government is not. He won't. He shows no willingness to alter his ways, even as most British Columbians begin to agree with Oksana Exell, the province's director for the Canadian Federation of Independent Business, who recently charged, "This government doesn't seem to have an agenda. It has pissed away its goodwill."

Ever since taking office, Vander Zalm has enunciated policies at the drop of a microphone, with little benefit of forethought.

Meanwhile, the province's button salesmen are being kept busy (one proclaims: "Gay Florists Are Against Vander Zalm"). The T-shirt merchants are flogging a model that has a smiling, hairy monster rising from a swamp, with the caption: "It came from Holland!" The premier appears unruffled, continuing to push his gardening video, host his Sunday radio phone-in show, market authenticated copies of his wife's headbands at his Fantasy Gardens gift shops and lecture the survivors in his cabinet room, which has become an echo chamber. Hard days for The Zalm. Yet one achievement cannot be taken away from him: no one else could have made Bill Bennett look so good.

SOME LIVES AND places are interchangeable. But only British Columbia could have produced William Vander Zalm, who has just put himself and the province out of their misery by resigning and calling a Social Credit leadership convention. Most Canadians valued the premier for providing some badly needed comic relief in the current paranoia of Canadian politics. But British Columbians knew better. Vander Zalm was, after all, a child of the same Pacific rainforest that claims such improbable mythical beings as the high-dwelling Sasquatch and Ogopogo, the underwater serpent of Okanagan Lake.

Vander Zalm's major fault as a politician is that he has no ideology and the attention span of a neurotic squirrel. He never managed to articulate a comprehensive platform beyond the general message that voting for him would keep "the socialist horde" at bay. Yet his political message was there for all to absorb: vote for me and everything will be "faaaan-tastic."

Vander Zalm may be the only Canadian politician who staged a successful *coup d'état* against himself. Because Social Credit is not a party but a political label, it requires not only campaign funds, but also legitimacy. The source of both those commodities is the Vancouver business community, and it was his deliberate self-alienation from that power-brokering group that contributed most to the premier's downfall.

The Howe Street boys, as they're known on these far shores, were willing to put up with Vander Zalm's nutsy excesses as long as he gave them a policy voice. But when Finance Minister Melville Couvelier resigned his portfolio, the last link was severed.

British Columbia can only be understood as a frontier—raw and unpredictable—an appendage to the country, rather than part of it. Frontiers are places (or states of mind) to escape to, lands (or ways of life) to lose and find yourself in, and they operate according to their own rules.

There is not much evidence in the Pacific coast province of the down-home neighbourliness of the Maritimes, the self-obsession of Quebec, the superiority of Ontario, the Hallmark optimism of Manitoba or the howdy-doodyism of Alberta. This is one tough place, where it rains most of the time and you're never sure whether it's God trying to wash the province clean of its sins or sweep it into the sea.

It's not a very Canadian place. There's no vestige of the Protestant ethic that made this country great, little modesty, none of the deference to authority that characterizes the Canadian everywhere else. People play as hard as they work, though the cost of making it in British Columbia comes as high as it does anywhere else—right out of the marrow.

Most of British Columbia's most successful citizens are proud of the sweat that went into their fortunes, and instead of trying to hide their accomplishments, they're busy finding new ways of showing off—flaunting their biceps, women and cash.

One of the few sensible things Vander Zalm ever said was that if Quebec could define itself as a distinct society, British Columbia had at least an equal claim to be allowed to do so. It's a valid argument, and since I moved here, I've often wondered what precisely makes British Columbia and its politics so unique. I've discovered the main difference is how sharply everything is polarized. British Columbians constantly live on the edge; there is seldom a middle way, little moderation or compromise.

The province alternates between the most left-wing and most right-wing administrations in the country; it has Canada's highest percentage of unionized workers and the most repressive labour legislation in the Commonwealth. Also, there is a strange way of settling quarrels. When Barry Tobler of North Vancouver ditched his girlfriend, Sylvia Lewis, she did not settle for getting mad or getting even; she doused him with Grand Marnier while he was sleeping and set him on fire. Even religion fails to calm people. When Vander Zalm installed a prayer room in the provincial legislature, where its members could contemplate their souls, it was immediately invaded by a coven of witches, a satanist and a couple of garden-variety Victoria pagans and finally had to be closed.

Tracing the roots of that attitude of confrontation and polarization is difficult. These are not a founding people. Few British

Columbians believe in history, even their own, if it involves loyalties or obligations. Yet there is a strand of thoughts and events
reaching back to the province's economic beginnings that helps
explain the genesis of all that polarization.

It all started in the bunkhouses—whether they housed
fur traders, railway builders, miners or loggers. They were
independently minded hombres who worked long hours in
life-threatening jobs. Powerless and frustrated, they cursed
their bosses and dreamed of overthrowing society as it existed
to create a new social order with more equitable rules. "They
were men from the north of England who brought to Canada
organizational skills and a marked propensity towards independent politics characteristic of the English and Scottish," wrote
Professor Robin Fisher, a University of British Columbia historian. Fisher added: "Equally militant were the many American
workers who provided the early constituency of radical unions.
The proliferation of company towns, the struggles of the hard-
rock miners, the mill-men and smelter-men within the bowels
of the earth, the rapid proliferation of militant employers' asso-
ciations and the frontier tradition of violence as a solution to
social conflicts, contributed to the 'heritage of conflict' between
capitalists and workers."

ON THE OTHER side of that early economic equation were the
bosses, rugged freebooters who owned their own mines or log

concessions and were determined to squeeze every ounce of muscle out of their sweating workforce. They held off the unions as long as they could, using federal troops or rented goons to settle strikes, giving not an inch in the battle for greater profits.

A contributing problem was that because of its rugged and chopped-up terrain, British Columbia has never had more than a relatively small agriculture sector, thus losing the solid and ameliorating influence that farmers usually bring to politics. "British Columbia is almost unique on this continent, if not the world, by having virtually no agricultural base," says Peter Pearse, a professor of Forestry at the University of British Columbia who spends most of his time heading national and provincial royal commissions. "An agrarian base can be a very moderating influence. People who come from the land can exercise a significantly stabilizing force in politics, but all we had was freewheeling entrepreneurs and the aggressive drifters who came here to work for them. The heritage of all that friction is that our right-wing parties are more reactionary than anywhere else, and our left-wing parties, more socialist—and there is nothing in between." Out of the historic struggles between primitive labour pools and their even more primitive bosses came the political, social and economic polarization that still pervades contemporary British Columbia.

If most Canadians view British Columbia as a strange and unpredictable place, most of the Pacific province's citizens reciprocate that sentiment. They have an image of Toronto as being inhabited mainly by pale-skinned androgynous creatures who eat porridge for breakfast and never have any fun. (They're quite happy to visit Toronto on alternate leap years as long as it's for no more than three days at a time.) They think Bay Street is populated by befuddled bankers, sweating corporate treasurers and vice-presidents in charge of environmental impact studies who spend most of their waking hours sticking pins in David Suzuki dolls.

No wonder that when they travel east, British Columbia's boosters are always being put down for acting like laid-back ambassadors from some overrated Shangri-La beyond the Rockies. They have a well-earned reputation for raving on mercilessly about their nonexistent winters and "painfully beautiful" scenery, dismissing any doubts as attacks on not just their taste, but their honour.

The eastern and western sensibilities seldom meet because most central Canadians still regard Canada as an Atlantic nation and view British Columbia, if they think of it at all, as a troublesome province on some distant second shore. That's a shame because if we have any viable economic future, a good part of it will have to be forged on the Pacific Rim, with Vancouver as its economic gateway.

William Vander Zalm's departure removes from power the most colourful of Canada's reigning premiers, but not much will change. British Columbia politics will stay as polarized as ever, and as improbable as it seems, the next premier could turn out to be equally goofy. After all, no modern B.C. politician has yet equalled the record of the province's second premier. He was a deranged itinerant photographer and journalist who changed his name from William Smith to Amor De Cosmos ("lover of the universe") and spent his final days pacing his cell in a Victoria insane asylum.

—1986, 1988, 1991

Lucien Bouchard: Revolution East

WHEN I FIRST arrived in Toronto from a war-torn Europe in the 1940s, it was a strongly bicultural community: British and Irish—except for the bankers, who were Scottish. I never did subscribe to the benevolent notion of Canada as a "cultural mosaic" which was supposed to differentiate us from the American "melting pot." The nation's ethnic structure had been set in place during the first decade of the century, when a million immigrants chose the western plains to make their last, best stand. It had been a perfect arrangement: the dominant WASPs got in on the kill of the massive construction projects and manufacturing boom that followed, while we "bohunks" (all of us refugees tended to be grouped as "DPs" or "Uke-aranians") had patronizingly been allowed to maintain our way of life—just so long as we ploughed the soil, did the most menial jobs and restricted public displays of our culture to folk dancing on Parliament Hill on

Dominion Days. This point of view was most brutally articulated
as recently as 1978 by Bryce Mackasey, a Trudeau cabinet minister, when he asked, "Where would we be without the Italians, the
Czechoslovaks, the Portuguese, the Greeks and Lebanese? Who
would do the dirty work, dig the subways, mine the mines and
sweep the floors?"

Where indeed. But since then, the sheer numbers of newcomers muted such prejudice. No ethnic or linguistic flavour
dominated the Canadian Crock-Pot. Every six years or so during the past four decades, nearly a million immigrants from
Asia, Africa and other non-white countries had arrived on
Canada's shores. The WASP and francophone bloodlines had
been overwhelmed by waves of newcomers of every class and
stock, dreaming big dreams about new lives in wide-open spaces.
Canada's founding societies remained in charge—as evidenced
by the all-white, mostly male leadership in politics and business—
but they were no longer in the ascendancy. A new and radically
different country was being born.

Perhaps the most profound revolution was the wane of the
WASPs. The White Anglo-Saxon Protestants who had once ruled
every aspect of Canadian life had, in most metropolitan dis-
tricts and economic sectors, been reduced to a visible minority.
Roast beef had become an ethnic dish. Canada had turned into
a multinational (or post-national) country, not in the abstract
of government edicts or sociological hocus-pocus, but in visible
facts plain to anyone walking the streets of Montreal, Toronto or
Vancouver.

The politically correct notion of Canada as the home of two nations had outlived reality. Only die-hard constitutional reformers still maintained that one society (Quebec) was distinct, while the other, by default, was indistinct and somehow interchangeable. To people outside Quebec, this "two nations" model had always been a sociological theory which meant not very much; to Quebeckers, it meant everything. To have their own language and culture officially recognized signalled the difference between being a proud society or just another marginal tribe with cultural curiosities.

It had been a wonderful dream, this Canada with two founding nations calmly coexisting as they evolved toward the twenty-first century. But by the mid-1990s, Canada had almost as many cultures as postal codes, and none added up to peace in our time. "The distinct society we're asking for," Quebec premier Robert Bourassa explained with impatient zeal, "is not a society of privileged citizens. It is a society with a different culture, a society with a different legal system, a society with specific institutions." But the same provincial premiers who had readily given precisely that kind of distinct status to the First Nations withheld it from Quebec.

Equality of treatment, which became the axis of the never-ending negotiations, was plainly incompatible with any form of officially sanctioned privilege based on language, ethnicity or length of tenure. The time had come to acknowledge that liberalism and tribalism were terminally incompatible. "For the tidal wave of new immigrants," wrote Michael Ignatieff at the time,

"Canada is more a land for the realization of private dreams than for maintaining the old compact between founding races. No common identity was provided for the millions of new Canadian immigrants other than a weak vision of mutual multicultural indifference."

The collapse of the two-nation theory outside Quebec moved debate on Canada's future to new ground. Deprived of its founding myth, Canada by the mid-1990s had become a land with a common past but not necessarily a common future. That troublesome new factor, which understandably triggered a revolutionary mode on both sides of the issue, was at the heart of Quebec's 1995 referendum: if Canada had abandoned its historical raison d'être as one country, should it become two?

———

THE MOOD OF English Canada had turned hard and uncompromising, reminiscent of the old Chicago blues refrain, "I told you I love you—now get out!" There had been too many false alarms. Confederation was supposed to have caved in when René Lévesque was elected in 1976 and again when he called the referendum four years later; the sun was never supposed to rise again once the Meech Lake Accord had failed; hell was going to freeze over when Canadians voted to reject the Charlottetown Accord two years after that. Ever since the Quiet Revolution of the 1960s, Quebec and the rest of Canada had been dealing with one another in a series of confrontations seeking, but never finding, the ultimate compromise between French dreams and English impatience. Federal politicians sacrificed their larynxes and careers and seized on equal-opportunity petulance, trying to find an answer to the eternal puzzle: what does Quebec *want?* More of everything and less of nothing was the simple answer. A more useful question might have been: what does Quebec want *to be?*

Quebec's case was put forward by Bourassa, who represented his seven million citizens with maximum clout and minimum risk for most of the decade. Being neither a convinced federalist nor or a convincing separatist, he was distrusted by both sides—the ideal Canadian political posture. He would usually come down on the side of Canada, but he also understood that Quebec could achieve the most through the theatre of the absurd. He was uninterested in rekindling the glory snuffed out on the Plains of Abraham; his were the politics of the bottom line and computer spreadsheets. His "profitable approach" viewed federalism as a chance to push his province into an equal technological partnership with the rest of Canada. Bourassa would meanwhile unequivocally declare that Quebec must be a nation without becoming a state—whatever that meant.

Despite his raging pragmatism—or perhaps because of it— Bourassa viewed the political process as a voyage of infinite and unexpected contingencies. The problem was how to create two "nations" and still have one state. The solution inevitably reduced itself to a formula resembling the famous quip of Montreal comic Yvon Deschamps: "We want an independent Quebec within a strong and united Canada."

Although they professed purity of thought and action, Quebec's nationalists believed in the most extreme of the six possible degrees of separation: independence, sovereignty, autonomy, special status, separation and sovereignty-association. According to the polls, the independence option most accept-able to Quebeckers was sovereignty-association. It was also the least practical. Its most telling critique came from the constitu-tional gadfly Senator Eugene Forsey, who dismissed the idea as "a horse that won't start, let alone run; you can no more nego-tiate sovereignty-association than you can negotiate sour sugar, dry water, boiling ice or stationary motion." Forsey was right. Even in a country that officially described itself at birth as a "self-governing colony," sovereignty-association was an unworkable oxymoron. As former Ontario premier Bob Rae never got tired of pointing out: "We already have a political union with Quebec. It's called Canada." These were solid, rational arguments—but nobody promised that common sense would carry the day. "Quebec has no opinions, only emotions," Sir Wilfrid Laurier had noted.

MOST REVOLUTIONS ARE dedicated to the destruction of the ruling classes who control the means of production. Quebec's Quiet Revolution, started under Jean Lesage in 1960 and still simmering thirty-five years later, had precisely the opposite effect in mind. The idea was for the province to create its own elites to grab control of its major institutions, so that Quebeckers would seize command of their own economy and culture. Few Canadians outside Quebec realized how fundamental a change that required. For more than a century, the resident Catholic bishops and cardinals, cocooned in the splendid isolation of their celestial palace at the foot of Dominion Square, had decreed that material matters be left to the English. This produced an impenetrable Anglo network that operated out of Montreal's Mount Royal Club. It was supported by the more mundane power wielders at the Mount Stephen and Saint James clubs. (The Saint James had two classes of members: those who wished they belonged to the Mount Royal and those who were glad they didn't belong to the Mount Stephen.)

It was during the Quiet Revolution that a genuine Quebec middle class began to emerge, consisting of an adventurous few who branched out of the traditional career paths of priests, lawyers or doctors. The Anglo institutions had paid no attention. Of Canada's Big Five banks, for example, only one—the Montreal—had a French-Canadian executive of vice-presidential rank or higher. (He was a talented, bilingual MBA graduate with the wonderfully appropriate name of Pierre MacDonald.) The new Quebec business tycoons, mostly trained at Montreal's École des Hautes Études Commerciales, were the natural successors of the notaries and bishops. Within one generation, corporate CEOs had become Quebec's role models, and a new and vibrant bourgeoisie had taken over. This was dramatically documented in the spring of 1995, when the authoritative business magazine

Affaires Plus published its annual list of the fifty most powerful Quebeckers. All but four of those named belonged to well-established Quebec families; of those who didn't, two were Jewish. WASP influence had not just waned; it had vanished.

Such circumstances—including the fact that for all but twelve of the previous forty-seven years, Canada's prime minister had come from Quebec—made it difficult for the separatists to maintain the myth that Quebeckers were somehow subjugated by *les maudits anglais*. That didn't stop them, of course. Just before the 1994 provincial election, Parti Québécois vice-president Bernard Landry complained in the Parisian magazine *L'Express* that Quebec "is the western world's last colonized nation." He added, with a straight face, that "its population has endured a cataclysm comparable to the Chernobyl nuclear catastrophe." (A slight overreaction to the impending loss of les Nordiques, *n'est-ce pas, Bernard?*)

———————

MY COMPANION WAS one of those wonderful Montrealers of a certain age and pleasant disposition connected with the political elites in Ottawa and Quebec City and trusted by both; partly because they shared his passion for minor French cheeses but mostly because he had been a useful interlocutor between the two cities and two cultures. In many ways he was the last of his kind. Independently wealthy, he had spent most of his life in public service, just as second sons of Anglican vicars in nineteenth-century England once joined the army—both as a duty and as an interesting way to spend one's life. Unlike most Canadian politicians and bureaucrats, he retained a firm notion of what his country was and ought to be; he wanted to help create a very different Canada, but a Canada all the same.

We had not seen each other for a couple of years and were sitting at the bar of the Atlantic Pavilion on Sherbrooke Street, trading apprehensions about Canada's future. He said something after our third cup of coffee that I could hardly credit having heard. "The thoughtful Quebec nationalists," he remarked, with the casualness of a weather forecast, "not only take separation for granted but they have a kind of lingering regard for English Canada because they know they weren't treated all that badly. They're saying now that the English shouldn't be absorbed piecemeal into the United States through the gravitational economic pull that will strengthen dramatically once Quebec leaves. They believe we should start the process of a calculated liquidation of English Canada by negotiating sovereignty-association with the U.S. at the same time Ottawa would be signing a similar treaty with Quebec. That way we'll preserve some clout, instead of ending up as nine states represented by 18 out of 118 senators in the U.S. Senate."

I would have dismissed that chin-dropping comment as both silly and wildly premature from any other source. From my friend, who had waged many political battles to keep the nation together, it seemed a warning worth heeding—especially considering it had been given before the elections of the Bloc Québécois to

Opposition status in Ottawa and the Parti Québécois to majority government in Quebec City.

The warning was certainly supported by the ideological evolution of Jacques Parizeau from an enlightened professor into a die-hard revolutionary. The first time I met Parizeau was in the 1960s, when he was a member of Premier Jean Lesage's entourage. As I walked into his office, he was doubled over at his desk in a fit of belly-pumping laughter over the premier's pretensions. Parizeau explained that Lesage had just ordered him to write a speech for a rally that night at Lévis, across the river from Quebec City, "specifically designed to impress Harold Wilson." (Wilson was then prime minister of the United Kingdom, and Lesage required British parliamentary approval to abolish the Quebec legislature's upper chamber.) Parizeau rightly considered his assignment absurd. He was an intellectual, throwing off such barbs as, "I was aware of the quarrel between Reynaud's mistress and Daladier's mistress in France and its influence on French national defence before knowing who the prime minister of Canada was." His bias against the English dated back to 1969, when he crossed Canada with a friend. They were chatting in French at a Winnipeg bar when somebody yelled at them to "Speak white!" He broke his right hand in the ensuing fist fight, and its little finger still juts out at an awkward angle.

In the next decade, Parizeau became more confident, more powerful, more articulate and much more cynical. His idea of Quebec's aspirations seemed to extend no further than exacting revenge for the British conquest of Quebec in 1759. He had become such a true believer that he gave the impression of not caring a whit how independence was achieved or how Quebeckers might suffer in the process. His jaded approach was captured in his remark to the *Los Angeles Times*: "Get me a half-dozen Ontarians who put their feet on the Quebec flag and I've got it."

The firebrand separatist preached the unlikely gospel that independence could come about so smoothly that hardly anyone would notice. The only real change, one assumes, would be that President Parizeau would arrive at the United Nations, the fleur-de-lys proudly fluttering from the fender of his tug-size, black Cadillac, to bore the Assembly with one of his avuncular lectures, blowing through his moustache, as he painted the glories of Quebec's new freedom. As Norman Webster, the wise Montreal *Gazette* and *Le Devoir* columnist, noted: "Jacques Parizeau isn't trying to fool all of the people all of the time, just fifty-one per cent of them ... once."

———

DESPITE THE AMPUTATION of his lower leg due to flesh-eating disease, the federal politician and one-time bosom buddy of Brian Mulroney, Lucien Bouchard, came to dominate the post-Parizeau strategy of separatism and propelled its progress. A master of desensitizing Canadians to the possibility of Quebec independence, he became the dark angel of federal politics. A complex, paradoxical figure, his loyalties were as changeable as the hues of a pigeon's pout. He had been a loyal Liberal, influential enough to be named vice-chairman of the party's Quebec political commission by Pierre Trudeau in 1968; he then switched to being a loyal follower of the Parti Québécois from 1973 to 1984, but changed allegiances again and became a loyal Canadian when Mulroney offered him a plum ambassadorship in Paris. Bouchard's four years as Canadian ambassador to France were notable for three reasons: he successfully mounted the 1985 and 1987 summits of *la Francophonie*; the embassy's expenditures under his stewardship shot up 71 percent; and while representing Canada, he abandoned his wife, Jocelyn, to conduct a flaming affair with CBC French-language TV star Denise Bombardier, who left her husband and young child behind in Montreal to live with him in an apartment off Paris's Embassy Row. His greatest protocol *faux pas* was to propose a toast at the first gathering of the embassy's two hundred employees: "To Quebec-France relations!"—quickly correcting himself to celebrate "Canada-France relations!"

Upon his return to Ottawa, he became a Mulroney Progressive Conservative, occupying the senior positions of secretary of state (which meant, ironically, that he presided over the 1988 Canada Day celebrations), environment minister and political minister for Quebec. He abruptly abandoned the Tories at the most crucial juncture of their mandate in 1990 to become the leader of his own separatist party. Asked by a reporter from *Le Journal de Montréal* about Parizeau, who had once been his closest ally, Bouchard answered: "I have great admiration and affection for him—to the extent that one can have affection for others in politics." It was a revealing reply, hinting at a bedrock belief that people in politics merely used one another and that no real friendships were possible.

His bond with Mulroney ought to have been the exception. The two men had been friends since law school at Laval, where they were self-described soulmates. Their lives had become intertwined at every turn. In 1974 Mulroney had helped Bouchard by having him appointed chief counsel to the Cliche Commission looking into violence on the Quebec labour scene. A decade later, the freshly coined prime minister of Canada appointed his pal to the country's most glamorous overseas posting, ambassador to France. When asked how the French would respond to such an inexperienced diplomat, Mulroney replied: "When they're talking to Lucien Bouchard, they're talking to Brian Mulroney." At the gala dinner in Quebec City during the 1985 Shamrock Summit, Mulroney had proudly introduced Bouchard to U.S. president Ronald Reagan as "the most eloquent French Canadian I know." When Bouchard's son, Alexandre, was born, his first call was to his friend Brian. Brian Mulroney didn't flinch in his loyalty to Bouchard, but Mila had her suspicions: "When he left Jocelyn and married Audrey in 1989, Brian had a little reception for the family at 24 Sussex, but I chose not to be there. I didn't like the way it had been handled. After the split Audrey would go to my hairdresser, and it was funny how we kept being scheduled at the same times. Once she came into the room where I was having my hair done, with tears in her eyes, and told me: 'I'm really sorry about what happened.' I said, 'Look, Audrey, I have no problem with you and I wish you and the baby all the best, but as far as I'm concerned, Lucien does not exist.'"

———

FOR MULRONEY, THE SPLIT WITH BOUCHARD during the last days of the Meech Lake negotiations was particularly painful because it violated his sacred creed: "You dance with the one what brung ya'." Nothing hurt him more during the decade he spent in office. Mulroney knew that politics and gratitude were strangers, but the split between the two men ran so deep that he instructed Mila that, should Bouchard show up at his funeral, she must stop the service until he left the church.

"He was a man of multiple personalities and each had its own agenda, often contradicting the others," recalled Arthur Campeau, who was an Ottawa international environment adviser. "I would start a meeting with one Bouchard and end it with another. He was given to shifting from one frame of mind to a different one without even realizing that he had, reinventing history as he went along. While environment minister in times of fiscal restraint, he never bothered justifying his expenditures because his friend Brian would make sure he had his way. He had many mood swings. This enabled him to convince himself of the Big Lie: he was absolutely certain, for example, that he never betrayed Mulroney, but that it was the other way round."

Bouchard depended on Mulroney to get himself elected the first time but campaigned forcefully and successfully in 1992 to defeat the Charlottetown Accord, and in 1993 elected fifty-four members of his Bloc Québécois. He saw an independent Quebec as a practical option, not as a miraculous solution or nostalgic dream. "We are seeking sovereignty," he told the first annual convention of the BQ in Montreal on April 7, 1995, "because it is absolutely essential, like the ripening of a fruit, like reaching adulthood, like the opening of a river into the ocean. *It is necessary, because we are a people.*"

The definitive summary from inside the Mulroney circle of the Bouchard defection was the biting comment of Stanley Hartt, then the PM's chief of staff. "Lucien turned himself into a human car bomb, designed to go off at a time and place when it would do the most damage," Hartt told me. "He acted when he did because he saw, for the first time, that there was a way for the Meech provisions to work and thus disarm Quebec separatism. The tactic of not coming to see his friend to talk things over was deliberate. He saw a chance to make himself both a hero and a martyr at the same time and a chance of eventually catapulting himself into being Parizeau's successor. That's what he did. I don't know anybody else like that. And I'm glad."

—1995

David Radler: The One Who Got Away

WHEN DAVID RADLER became known as Canada's most treacherous turncoat, it was over the stunning repudiation of his thirty-six-year partnership with Conrad Black, the portentous power broker who was found guilty at trial of fraud and obstruction of justice. Though he may not admit it in court, Radler was more than Black's fiduciary partner. He was his alter ego, his hatchet man, the guy who devised most of the fancy manoeuvres that created the world's third-largest media empire, then helped to turn it into a junkyard of broken dreams and shattered promises.

Unlike Black, who courted the spotlight, Radler refused most interviews, pretending he was a simple man of God on a private mission with no name. I was one of the exceptions. He would often take me to lunch (usually hot dogs and a Diet Pepsi) and a few times invited me to his house on Vancouver's prestigious Marine Drive, mostly for Jean Charest fundraisers. To my surprise, this corporate fire-eater's home was decorated with a sensitively chosen Group of Seven collection.

As we began to talk, it came out that his father had owned Au Lutin Qui Bouffe, a popular Montreal restaurant in the 1960s that attracted patrons by having tiny piglets run around the floor. David's first job following his graduation from Queen's was to create a handicrafts marketing program for the Curve Lake Indian Reserve, north of Peterborough, Ontario, which he did so successfully that he later developed similar schemes for thirty other First Nations bands. He joined Black in buying the *Sherbrooke Daily Record,* where he is remembered mainly for the day an employee came into his office with a list of grievances. Instead of listening to him, Radler had two cents taken off his next paycheque for wasting a sheet of paper.

When I asked Radler how he picked the newspapers he chose to buy, his explanation was simple. He would move into a likely property and count the desks, calculating how many reporters he could afford to fire to still provide enough editorial matter to separate the ads.

———

WHEN THE HOLLINGER operation went international, Radler took over the U.S. operation, which consisted mostly of the kinds of small papers whose sale was later to come under scrutiny by the courts and SEC investigators.

David Radler was lively and interesting, but his notion that cost-cutting constitutes great publishing was questionable. The investigators took note of the stunning accusation made by a former publisher of the *Jerusalem Post*. With scarcely controlled fury, he claimed that when the paper was under Radler's wing, he confiscated a fund voluntarily collected from readers to help impecunious Israeli citizens and used the money to finance his campaign to wrest an honorary doctorate from a Jerusalem university. (Radler regarded the *Post* as his exclusive domain, and when Conrad asked to see the paper, Radler obliged by arranging for him to receive it. By a sea mail.) He held Black in little awe and less respect. He once confided to me that he thought "Conrad has a psychological age of eighty."

Radler is the toughest-minded executive I ever encountered. Only facing up to the maximum risk of thirty-five years of jail time brought him to heel. When he agreed to plead guilty to a single count of fraud, he knew the jig was up and that only by co-operating with the authorities would he have a chance to limit the damage. He has come a long way from the Curve Lake Indian Reserve.

—2005

Kinky Friedman: That Bad-Ass Country Singer

HE FIRST APPEARED on my radar screen in the mid-1970s, when Kinky Friedman and his six-piece band, the Texas Jewboys, recorded sassy music that wasn't merely outside the box but outside the stadium. Kinky's repertoire included the occasional serious, extended tribute to the victims of the Holocaust ("Ride 'em Jewboy"), but more often, the band played anti–women's liberation songs such as "Get Your Biscuits in the Oven and Your Buns in the Bed." Kinky crossed over the line with his crude send-up: "They Ain't Makin' Jews like Jesus Anymore." (Sample lyric: "'You know, you don't look Jewish,' he said, 'near as I could figure / I had you lamped for a slightly anemic, well-dressed country nigger.' / . . . / They ain't makin' Jews like Jesus anymore, / They ain't makin' carpenters who know what nails are for.") At the time, Kinky was being accused of corrupting the youth of America or at least those who listened to his music. He contradicted such charges by brazenly pointing out: "I never say the word 'fuck' in front of a c-h-i-l-d."

His band members enjoyed being outrageous but missed the fringe benefits. "Why don't we ever attract groupies?" complained Major Bowles, the band's drummer. "All we get is Jewish sociology professors taking notes."

Kinky performed at the Grand Ole Opry in Nashville, was part of Bob Dylan's 1976 Rolling Thunder Revue tour and played opening acts for his buddy Willie Nelson. But by the early 1980s, his career sank in a quagmire of drugs, cocaine being his poison of choice. "He was high on 27 different herbs and spices," recalled Jimmie "Ratso" Silman, a Washington TV cameraman who once played backup guitar for the Jewboys. "Friedman was a different person back then, fairly repellent as a human being." When Kinky quit the drug scene, he had a simple explanation. "I stopped doing cocaine," he recalled, "when Bob Marley fell out of my left nostril."

Friedman visited Vancouver while I lived there in the 1980s, but by then he no longer had a band. "While we were doing a gig near Austin, I went for a walk," he explained. "That was when I realized how ambivalent I felt about my music, and then it hit me. Anybody who knows the word 'ambivalent' had no business being a country singer." Instead, he began writing satirical detective novels with such bizarre titles as *Armadillos and Old Lace, God Bless John Wayne*, and *The Love Song of J. Edgar Hoover*, and nearly all of his eighteen books became minor bestsellers. They were just as earthy as his songs. In one scene he described the time one of his characters was in a motel making love to a new female friend when a bellhop who refilled mini-bars entered his room without bothering to knock. The lover was not amused. "Can't you see that I'm in the middle of somebody?" he complained.

His writings were peppered with references to sex that not merely transcended but set back political correctness: "Every time you see a beautiful woman, just remember somebody got tired of her. But I could imagine a number of things that would look good on her. One of them, would be myself. She's the kind of girl that older dentists find attractive. Has a nice set of teeth, a fair set of knockers and a lousy set of values."

Not surprisingly, Bill Clinton, then in his Monica phase, was one of Kinky's most ardent fans. Kinky was invited to the White House, where they exchanged escapades. Friedman even composed and recorded a down-and-dirty ditty that he was convinced would absolve the president from charges of extramarital sex. The first line of the lyrics was self-explanatory: "Eatin' ain't cheatin'."

———————

OVER THE YEARS, I sort of forgot about Kinky, only occasionally played his past hits or leafed through his books. The man was refreshingly incorrigible, but once the shock value wore off, his humour commanded a brief shelf life. It came as a rude awakening, therefore, when I heard that this aging reprobate was running in the 2004 U.S. election on an independent ticket for governor of Texas. In the process, he had unexpectedly emerged as one of the most newsworthy candidates of the American election campaign. Because of a four-way split in the gubernatorial vote among mediocre rivals, polls showed him at 20 percent, and he actually stood a chance of winning. He hadn't changed his tune but his one-liners had grown more mellow. "I'm a bastard child of twin cultures," Kinky commented during a campaign speech, "Jewish and cowboy, that have nothing in common except they like to wear their hats indoors."

At the start of his campaign, Friedman received twice as many write-ins from registered voters belonging to neither of the oldline parties as were required to get his name on the ballot as an independent candidate. Serious Texan political observers started to predict the long-shot possibility of a Friedman upset. That was a dramatic switch from Kinky's initially jocular approach to his candidacy. At first, he insisted that the main reason he wanted to move into the governor's mansion was that he'd run out of shelf space. He also promised that as the state's first Jewish governor, he would reduce speed limits to 54.95 mph. Word leaked out that he had already promised to appoint at least eight of his cronies as wardens of Texas's women's prisons.

But at some point, Kinky got serious and realized that if he could harness the state's prevalent political discontent and mobilize the 71 percent of citizens who didn't vote last time in mid-term elections, he might have a chance. The landscape seemed ideal for a non-politician. "Given the choice," declared his campaign manager, "Texans are just as likely to vote for somebody they can believe in, who talks straight to them and understands their frustration."

But just how sincere can Kinky really be, not just about going straight but about holding the Lone Star state's highest elected office? "If you ask him whether this is a joke, if you even suggest it's a joke, he'll lunge at you," reported Evan Smith, editor of the *Texas Monthly* and one of the state's top political commentators. Smith described the ex–cowboy singer's fierce independence as his greatest strength: "He's independent of everything and of everybody," Smith wrote. "Sometimes even independent of his own brain. Certainly, his mouth is independent of his brain. But the fact that he's willing to take on the establishment, however he defines it on any given day, means he has tapped into the people's dissatisfactions. His candidacy sent shivers up the spine of career politicians everywhere."

During his campaign, staged mostly in bars and at picnics, Kinky treasured most the comment from an anonymous farmer who came up to him and whispered: "You ain't worth a damn, but you're better than what we got." Still, Friedman began to sound more like a conventional politician, a stuffy echo of the former Kinky, who never met a conventional idea he couldn't publicly skewer. He began singing a new tune. "My plan is to appoint the very best people that I can find, get out of their way and let them do their job," he grandly declared. "I want people who have a passion about Texas and who care about her and who will do the right thing. It's a plan that's never been tried here before. It's time for a fundamental change. We can make Texas number one in renewable fuels—which is a hell of a lot better than being number one in executions, property taxes, and dropouts."

It wasn't until you got to the small print of his platform that Kinky's true character re-emerged. One example: Texas has the longest border with Mexico, and Friedman's solution to illegal immigration—his "Five Mexican Generals Plan"—was as original and off-the-wall as any of his books or songs. "When I talk about the Five Mexican Generals plan, people think I'm joking but I'm dead serious," he maintained. "I will divide the border into five juris-dictions, assigning one Mexican general to each and provide him with a $1 million trust fund. Every time a person crosses illegally into the U.S., we'll subtract $5,000 from the fund." Friedman's plan would have placed the responsibility of securing the border on corrupt Mexican military leaders instead of inept American border guards. It might even have worked; nothing else has.

His pledge to eliminate Houston's pathetic ranking as the worst air-polluting city in the United States was considerably less imaginative. If elected, Kinky planned to build coal-fired elec-tric generating plants in the Dallas–Fort Worth area, so that the prevailing southerly winds would tag that city as being the state's most polluted area. Houston would automatically slip into No. 2 position, thus fulfilling his election promise. Alone among the candidates, he supported gay marriage ("I believe they have the right to be as miserable as the rest of us") and proposed to finance public education by legalizing gambling terminals in bars. He planned to call the program "Slots for Tots."

His most controversial appointment, should he win, would be to name his buddy Willie Nelson as head of Texas's Energy Commission. "People find that very humorous," he admitted.

"But I believe very strongly that musicians can run this state better than politicians. We won't get a lot done in the mornings, but we'll work late and we'll be honest."

Born in Chicago sixty-one years ago as Richard Friedman, he became a chess prodigy at seven, the youngest player to take on then–U.S. chess champion Samuel Reshevsky. He lost the match, but the chess master praised his game. The youthful Friedman graduated from the University of Texas, where he was permanently dubbed "Kinky," which best described his Jewish Afro hairdo. (Friedman himself refers to his hairstyle as "my Lyle Lovett starter kit.") He joined the Peace Corps in 1966 and was assigned to Borneo, where "I was supposed to teach agriculture to people who had been farming successfully for 2,000 years."

If Friedman had a hobby—aside from insulting anyone within hailing distance—it was taking care of pets in the shelter he runs. "On the whole, I prefer cats to women because cats seldom if ever use the word relationship," he declared. "I seldom meddle in cats' personal affairs and they rarely meddle in mine. Cats are a fairly right-wing group politically. They are lovers of the status quo. They don't like anything that might represent change. They hate marriages, divorces, moving days, graduations, bar mitzvahs, bill collectors, rug shampooers, painters, plumbers, electricians, television repairmen, call-out masseuses, Jehovah's Witnesses and just about everything else, most of which I agree with them about. They have great insight into human character. Cats, as a rule, don't like lawyers."

"Kinky's problem," a *New Yorker* profile claimed, "is that he considers himself a serious soul who has never been taken seriously." In front of a liberal crowd, Kinky wooed the voters with the racist and sexist epithets that came to him naturally. And that was the dilemma reducing his chances: if he remained true to himself, he risked not being taken seriously; if he abandoned his persona and tried to become a regular contender with shopworn ideas and no outrageous asides, most Texans would opt for one of the other, certifiably regular candidates. (Although he would be the first Jewish governor, Kinky seemed nervous mainly about the Baptist vote. It wasn't that long ago that he advised the church's clerics to keep the heads of new converts under water much, much longer during baptism ceremonies.) In his serious moments, Kinky claimed he was running "against the system, against the stagnant status quo and all the politicians who've been there so long they have forgotten why they're there."

Politics didn't change the man. He still puffed Groucho Marx cigars (Montecristo No. 2s), sported Frank Zappa–like facial hair, dressed entirely in black and owned only two shirts. But he was well aware that he would be elected on November 7 only if there occurred a bizarre alignment of stars in the heavens and he was the beneficiary of the devil's own luck on the ground. "If I lose this race, I will retire in a petulant snit," he predicted, and it was a promise he aimed to keep. (He did lose and did stage a monumental snit.)

Too bad they ain't makin' Jews like Kinky anymore.

—2006

John Diefenbaker: Renegade Out of Power

IT'S AN HOUR before closing time and the Princess Café, a fluorescent-lit Chinese and Canadian food emporium on Central Avenue in Prince Albert, deep in the heart of northern Saskatchewan, is nearly empty. A truck driver with a crewcut and knotty, walnut skin is talking to a kid in a Hawaiian shirt. In one corner sit three Indians with closed faces, not saying anything, just sipping giant Diet Cokes, and in their silence you feel as though the fumes of their loneliness were leaking out of them and polluting the dingy atmosphere.

The kid is talking politics. "I'm for Dief. He don't agree with nobody. He's his own man."

The truck driver leans into his coffee. "Yeah" says he. "Show John the grain, and he'll go against it."

———

IT IS TUESDAY night of the week before polling day, and his tiny retinue of handlers is nervous. It is the last rally of John Diefenbaker's last campaign. Will the old man fill the hall, even with Peter Lougheed being flown in for the occasion from Edmonton? Can he hold his audience's attention? Will he use the meeting for one final, bitter assault on everyone in sight? Can he be trusted?

By eight o'clock nearly four hundred supporters have filled the chairs of the Sheraton Marlborough Hotel, and suddenly, marching behind a piper and the Alberta premier, comes The Chief. He looks like a comatose veteran of the Boer War, but he can still change the temperature of any hall he enters, even this plastic ballroom with its red ceiling and crematorium cheerfulness.

This is Diefenbaker as icon. Canadian history on the hoof.

Lougheed is all tact and heart in his introduction, careful not to upstage the ancient warrior's political swan song. There is a kind of forlorn elegance about the ex–prime minister, slumped on the platform, waiting his turn, trembling with age. But once he's up, the blood fills his limbs. His voice is strong, his manner confident and, contrary to the fears of his stagers, he performs with style and grace.

"They say I'm too old," he bellows, mimicking his Liberal and NDP opponents. "I'll take those birds for a three-mile race any time . . . providing they first agree to an examination [*pause*] from the neck up!" (Asked later in private how he's really feeling, Diefenbaker's eyes twinkle as he confides: "Like a twenty-minute egg [*pause*], but the doctors scared the hell out of me. They said I was as sound as the Canadian dollar.")

He stands, right hand on hip, left forefinger pointing, the clipped participles and long, open vowels lending his speech biblical cadence. His notes keep falling off the lectern, but it makes not the slightest difference. His trains of thought seldom survive more than a sentence. ("Where is Canada going? My friends, I never had a family. The one thing denied me.") The galloping non sequiturs and fractured metaphors are aimed at anything that traverses his thought patterns. But politically, Liberal PM Pierre Trudeau is his target.

He blames Canada's horrendous inflation rate directly on the Liberal leader's extravagances in refurbishing his official summer residence at Harrington Lake. ("When I was prime minister, we spent twenty-five dollars a year. Olive made the curtains.") He goes on to accuse Trudeau of approving secret loans to Idi Amin, showing little respect for the Commons ("Parliament is but a memory") and being arrogant ("if Trudeau goes back, Canada ends").

The exaggerations grow tiresome, but his timing remains perfect. "There is nothing," Diefenbaker confesses in a dropped voice, "nothing more lonely than being a former prime minister. Being the only one . . ." The long pause reduces the room to hushed reverence. Then comes the punch line: "But after next Tuesday night, I'll have company!" The good, windblown faces in the audience crack up, and one finely coiffed Baptist matron in front of me laughs so hard her hairpins pop out.

The electricity flows through his listeners. Other parts of Canada might be a political graveyard or minefield for him, but here they still love the Old Chief. This is Diefenbaker Country, and will be long after he's gone.

His performance grows boring only when he insists on reeling off an endless litany of his past manifestations of courage, almost back to the time he didn't flinch when he was getting a smallpox vaccination in grade school. The speech unrolls for fifty minutes, like some wild, finger-painted fresco. The climax comes when Diefenbaker recites the moving coda from his Bill of Rights.

There isn't a dry eye in the house.

I am in the audience, hiding behind two fat farmers so that the Chief can't see me, since my book about him has been published, and although he swears that he has never read it, he attacks me for seventeen factual errors in the first chapter. The hall is still as his eyes bore into me. Then he sticks out an accusing finger: "*THERE HE IS*," he bellows. "*THERE HE IS, THAT HIRELING OF LIBERALISM—WHO WRITES PSEUDOBIOGRAPHIES FOR MONETARY GAIN!*"

Only the last part is true, but as a fellow abuser of fancy metaphors, I must salute him as "best in show."

———

AT EIGHTY-THREE, DIEFENBAKER retained two ambitions: to plant Prince Albert's Diamond Jubilee flag at the

North Pole and to outlast Sir Wilfrid Laurier's forty-five-year record as a sitting MP.

In private he is quietly preparing the pageant of his passing. He has set $100,000 aside for a home for disadvantaged children in Prince Albert to be named after Olive, but his main preoccupation is with the details of his burial. After a state funeral in Ottawa, John Diefenbaker's remains will be carried across the country to Saskatoon aboard a special, slow-moving train ("just like Churchill's"). Unyielding beyond the end, he has drafted one very specific provision for the ceremony: his casket is to be draped with the Red Ensign that he fought so hard to preserve as the flag of the country he loves—instead of the "Pearson Rag" he hates.

It was easy enough to make fun of the man, to caricature his crusades. But it was his stride and stance, his sheer guts—the brew of his laughter and the dint of his compassion—those were the qualities that made John Diefenbaker a politician apart. Like P.G. Wodehouse's fictional butler, Jeeves, he entered any room "as a procession of one."

Although Diefenbaker seldom stopped talking about himself, his essence remained a mysterious mixture of vanity and charm, vulnerability and brass, outrage and mischief. He single-handedly transformed Canadian politics into the country's leading spectator sport. The dilemma of most Canadian politicians is how to stress the marginal differences between themselves and their rivals so that they can conceal their basic similarities. Diefenbaker's problem was exactly the opposite:

how to place enough restraints on his combative nature so that he would sound more like his electable and less individualistic contemporaries. Even in his declining years, he remained a political giant ambling on his knees in a land of midgets.

Most leaders find themselves in conflict with their times either because they remain reactionaries who try to resurrect the past or because they attempt to become visionaries and find their aim exceeds their grasp. Diefenbaker suffered the rare distinction of being both. His intellect was frozen in another time; his heart was an open city. He was born only four years after Sir John A. Macdonald died; his life spanned Canada's history. He could draw on memories of times when Red River carts still creaked along the Carlton Trail and buffalo bones littered the Prairies. During a 1962 campaign stop at Melville, Saskatchewan, I happened to be standing behind him as he asked a group of old-timers in what year they had come west. When the eldest replied, "April of 1903," a delighted Diefenbaker shot back, "We came in August!"

No Canadian politician ever rose so steadily through a succession of defeats. He was soundly beaten in five election campaigns—municipal, provincial and federal—before finally squeaking into the House of Commons as a member of the Conservative Opposition in 1940. He won endless converts on his perpetual circuits of speech making across the country, but inside the higher Conservative party hierarchy, he was dismissed as "that Bolshevist from the West." At the same time, the Liberals harassed him by redistributing his seat out of existence and even descended to the petty ploy of converting the house next to his Prince Albert home into an interim residence for unwed Indian mothers. But Diefenbaker knew how to wait, and he had a nose for power. In 1956 he fooled the pundits by capturing the Tory leadership and the following year managed to win a minority mandate.

ELECTIONS SAVAGE a man's pride and poise, but Diefenbaker loved to campaign. In 1958 he decided to transform himself into an incarnation of the Canada he knew. The asylums are full of people who imagine themselves to be Napoleon—or Jesus Christ—but Diefenbaker persisted in becoming Captain Canada—a personification of the national will for whom all things were possible. Trumpeting his "Vision" of northern development, he went on a charismatic rampage that made his audiences quiver. They cheered every time he paused for breath. In Fredericton a crush of swooning women held their children up to touch him. When Ed Morris, then a Conservative candidate in Halifax, was introducing the PC leader, he began by saying: "My friends, what shall we say of this great man?" A voice from the back rows carolled out: "Dear John . . . Dear John." Morris bowed his head. "Yes," he intoned. "We may as well say, 'Dear John . . .'" Two thousand men and women stood up to roar their approval. (Not everybody got his signals right. At a ceremony in West Vancouver's Park Royal, an Indian chief called Mathias Joe presented a walking stick to the PM with the tribute: "John Diefenbacon, you're the thunderbird of our country.")

On that triumphant election night in 1958, Diefenbaker won 208 seats, wiping out the Liberals in six provinces. It was the largest mandate ever given a Canadian prime minister. Even if his French couldn't get him past a Berlitz receptionist, Quebec accorded him 62 percent of its votes—just one point behind true-blue Ontario. In the golden months that followed, Diefenbaker acted less like a politician than a force of nature. During a Commons question period on July 2, 1958, when he was asked by Hazen Argue (then of the CCF) what his government intended to do about drought on the Prairies, Diefenbaker matter-of-factly replied, "Yesterday and also the day before when I was in Brandon, several localities received rain for the first time." A couple of Liberal backbenchers giggled nervously. But to most members of Parliament, it seemed only mildly ludicrous that this all-powerful leader could order blessed raindrops down from the sky. He took office when he was just short of sixty-two, too late to erase the habits of all those lonely years as a struggling attorney in the tomorrow country of northern Saskatchewan. His magnificent victory at the polls condemned him to a permanent sense of anticlimax; he interpreted the people's acclaim as adequate proof of his greatness and became intoxicated with the trappings rather than the substance of his office. In a sense, it was not power but the absence of power that had corrupted him. He had spent thirty-seven years in the political wilderness, denied what he felt to be his rightful place. All that apartness, all that contempt, simmered up to dominate his every act.

———

HIS GOVERNMENT INITIATED many enlightened mea-
sures, but as PM he remained preoccupied with settling old scores.
He never absolved anyone of the slightest rebuff. On April 4, 1967,
when the Liberals announced that they had named the popular
Conservative House speaker Roland Michener to be Canada's
twentieth governor general, Diefenbaker alone failed to applaud
the appointment—because Michener had ruled him out of order
during a procedural wrangle eight years earlier. Before he became
prime minister, Diefenbaker had heard his party vilified so often
for being too cautious that, once in power, he indulged freely in
populist radicalism, which was his natural instinct. (That was why
I called him a renegade to his party's established political stance.)
His conviction—born in Saskatchewan during the droughts of the
thirties—that the economically underprivileged can help themselves only through collective political action found its expression
in his concept of social justice, based on the commendable notion
that every Canadian has the right to expect equality of opportunity. During six years in office, his administration spent almost as
much money as all governments between Confederation and 1946
combined (including the cost of two world wars) in a wild jumble
of programs designed to help develop the North and assist farmers, fishermen and other low-income groups.

Afloat on a sea of generous impulses, Diefenbaker seldom
understood the details of his own policies. In the 1965 campaign,
for example, his party strategists worked out an elaborate scheme
for allowing urban house owners to deduct municipal assessments
from federal income tax. Diefenbaker tried vainly to explain what

it was all about until he gave up in Winnipeg by lamely conceding he thought his plan "might be limited to home-occupied houses"—whatever that was.

Instead of advancing any set of identifiable principles, his brand of politics turned out to be little more than a drawn-out sequence of morality plays staged to combat imagined forces threatening his downfall. Whether his audience filled a tiny Legion hall in northern Saskatchewan or an auditorium at one of the thirty-five universities that granted him honorary degrees, he used every public occasion to hurl defiance at the nameless adjudicators of Canadian society's great power blocs. He thus caught himself in his own trap of demanding to be loved for the enemies he had made.

He was at his best among his own people on the Prairies and campaigned on every conceivable occasion, whether there happened to be an election in the offing or not. It was Diefenbaker's eyes that were his saving grace, acting as jovial monitors of his innermost emotions, mocking the pomposity of his own performances. But at his nightly rallies, he would turn on his audiences like some medieval necromancer dispensing rhetorical fire. With an energy born of gloating, he would dance out his joy at the wickedness of his political opponents. When he accused the Liberals of "shedding tears of falsehood," his audiences knew what he meant, and when he confessed that his errors as prime minister were "mistakes of the heart," they rushed to forgive him. He was the champion of every boy who ever had a pimple, the candidate of every woman sustained by romantic visions of deliverance from her humdrum realities.

His language was a splendid artifice, the words fanfaring his message in the cadence of Southern camp meetings, where the language of exhortation, graceless by choice, took the place of logical discourse. "Join with me," he pleaded. "Join with me to catch the vision of men and women who rise above these things that ordinarily hold you to the soil. Join with me to bring about the achievement of that Canada, one Canada, the achievement of Canada's destiny!"

During the Brantford, Ontario, rally that wound up his 1963 campaign, he clarified once and for all just exactly how he obtained his best advice: "I ask myself, 'Is a thing right?' And if it is, I do it." To identify not only his audience, but also himself with the aspirations of the "average Canadian," Diefenbaker tried to ally his own past with every part of the country. That never sounded more preposterous than in a Halifax speech when he established his family contact with the Atlantic port by earnestly proclaiming: "Had it not been for the trade winds between here and Newfoundland, my great-great-grandmother would have been born in Halifax."

BUT ALL THAT thunder had little to do with the art of governing the country, and gradually it became clear that Diefenbaker viewed legislation more as a posture than a process; his government never demonstrated any clear purpose except to retain power. His administration's final collapse in 1963 (with seventeen ministers leaving through various exits during its last ten months) was like the ruin of some great papier mâché temple built for a Hollywood spectacular when the rains come down and wash the whole Technicolor mess into the sea. By the time Diefenbaker had lost his last election as leader in 1965, his once great Conservative party had been hived into a coalition of the discontented and the dispossessed, with only one Tory MP (Lincoln Alexander) surviving in the fifty constituencies of Canada's three largest cities.

Politics is a process of elimination. But John Diefenbaker refused to be eliminated.

In the last decade of his life, he moved off into a private world, becoming a figment of his own imagination, the starved topography of his face illuminating the nation's TV screens as he gloomed about whatever was happening at the time. But occasionally the humour still bubbled up, as in the joke he would tell his Prince Albert cronies about the swimming pool Pierre Trudeau had built in the PM's official residence: "He's a great swimmer; a great athlete. But just after construction finished, he got stuck on some of the underwater furniture. Standing alongside, looking down at him was a chap with a sign LIFEGUARD on his hat. Trudeau finally got out and said, 'Aren't you the lifeguard here? Why didn't you help me?'

"He replied, 'I can't swim.'

"Trudeau then asked him: 'How the *griggins* did you get the appointment?'

"'I'm bilingual!'"

Diefenbaker's partisan fevers never subsided. In the fall of 1971, he was suddenly taken ill during a visit to Wales, and

Trudeau extended the courtesy of sending a government jet to bring him home. The ex–prime minister was loaded aboard on a stretcher, but during the journey, the attending doctor filled him with six pints of blood and enough iron pills so that by the time the plane landed in Ottawa, he was able to stride down the ramp—and immediately called a press conference to attack the Liberals' overspending habits—especially their pernicious use of government planes for private trips.

Through John Diefenbaker's long career and longer lifetime, it was always possible to admire the man's instincts without respecting his performance. His was the most primitive of partisanships. He shattered the bedrock of Canadian political traditions: the idea that the Conservative party was an instrument of Toronto's Bay Street; the long-accepted convention that political leaders in this country should talk grey and act neutral; the very notion that prime ministers must lick the velvet hand of the business elite.

When a great man dies, some promise of a country's life is buried with him. That sentiment was most dramatically caught in the terse obituary haughtily declaimed over French national television in 1970 by Prime Minister Georges Pompidou: "General de Gaulle is dead. France is a widow."

Canada may not be widowed, but we were no less bereaved. John George Diefenbaker's passing begged to be taken more as a symbol than an event. We mourned his death as we might grieve the loss of our own youth, for a way we were and could never be again.

WHEN I FIRST heard of John Diefenbaker's wish that his body be carried by train across the country he loved, I had two strong reactions. The first was to recall a phrase from the official program of Sir Winston Churchill's funeral, designating how his body should travel on a funeral barge along the Thames "with the pomp of waters un-withstood." Somehow, that description fitted perfectly The Chief's own final journey as his unrepentant remains were borne from Ottawa to Saskatoon.

My second reaction was to relive the five elections I had covered from aboard the Diefenbaker train, tumbling through the night of time in a press car filled with the noise of tapping typewriters and tinkling glasses. I particularly remember the 1965 campaign, when we all knew he couldn't win, but Diefenbaker kept searching for some totem to further his fortunes. When a supporter in Richmond Hill, Ontario, gave The Chief a canary, he spent hours coaxing the bird to sing, convinced that this was the omen he had been waiting for. The bird just sat there staring back at him. But a week before polling day, when Diefenbaker's back was turned, a railway steward took pity on him and did a passable canary imitation. The Chief got very excited, and the incident noticeably boosted his energies for the final push.

Diefenbaker was at his best moving through the knots of Prairie farmers who turned out everywhere to greet him, looking into men's eyes and women's feelings, absorbing their sense of shared loneliness, the fear of living at the margin of things. There, among his own people, The Chief became the breathing reminder of a simpler age when God was alive, one man's courage could still change history and rural Canada ruled the roost.

At Stettler, Alberta, two raggedy kids were holding up a huge hand-painted cardboard sign with the letters "DEIF FOR CHEIF." At Swift Current, Saskatchewan, twenty blue-gowned ladies on the back of a truck broke into "Land of Hope and Glory" and sang "Mademoiselle from Armentières" (in English) for an encore.

At Taber, Alberta, Diefenbaker told an audience of hushed schoolchildren: "I only wish that I could come back when you're my age to see the kind of Canada that you'll see. So dream your dreams; keep them and pursue them." When we stopped briefly at Morse, Saskatchewan, a local band of musicians was out on the platform, serenading Diefenbaker with their ragged version of "The Thunderer." None of us could file our stories because the telegrapher was playing the drums.

Later that day an old man sat patiently by the tracks as The Chief's train rattled by, held up a homemade sign in the twilight: "JOHN, YOU'LL NEVER DIE."

He was right.

—1963

Sources

Hitchhiker's Guide to the Mind of Conrad Black

From *The Establishment Man: A Portrait of Power*

Toronto: McClelland & Stewart, 1982

Sir George Simpson: The Birchbark Napoleon

From *Caesars of the Wilderness*

Toronto: Viking (Penguin), 1987

Reprinted by permission of Penguin Group Canada.

The World According to Garth

From "The World According to Garth," *Globe and Mail*, March 27, 2009

Sir Herbert Holt: The Tycoon Who Tried to Buy Canada

From *Flame of Power: Intimate Profiles of Canada's Greatest Businessmen*

Toronto: Longman's, Green & Co., 1959

The Murder of Harry Oakes: Why Nobody Cried

From *Flame of Power: Intimate Profiles of Canada's Greatest Businessmen*

Toronto: Longman's, Green & Co., 1959

Peter Nygard and His Twenty-Five Best Naked Friends

From *The Acquisitors*

Toronto: McClelland & Stewart, 1981

My Adventures in Bronfman Country

From *Here Be Dragons: Telling Tales of People, Passion and Power*

Toronto: McClelland & Stewart, 2004

Reprinted by permission of McClelland & Stewart.

Victor Rice: The Executive Who Fired Fifty-Two Thousand Workers

From *The Canadian Revolution, 1985–1995: From Deference to Defiance*

Toronto: Viking (Penguin), 1995

and "Victor Rice Gives Capitalism a Bad Name," *Maclean's*, August 27, 1990

How Robert Campeau Caught the Biggest Fish

From *The Canadian Revolution, 1985–1995: From Deference to Defiance*

Toronto: Viking (Penguin), 1995

Nelson Skalbania: Not a Poor Country in the Balkans

From *The Acquisitors*

Toronto: McClelland & Stewart, 1981

and "The Downfall of Jesus Christ Superstar," *Maclean's*, March 3, 1997

K.C. Irving: How Could He Top the List?

From "How Could K.C. Irving Make the List?" *Maclean's*, July 13, 1998

The Eatons: Spoiled Kids Who Destroyed an Empire

From *Titans: How the New Canadian Establishment Seized Power*

Toronto: Viking (Penguin), 1998

and "From Dynastic Myth to Mere Mortals," *Maclean's*, March 10, 1997

Lord Strathcona: Lord of All He Surveyed—and Then Some

From *Flame of Power: Intimate Profiles of Canada's Greatest Businessmen*

Toronto: Longman's, Green & Co., 1959

Bud McDougald: The Tycoon Who Never Gave an Interview

From *Sometimes a Great Nation: Will Canada Belong to the 21st Century?*

Toronto: McClelland & Stewart, 1988

The Day Confederation Life Went Bust

From *The Canadian Revolution, 1985–1995: From Deference to Defiance*

Toronto: Viking (Penguin), 1995

Tom d'Aquino: The Man Who Sold the Farm

From *Canadian Business*, October 12, 2009

Brian Mulroney: Wooing New York Millions

From *Sometimes a Great Nation: Will Canada Belong to the 21st Century?*

Toronto: McClelland & Stewart, 1988

René Lévesque: Meeting the Wall Street Cowboys

From *Sometimes a Great Nation: Will Canada Belong to the 21st Century?*

Toronto: McClelland & Stewart, 1988

Kim Campbell: Ah, We Hardly Knew Ye

From *Defining Moments: Dispatches from an Unfinished Revolution*

Toronto: Viking (Penguin), 1997

Louis Riel: The Mad Rebel Who Was Our Founding Father

From "A Well-Deserved Honour for Riel," *Maclean's* March 23, 1992

Jack Pickersgill: "Sailor Jack" and the Politics of Patronage

From *The Distemper of Our Times: Canadian Politics in Transition, 1963–1968*
Toronto: McClelland & Stewart, 1968

Bill Vander Zalm: The Kamikaze Premier

From *Sometimes a Great Nation: Will Canada Belong to the 21st Century?*
Toronto: McClelland & Stewart, 1988
and "Beyond Fantasy: Vander Zalm Ends a Bizarre Chapter in the Politics of Extremes in British Columbia," *Maclean's*, April 8, 1991

Lucien Bouchard: Revolution East

From *The Canadian Revolution, 1985–1995: From Deference to Defiance*
Toronto: Viking (Penguin), 1995

David Radler: The One Who Got Away

From "Conrad Black's 'Torpedo,'" *Maclean's*, August 29, 2005.

Kinky Friedman: That Bad-Ass Country Singer

From "Will the Governor of Texas Be Kinky? How Kinky Friedman, the Former Leader of the Texas Jewboys, Became a Real Candidate for the Governorship of Texas," *Maclean's*, September 1, 2006.

John Diefenbaker: Renegade Out of Power

From *Renegade in Power: The Diefenbaker Years*

Toronto: McClelland & Stewart, 1963

Index

Edmonton Oilers, 192, 193
Edward, Duke of Windsor, 86
Edward VII, 72–73
E.I. du Pont de Nemours and Co., 142
Eleuthera Island, 115
Elizabeth, Queen of Romania, 206
Elliott, Maxine, 113
Enders, Gaetana, 28
Enders, Thomas O., 28
England, 24, 60, 64, 80, 83, 231–33, 281
Ermatinger, Edward, 70
Esquimalt, 301–3
Establishment, Canadian, 160, 163, 173,
    238, 242, 247
Establishment Man: A Portrait of Power, The
    (Newman), 11
European Union (EU), 258
Exell, Oksana, 307
Exhibition Stadium (Toronto), 145

F
Fairclough, Ellen, 297–98
Famous Players Corporation, 97
Farrell family, 181
Farrow, Moira, 181
Federal Plan Commission, 91
Federated Department Stores, 156, 162,
    163, 167, 168
Ferragamo, Vince, 197
Fildes, Christopher, 251
Financial Post, 151, 157
Financial Times of Canada, 151
Finland, 123
Finlay, John, 13–14
Fisher, Robin, 311
Fleming, Donald, 297
Foch, Ferdinand, 30
Foreign Investment Review Agency, 267
Forsey, Eugene, 320
Fort Chimo, 218
Fort Edmonton, 56
Fort Garry, 221, 222
Fort Langley, 55, 70
Fort McPherson, 63

Fort Timiskaming, 50
Fortune Book Club, 140
Fortune magazine, 19, 157
Foster, Ann, 59
Foster, Clem, 107
Foster, George, 235
Fox Creek (Alberta), 186
F. Perkins Ltd., 146–47
France, 13, 21, 29, 33, 34, 64, 67, 80, 90,
    324, 326, 327, 355
Franco, Francisco, 24
Francophonie, la, 326
Fraser, Colin, 54
Fraser, Fil, 141–42
Fraser, Simon, 216
Fraser River, 216
Fredericton, 204
French Canada, 23
French Half-Breeds, 221
Friedman, Kinky (Richard), 8, 335–42
Frum, David, 24

G
Gardiner, A. G., 231
Garrow, E. A., 91
Gates, Robert, 152
Gazette (Montreal), 197, 325
George V, 90, 214, 215
Germany, 17
Gladstone, William Ewart, 68, 220
Glencoe, 295
Globe, 106, 109
Globe and Mail, 39, 41, 67, 106
Globe and Mail's Report on Business, 166
Gobuty, Michael, 195
Godard, Jean-Luc, 37
Godin, Sévère, 84, 87, 96
Gold Rush, 48
Goodman, Roderick, 128–29
Gordon, Daniel M., 213
Gordon, Walter, 298
Gousseland, Pierre, 13–14
Grace family, 268
Graham, Alan, 247

Sommer, Elke, 122
Sorrow and the Pity, The (film), 33–34
South African War, 233
Southwest Marine Drive, 181
Sovereign Life, 247
Soyka, Fred, 247
Spain, 24
Spanish Armada, 13
Spectator (London), 251
Spry, Irene, 59
Square Mile, 214
Stanley, Henry, 36
Stanley Park, 183
Steele, S. B., 233
Stephen, George, 226–29
Stephenson, Signy Hildur (Mrs. John
    David Eaton), 206–7
Sterling Newspapers, 13, 14
Stern, Howard, 263
Stettler (Alberta), 357
St. Eve, Amy, 40
Stewart, Brian, 17–18, 34–35, 37
Stewart Forest Products, 186
St. George's Hospital (London), 112
St. Gilgen (Austria), 169
Stimpson, Fred, 188
Stirling, Geoff, 298
St. James Street, 83
St-Laurent, Louis, 286, 287, 292–93, 296
St. Lawrence, 73
St. Paul, Minneapolis & Manitoba
    Railroad, 227
St. Paul & Pacific Railway, 226
Strathcona, Lord (Donald Alexander
    Smith, Baron Strathcona and Mount
    Royal), 211–36
Strathcona Trust for Physical and
    Patriotic Education in Canada, 235
Stresemann, Gustav, 17
St. Stephen's Anglican Church, 71
Stuart, John, 60, 216
Stuart Lake, 55
Sutherland, William, 73
Suzuki, David, 313

Swastika, 103, 105–7
Sweatman, Alan, 123
Sweezey, R. O., 84
Swift Current (Saskatchewan), 357
Sylvanite Gold Mine, 107
Szász, Endre, 180

T
Taber (Alberta), 357
Tadoussac, 217
Tan Jay, 124
Tan Son, 37
Taylor, E. P., 4, 147, 237, 239
Taylor, George, 59
Taylor, Margaret, 55, 59, 60
Taylor, Thomas, 55
TD Tower, 137
Telegraph-Journal, 202
Tennyson, Lord Alfred, 220
Texas, 338–42
Texas Jewboys, 335, 336
Texas Monthly, 339
Thomas, Peter, 186
Thomson, Dick, 160
Thornbrough, Al, 147, 148
Time and Chance (Campbell), 273
Timothy Eaton Memorial, 207
Tobler, Barry, 310
Toburn Gold Mines Limited, 108
Today Show (TV show), 141
Toigo, Peter, 307
Top Twenty Club, 306, 307
Tories, 1, 2, 212, 229, 231, 275, 277, 288,
    290, 295, 326, 349
Toronto, 19, 75, 94, 120, 164, 165,
    312–13, 315
Toronto Club, 12, 26, 41, 241, 242
Toronto Daily Star, 206
Toronto Islands, 92
Toronto Star, 89, 113, 128, 129
Tough, George, 106, 107
Tough, Jack, 106
Tough, Rob, 106
Tough, Tom, 106